# WHAT'S YOUR WHY?

I0626873

## UNLOCK YOUR DESIRED LIFE BY FINDING CLARITY

An Anthology created to help you navigate
your focus for intentional living

Compiled by Lady Amb. Dr (h.c.) Robbie Motter and
Rev. Amb. Dr. (h.c.) Christine Park, D.D.

HAVANA BOOK GROUP LLC.
HAVANABOOKGROUP.COM

HAVANA BOOK GROUP LLC
2173 SALK AVE, SUITE 250
CARLSBAD, CA. 92008

COPYRIGHT 2025 All rights reserved.
ISBN: 979-8-9927525-8-8

# WHAT IS YOUR WHY?
*Ambassador Dr. (h.c) Randi D. Ward*

You are here on Earth for a special reason---your unique why.
You work hard to create a way of life you can happily live by.
Your specific WHY'S are created by you and you alone.
Each WHY will then become an important steppingstone
To guide your life and create the person you will become
And also enable you to deal with issues you must overcome.

While you are here on earth, you strive to make a difference.
You dream of helping others and being a positive influence.
Your WHY may be to inspire others
through creative expression
Or provide comfort or healing via a chosen caring profession.
Maybe you want to help the economy
by supporting community growth
Or simply to fulfill your own potential
via self-improvement and growth.

Your WHY may involve lifelong learning to expand your mind
So, you can lead with integrity and actions
that are sincere and kind.
Maybe creating the best environment
for your family is your desire,

So, your children can achieve dreams and goals that are higher.

You may want to be the voice for those
without the power to speak

Or lend a helping hand to lighten
the burden of those who are weak.


Maybe you yearn to create something unique
to help our society

So, you can also receive special recognition
or some form of notoriety.

There are countless reasons why
we humans have so many WHY'S.

It is extremely essential for us to be able to clearly recognize

Our exceptional talents and gifts
so we can fulfill our heart's desire,

That WHY is what drives our passions
and sets our souls on "fire."

# PREFACE

*By Lady Amb Dr. Robbie Motter (h.c.)*
*Founder & CEO, Global Society for Female Entrepreneurs*

What's your why?

It's a question that has echoed throughout my life — from the moment I found myself on my own at 14, navigating a world without a safety net, to today, where I proudly lead a global community of purpose-driven women through the Global Society for Female Entrepreneurs.

This book was born from a vision to inspire others to pause, reflect, and reconnect with their deepest truths. In a world full of distractions and expectations, it's easy to lose sight of what truly drives us. But when we ask why — when we dare to go inward and listen to the whispers of our soul — we uncover the fuel behind our resilience, our passions, and our ability to create impact.

What's Your Why? is not just a collection of stories. It is a movement, a collective heartbeat of fifty-three incredible co-authors who bravely share their journeys, awakenings, and revelations. Each chapter offers a glimpse into the soul of someone who has faced challenges, sought clarity, and found power in purpose. This book is your invitation to do the same.

For the first time ever, we will launch this book in Africa at the LOANI "All Means All" World Conference in July 2025 — a historic moment where we will raise our voices together and celebrate our shared commitment to intentional living. I and our publisher Angela Covany, Havana Book Group Publishers, and all our contributing author's couldn't be more proud of this global collaboration and the powerful legacy it represents.

My hope is that as you read these stories, you find the courage to ask yourself:

What is your why?

And once you find it — go live it boldly, beautifully, and without apology.

Together, we rise.

With purpose and love,
Lady Amb Dr. Robbie Motter (h.c.)
Founder/CEO
GSFEUS.COM

# FOREWORD
## Rooted in Purpose, Rising in Power
*By Professor Caroline Makaka*
*Founder & President, Leaders of All Nations International*

In every era, a spark emerges—a moment that awakens hearts, ignites change, and calls us to rise higher. This book is that spark.

"What's Your Why? Unlock Your Desired Life By Finding Clarity" is more than a collection of stories; it is a living movement. Within its pages are visionaries, leaders, and everyday heroes from across the globe, each sharing not just what they do, but why they do it. In that "why" lies the true essence of leadership: purpose.

In a world that often rewards outcomes over journeys and image over integrity, it is revolutionary to pause and ask: Why?

Why do we rise each morning and choose purpose over passivity?

Why do we continue to lead when the path is steep?

Why do we serve, build, and uplift—even when no one is watching?

The answer lies in our "why." It is the soul's compass. The engine of transformation. The birthplace of legacy.

At the heart of this global movement is a woman who embodies this truth: Lady Ambassador Dr. Robbie Motter (h.c). A trailblazer and unwavering advocate for women and unity, Lady Robbie has spent decades building bridges where others saw walls. As Founder and CEO of the Global Society for Female Entrepreneurs (GSFE), she didn't just start an organization— she cultivated a global sisterhood. A sanctuary where women rise together, lead boldly, and thrive without apology.

Her mantra, "We don't compete; we complete each other," resonates through every page of this book. It is a powerful call to collaboration over comparison, unity over division, and connection over isolation.

This book is her legacy in motion—a platform for voices to rise, truths to be shared, and leaders to lead with authenticity. In sharing our stories, we offer others the courage to stand in their own.

## Why This Book Matters

The power of the story cannot be overstated. Stories don't just entertain—they heal, teach, inspire, and connect. In a world fixated on perfection, this book offers something richer: truth, vulnerability, and raw humanity.

Each contributor brings a unique background—diverse in geography, profession, and life experience—but all are united by a commitment to purpose. From entrepreneurs to educators, artists to advocates, survivors to changemakers, these voices reflect the full spectrum of human brilliance and resilience.

This book is not just for leaders. It's for the dreamer unsure of her voice. The mother balancing ambition and caregiving. The survivor learning to speak again. The teacher, healer, refugee, innovator—this book is for you.

Whether read in a boardroom or under a starlit sky, these stories serve as mirrors—reflecting our own truths, strength, and potential.

## The Legacy of Lady Robbie

Lady Robbie Motter's lifework has transformed thousands. Through G.S.F.E, she's created a global ecosystem where leadership is defined by equity, empathy, and empowerment. Her impact is not measured in titles, but in lives lifted and futures ignited.

She reminds us that leadership doesn't demand perfection—it demands presence. Her life is a living lesson in asking boldly, giving freely, and rising together. This book is an extension of that mission: a call for others to step into their light and own their "why" with courage.

## The Ripple Effect of Purpose

When we lead from our "why," we stop seeking validation and start building impact.

We love each other more deeply.

We serve more selflessly.

We connect more intentionally.

The heartbeat of this book is the purpose that sends ripples into the world—ripples that build schools, birth movements, start businesses, feed communities, and change lives. You will feel those ripples on every page.

I, too, have been shaped by purpose. Orphaned young, I faced grief that could have consumed me. I chose not to be defined by loss. I chose to give. From that pain came a mission to uplift others. Today, as Founder of Leaders of All Nations International and creator of the We Are the Change movement, I live to ignite light in others. Many in this book share similar journeys—rising from adversity to become beacons of hope.

## This Book Is a Movement

Our Why is not an end—it is a beginning. A rallying cry for those ready to lead with heart. Every contributor here represents more than a story; they represent a community, a cause, a calling. Their words are seeds of transformation. And with every reader, those seeds take root.

We are entering a new era of leadership. One defined not by authority, but by authenticity. Where vulnerability is a strength, unity is the strategy, and purpose is the power. The voices in this book aren't waiting for permission; they are breaking barriers, building tables, and rewriting what leadership looks like.

Let these stories challenge you. Let them remind you that your voice matters. That your "why" matters, and that the world is waiting for both.

## In Conclusion

To every reader—this book is for you. Let it awaken your purpose, stir your courage, and help you rediscover your voice.

To Lady Robbie—thank you. For your vision, your heart, and your unshakable belief in the power of people and purpose. You are a lighthouse guiding so many home to their "why."

As Dr. Martin Luther King Jr. said:

"Our lives begin to end the day we become silent about things that matter."

Let us never be silent.

Let us rise—together.

Because one story can change a life.

And one purpose can change the world.

With unwavering gratitude and shared purpose,
Professor Caroline Makaka
Founder & President, Leaders of All Nations International
Creator, We Are the Change World Movement

# Chapter Overview

The Power of Purpose: Discovering Your Why
Amb. Dr. (h.c.) Angela Covany ........................................22

Born to Belong: Turning the Mess into a Movement and
a Legacy in Motion
Dr. Angelica Benavides ...............................................28

My Journey: The Foundation of My "Why"
Dr.(h.c.) Angeline Benjamin .........................................36

Why? You Can't Die With The Music Inside You!!!
Angeline Joji ........................................................48

Understanding Why I've Made Some of The Choices and
Decisions I've Made in my Life.
Barbara A. Berg, L.C.S.W. ...........................................60

Natural Self-Discovery and The Road to Finding Your Why
Belinda Foster .......................................................72

Creativity With a Purpose
Bella Castillo .................................................................................82

My Why: A Life of Purpose, Power, and Global Impact
Professor Caroline Makaka, PhD.................................................94

From Surviving to Soaring: Why I Became a Holistic
Prosperity Navigator
Amb. Charles Hai Nguyen ........................................................104

Driven by Love: My Journey to Finding My Why
Ambassador Dr. (h.c.) Charmaine Summers ...........................118

The Fabric of Unity: Ochea's Journey
Amb. Dr. (h.c.) Chebra "Ochea" Dorsey...................................130

The Unfolding of my Why: Embracing Purpose in
Every Step of the Journey
Amb. Dr. Cherilyn Lee, PhD, PA, CHNP..................................138

Shifting Seasons of Purpose
Reverend Amb. Dr. Christine Park, DD (h.c) ..........................144

Seemingly Simple Encounters
Cynthia Wilson Pleasant.............................................................152

What's My Why? Self-defense (From a Woman's Point of View)
Dr. (h.c.) Debbie Love ..................................................164

Beyond Grief: A Mothers Love Transformed Into
Action For Change
Amb. Dr. (h.c.) Dorothy Wolons ....................................174

My Why: A Journey from Mango Trees to Majesty
H.R.M. Prof. Dr. Queen Eden Soriano Trinidad........................190

My Why: A Journey of Empowerment through the Arts
Emiko Ishii.................................................................198

My Why: Glorifying God Even Through Life's Deepest Valleys
Grace Richardson ........................................................204

Exploring Uncharted Paths
Holly Porter ...............................................................216

Honor The Child In Each And Every One Of Us
Dr. Iréné Lara, PsyD, Reiki MT, LCSW ..............................226

Defying Naysayers: Fueling My Why by Proving Them Wrong
Jackie Phillips..............................................................234

My Why
Dr. Jaya Sajnani.................................................................244

Breaking the Silence: The Why Behind M.A.L.H.Y.
Amb Dr. Jessica CH Smith President of MALHY.....................252

WHY???
Dr. (h.c.) Kaye Sheffield, MS, CCC-SLP ............................260

Rising From the Ashes Like a Phoenix
H.C. Dr. Doula Lakeysha Mattis.........................................268

What is my WHY?
By Dr. Latrice Jones (h.c.) ................................................278

Love, Just Love
Laura Dunn.......................................................................290

When Life Rewrites Your Why
Lauren Raguzin .................................................................298

What Is My Why?
Lady Ambassador Dr. Lenora Peterson-Maclin,
Ph.D., H.E. ......................................................................312

Why I Empower Midlife Women to Defy Age
and Design Their Destiny
Dr. (h.c.) Lynnette LaRoche ....................................................318

The Values and Beliefs That Guide My Choices
Amb. Dr. (h.c.) Marcy Decato .................................................330

What's Your Why?
Dr. (h.c.) Marietta Aguido Reformado ...................................336

A Shared Vision of Wellness and Beauty
Melissa Khan ............................................................................346

What's Your Why: Coaching Beyond the Field
Dr. (h.c.) Coach Mikki St. Germain .......................................352

What's My Why?
Minh Dannerstedt, Ph.D. ........................................................358

Why is My Why
By Pastor Dr. Monica "Monica Go" Gomez ........................... 366

Lady Amb. Nanette Meneses' Why: A Journey of Miracles,
Resilience and Empowerment
Lady Amb. Nanette Meneses ...................................................374

Fuel by Passion: The Drive Behind Our Purpose
Ambassadors and Drs. Randi D. Ward and
Chaudhry Masood Mahmood Bhalli..............................................386

What's My Why
Rima Aboulhosen....................................................................396

Finding My Why: A Journey of Transformation
Lady Amb Dr. Robbie Motter h.c. ..............................................406

A Right Now Passionate WHY
Sandie Fuenty ........................................................................406

It's Time: Suit Up and Show Up—The World Needs You
Now More Than Ever
Shannon Leischner ..................................................................424

Three Women, One Purpose: Discovering Our Why
Dr. Stephanie Ellison-Keys, with Georgia Cannon-Alleyne
and Lynnette Steele ................................................................434

Legacies on Lakeshore: A journey of Love, Service, and
Inspiration
Stephanie Steenstra.................................................................442

What's My Why?
Sue Phillips .................................................................................454

My Big Why: A Passion for Uplifting and Healing Others
Dr. (h.c.) Susie Mierzwik.........................................................464

What Is My Why?
Tonya Holley-Powell ................................................................472

Chronicles of a Village Girl from Mathakwaini Village: A
Journey of Resilience and Purpose
HH Amb. Dr. Winfred Wanjiku Gitonga...................................480

Raising the Collective Vibe: Finding the Divine Within
Dr. Zulmara Maria (h.c.) ..........................................................492

# The Power of Purpose: Discovering Your Why

*By Ambassador Dr. Angela Covany (h.c)*

Why? Why do anything?

Why did the good Lord wake you up this morning?

It is because you have purpose. You are blessed beyond measure, and you are the only one who can be you. You bring your own strengths and compassion to the table wherever you go. You bring happiness to rooms where others need a smiling face.

Every person has a story of resilience, strength, and hope that can—and will—inspire others when shared. This life is challenging to navigate. Everyone struggles, no matter how strong we are; life has a way of pulling us down. It is through the sharing of our experiences that we find light. We realize we aren't so different—our struggles are more similar than we think. We are always given lessons and blessings. Through others, we are given hope, guidance, and perspective.

It is through self-reflection and our own inner compass that we find our purpose. I believe your purpose finds you right where you are, with your own set of skills, natural talents, and mindset.

My purpose has always been to be of service to those around me. From childhood, I looked for the silver lining to share with others. I learned to see the glass half full. In my teenage years, I developed an open mind, learning to appreciate the gifts of each day and the treasures hidden in our memories.

My twenties and thirties were filled with the joy of motherhood and marriage. During that time, my "why" centered on being the best mother and wife I could be. Life doesn't come with a blueprint—only wisdom with the awareness and maturity we gain over time.

It was in my forties that I reached a higher understanding of purpose. I'm here to lift others. I'm not perfect—never will be—I am human. For much of my life, I felt the pressure to earn perfect grades, be an excellent chef, and overachieve in all areas. However, as I've grown older, I've learned I don't need to be perfect—I just need to be me.

When we stop trying to be what others expect us to be and start looking at life through the lens of self-worth and confidence, our true path illuminates before us.

I was raised by a mother who taught me the power of words—spoken, written, or sung. She once asked me to research lyrics before singing them, emphasizing integrity and the power in the message. My father believed your word was your bond, and I carry that into everything I do. My children know that if I say I'll do something, I will.

The thoughts you tell yourself become your reality. The way you speak to yourself impacts your life. Words hold incredible value. Your words and actions become your legacy and your lasting imprint.

If you don't like the path you're on—change it. Find your inner strength. Find your purpose. Find your "why."

Today, I have many "why's."

Professionally, I've built a company that offers a platform for others to create legacy through the written word—a legacy that will outlive them. I call it Timeless Legacy.

Personally, I've been blessed with children, grandchildren, and family I treasure daily. They motivate me to wake up each morning with gratitude and ask God for strength to face the day

with a smile and a joyful heart.

I am also blessed with friendships that have become family—so many beautiful souls.

## Amb. Dr. Angela Covany (h.c)

Angela Covany is the CEO/Founder of HAVANA BOOK GROUP PUBLISHERS LLC., a publishing company located in the United States. She currently serves on the Advisory Board of G.S.F.E. She was a former Director of the Global Society for Female Entrepreneurs (G.S.F.E) for the Temecula, California chapter and previously Co-director for Menifee, Ca. She has also been the Director for Ventura and Santa Barbara, California chapters of National Association of Female Executives (N.A.F.E). Both companies serve to empower women personally and professionally to reach their fullest potential. Angela is a #1 Best-selling Author, Artist, Illustrator, and Keynote Speaker. Some of her published works include "Silver Lining Abstracts", a contributing Author of "Entrepreneurial Women of Faith Anthology", "It's All About Showing Up: The Power is in the Asking", Volumes I, II, & III, "Holiday Express", "100 Most Successful Women from around the World", and her self-compiled Anthology entitled, "LOVE YOUR HATERS: How to harness the power of self-love and embrace the peace found in forgiveness", and "Expert World leaders: Reaching beyond Boundaries Volume 2". She has also been a contributing author in several other books. Angela has a passion to help others connect through written and spoken words. Her publishing company allows others to have a platform to help uplift, educate, and build living legacies. She feels a great sense of alignment in combining passion with purpose. From 2016-2022, Angela has been recognized with three Lifetime Achievement Awards by three seated presidents: President Barack Obama, President Joe Biden and President Donald Trump for her dedication to her community. Angela has been awarded by many city and state municipalities, recognizing the efforts has made to help others personally and professionally. Angela has been the recipient of the Most Inspirational People in the World from (SIMA Global Awards 2022) She Inspires Me Award. She has received the International Award "Beautiful Survivors Reaching Beyond Boundaries" from (LOANI) Leaders of All Nations International. She holds an International Lifetime Achievement Awarded in 2022. She has most recently been honored with an Honorary Doctorate Degree in Humanitarianism from (GIA) Global International Alliance for her desire to

continue to be a service driven leader and has been awarded recently with an Ambassadorship all of which she is humbly grateful for receiving.

Contact Information:

WWW.HAVANABOOKGROUP.COM

WWW.HAVANABOOGGROUPPUBLISHER.COM

WWW.HOWTOLOVEYOURHATERS.COM

HAVANABOOKGROUP@MAIL.COM

# Born to Belong: Turning the Mess into a Movement and a Legacy in Motion
### By Dr. Angelica Benavides

Let me be real with you: I used to hate school.

Not dislike. Not tolerate. I hated it.

Why? Because school didn't feel like it was made for me. I was that little brown girl with big dreams and an even bigger family—ten siblings, five boys, five girls, and me smack dab in the middle of all it is me. Born in Mexico but raised in the U.S., I felt like I didn't belong anywhere. I didn't speak the language well, and English felt like a puzzle I wasn't meant to solve. Every classroom reminded me: "You're behind. You're different. You don't fit in."

So, I survived. I smiled when I needed to. I tried not to raise my hand. I walked through the halls silently, wondering if anyone else felt like a ghost in their own story.

And then... life decided to give me the masterclass version of "You think school was tough? Watch this."

Seven years of battling illness. Not a cold. Not a minor hiccup. Cancer. And not the easy, one-and-done kind (is there such a thing?). No, mine came with scars, tubes, hospitals, and a price tag I never saw coming. It came with the loss of three homes, the heartbreak of bankruptcy, and the devastating moment when my husband walked away—with someone else.

I didn't just hit rock bottom—I set up camp there. But something miraculous happened in the rubble. I found **me**.

Or maybe... I built her.

Because that's what we do, isn't it? When life breaks you, you have two choices: stay broken or rebuild bolder.

So, I decided that if I lived through this—and oh, I planned to—I wouldn't live small anymore. I wouldn't shrink to fit into classrooms, relationships, or society's boxes that told me I wasn't enough.

Instead, I would live loud, bold, and on purpose.

So, what's my Big Why?

It's simple. **I refuse to let anyone else feel like they don't belong**. Not in school. Not in life. Not in their calling. I turned my pain into a platform and my struggle into a system that's now helping students, entrepreneurs, and visionaries around the globe write a new story—one where they are the main character, the author, and the movement-maker.

I founded a virtual academy for kids who feel like school isn't for them—because I was that kid. I became a contractor, partnering with educational reformers to transform systems that leave too many behind. And I created a **global book tour and movement** for people ready to tell their story, turn it into a message, and launch it into the world like the fireworks it was meant to be.

But let me tell you something I've learned on this journey:

**I can't do it alone.**

I tried. I really did. But healing, growing, and impacting lives isn't a solo sport. It's a team marathon with glitter, grit, and group chats full of late-night "we got this" pep talks.

So now I recognize others through the **World Impact Icon Certification**—because if you're brave enough to tell your story, you deserve to be honored for it. We don't just hand out certificates—we hand out belief, belonging, and badges of courage.

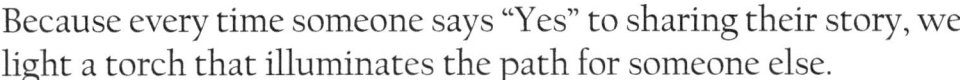

Because every time someone says "Yes" to sharing their story, we light a torch that illuminates the path for someone else.

**So how did I unlock my Big Why?**

Through people. Through showing up.

There's a beautiful phrase I learned from a powerful woman who inspires me deeply—**Ambassador Lady Robbie Motter.** She says, "Just show up." That sounds simple, right? But showing up when life knocks you down, when you're bald from chemo, broke from foreclosure, or bruised from betrayal—that's courage. That's the spark that ignites your purpose.

I've made it my mission to show up—even when I didn't feel ready, even when I didn't have it all figured out. Because every time I did, something magical happened: I connected. I asked questions. I found mentors. I found my people.

I no longer try to figure everything out by myself. When I get stuck, I ask. I research. I explore. I lean into my curiosity and reach out to those who've walked the path before me. That's where the wisdom lives—in community.

Yes, sometimes it's hard. I feel stuck. I struggle. But I don't stay there. I've built a toolbox full of strategies, affirmations, lessons, and truth bombs gathered across the seasons of my life. And I pull those tools out—one by one—when I need to light the way.

One of the biggest shifts I made was learning to ask for help.

For years, I wore my independence like armor. I thought I had to do it all on my own. But that mindset kept me small and exhausted. The truth is, I needed others. And when I finally let them in, I started to soar.

Once I discovered what I was truly passionate about—education, empowerment, and impact—I started building. Little by little, sometimes in baby steps, sometimes in chaotic leaps. Honestly?

It looked messy at first. It felt like I was creating a thousand little projects that didn't connect.

But now I see it clearly. Those "babies" I created? They're all part of the bigger picture. They're my movement in motion. My legacy is rising.

So, if you're still unsure of your Big Why—start showing up. Start asking. Start building. Seed the ideas. Water them with faith. And watch what grows.

Trust your intuition. Trust your purpose. Trust your soul.

And when it gets dark? Grab your flashlight. Pull out the tools. And remember: **You don't have to do this alone.**

**Your mess? It matters.**

Your story, even the parts that hurt to remember, even the chapters you wish you could skip—those are the exact pages someone else needs to read. Not just to relate, but to rise.

You may feel like your world is falling apart, but what if... just what if... it is falling into place?

What if that diagnosis, that divorce, that dark night of the soul isn't the end of your story—but the beginning of your movement?

Here's my truth: I'm passionate about living now. I dance more, laugh louder, and hug tighter. I travel the world not just for the stamps, but for the souls I meet who remind me why I do this. Through my **PowerTalk Live Show**, my **B-Global Magazine**, and every summit and international book fair I attend—I'm not building a brand. I'm building a bridge.

A bridge that connects survivors to speakers. Dreamers to doers. You... to your legacy.

And yes, we have fun while we're at it. Because healing isn't always heavy. Sometimes it's dancing in a pink wig after chemo or laughing through a late-night Zoom call with fellow visionaries. Sometimes it's telling cancer, "You may have taken my hair, but you can't touch my sparkle."

Let's face it—we're not just here to exist. We're here to live well, love boldly, and leave something behind that whispers to the next generation: "You can do this too!"

So, what's my Big Why?

**It's YOU.**

It's every person who's ever felt invisible, unheard, or unworthy. It's every story that's still stuck in someone's throat, waiting for the courage to come out. It's every future leader walking into a classroom thinking, "I don't belong here," and me standing at the door saying, "Yes you do. Let me show you how."

Let me end with this:

If you've been waiting for a sign, this is it.

It's time to turn your story into a spotlight.

Your pain into power.

Your trials into a torch that lights the way for someone else.

I can't do this alone. But together?

We can light up the world.

So, let's become **movers, shakers,** and **world impact makers**— even if we have to crawl some days, take small steps on others, sprint when inspiration strikes, or simply lean on each other to rise.

**Together, let's do this.**

 Because the world is waiting for our light, our love, and our legacy.

Let's rise. Let's roar. Let's impact the world—one story at a time.

## Dr. Angelica Benavides

Dr. Angelica Benavides, also known as Dr. B., is widely recognized as **The Ultimate Legacy Builder**—a global publisher, educator, humanitarian, and visionary leader dedicated to helping others turn their stories into movements that leave a lasting legacy. With over 30 years of experience in education and leadership, Dr. B has devoted her life to empowering individuals, transforming communities, and revolutionizing systems through storytelling, innovation, and collaboration.

She is the founder and CEO of **B-Global Publishing**, the voice behind **PowerTalk Radio**, and the editor-in-chief of B-Global Magazine—platforms that elevate global entrepreneurs, educators, and thought leaders. As the visionary behind the **WOW Women Network**, Director of **GSFE LATINX**, and **Marketing Executive Director and Latin Chairwoman for Leaders of All Nations International**, Dr. B creates spaces where voices are amplified, leadership is cultivated, and global impact is born.

Dr. B is also the **Co-Founder of Educational Luminaries**, a movement committed to revolutionizing education through strategic partnerships, leadership development, and cutting-edge literacy initiatives. Through the Educational Reform initiative, she works with a network of experts across multiple fields to redesign learning systems that meet the needs of today's students and tomorrow's leaders.

Her humanitarian work shines through the **Alive and Beautiful Foundation**, where she uplifts cancer survivors through runway celebrations, mentorship, and entrepreneurial training—turning pain into power and survival into purpose.

In 2025, Dr. B launched a **World Legacy Tour** to help individuals transform their personal stories into published books, brands, and create global movements. Her mission is to help others inspire, lead, and leave an imprint that echoes across generations.

Dr. B is not only a leader—she is a force of transformation, legacy, and global impact.

Contact Dr. Angelica Benavides:

support_staff@drbglobal.net

https://blinq.me/6XdEPTRPdsS5664TXbOI

# My Journey: The Foundation of My "Why"

*By Dr.(h.c.) Angeline Benjamin*

I will never forget the courage it took for my parents to make the life-changing decision to send my sister and me to a foreign country — a place where we had no friends, no relatives, and nothing familiar to hold onto. They sacrificed everything to give us opportunities they never had—to escape racial discrimination and build a life where success was determined not by our background but by our determination and hard work. Their bold decision became the foundation of my "why": to honor their sacrifice by building a life not measured by comfort or convenience, but by resilience, purpose, and the determination to make a meaningful impact.

From an early age, I absorbed the values of resilience, discipline, and ambition from my father, a true entrepreneur who rose from poverty to success through sheer perseverance. He didn't just build a business; he built a mindset — one rooted in self-reliance, calculated risk-taking, and empowerment. His philosophy was simple yet profound: "Teach someone to fish rather than simply provide the fish." He believed true success wasn't just about personal achievement but about helping others become capable and confident in their own journey. He also taught me the importance of finding someone who believes in you, someone who empowers you to reach the next level. Later in life, I came to understand the power of mentorship and coaching through this very lesson.

My parents' sacrifices instilled in me a deep sense of responsibility, not just to succeed, but to honor the opportunities I was given by making a meaningful impact. Their unwavering commitment to our future fueled my drive to pursue excellence, embrace challenges as opportunities, and ultimately, pay it forward by guiding others on their path to success.

This foundation shaped my career, leadership style, and passion for coaching and mentoring. It is why I believe so strongly in empowering others, fostering resilience, and unlocking potential—not by handing out success but by equipping people with the mindset, tools, and confidence to achieve it on their own.

## A Transformational Lesson in Leadership

One of the pivotal moments in my career came when I had to negotiate with a government health official regarding multiple food safety violations. In the past, my instinct might have been to defend my company's practices, justify the missteps, or push back against the concerns raised. But instead, I chose a different approach.

Rather than arguing, I asked: "How can we work together to resolve these issues? What support do you need from us to ensure these problems don't happen again?"

What happened next changed my perspective on leadership forever. The official, initially rigid, and uncompromising, softened. I realized they weren't seeking resistance—they wanted to be heard. They weren't looking for excuses—they wanted solutions. By shifting the conversation from opposition to collaboration, I built trust and found a path forward that benefited everyone.

That experience reinforced a powerful truth: real leadership isn't about enforcing compliance; it's about protecting lives. It's about cultivating a mindset of responsibility, care, and proactive action. When people understand why safety matters—not just as a rule, but as a commitment to the well-being of others—they take true ownership. It's not about following checklists; it's about fostering a culture where every decision is made with awareness and accountability.

This realization ultimately led me to transition from a compliance-focused mindset to coaching and mentoring. I came to understand that real success isn't just about following regulations—it's about fostering a mindset of accountability and purpose that leads to lasting impact. Today, I dedicate myself to helping others create and commit to priorities that bring real value to their lives. Because when we focus on what truly matters, we don't just improve processes—we transform people.

## The Power of Coaching and Paying It Forward

Another defining moment that reinforced my passion for coaching came when a restaurant manager I mentored faced a crisis. After months of working together, the manager fully embraced the principles of instilling a proactive mindset around food safety and risk management. That commitment was tested when a customer filed a serious complaint, claiming they had fallen gravely ill after dining at the restaurant.

Rather than reacting with fear or defensiveness, the manager took decisive, ethical action. Instead of waiting for an investigation to be forced upon them, they proactively contacted health officials, inviting them to review the case. Because the restaurant had a strong history of excellence, with consistently high inspection scores and a track record of addressing potential risks before they escalated, the officials expanded their investigation beyond the restaurant.

In the end, their findings revealed that the illness had not originated from the restaurant at all. Instead, it was traced back to the customer's home, where cross-contamination had occurred due to a pet known to carry harmful bacteria.

This experience reaffirmed my conviction in the value of coaching. It proved that authentic leadership is not about avoiding problems but about taking ownership, acting with integrity, and fostering a culture of accountability. Seeing the impact of coaching firsthand and how it empowered leaders to respond with confidence rather than fear solidified my decision to dedicate myself to mentoring others. It's not just about policies or procedures—it's about equipping people with the mindset and skills to navigate challenges with clarity, responsibility, and purpose.

## The Unexpected Start of My Coaching Career

After retiring from my corporate career, I was surprised to receive calls from franchisees I had once helped through difficult times. They didn't know I had retired—they assumed I had been laid off and wanted to offer me support, referrals, and job opportunities. I was deeply touched by their kindness. When I explained that I had retired and was transitioning into entrepreneurship with my husband, they respected my decision.

Then, two former operations managers, who had since moved to a new company, reached out, asking if they could hire me as a consultant to coach their team and establish a Quality Assurance department. My plan was to build my consulting business in the future, but I had not expected it to happen so soon. Before I even had the chance to promote my business, I had two contracts— both offering more flexibility and compensation than I had imagined.

Most importantly, I realized this was what I truly loved—

coaching others to achieve their goals.

## Finding My Calling

This clarity deepened when I took the Gallup StrengthsFinder assessment. The results, along with two other core values and personality assessments, confirmed what I had always known deep down—coaching, mentoring, and helping others grow is not just something I enjoy; it is my calling. It is in my DNA.

My calling is not about providing therapy or sympathy for those who need my coaching or mentorship. My goal is to empower them, provide them with the skills they need to achieve their goals, and show them the raw talents they possess, which can help them believe in themselves and gain the confidence to achieve almost anything they want to do. I often asked them: "Are you willing to invest yourself and do the work required to achieve the goal you set?"

The impact I strive to have on those I mentor extends beyond their personal success. My greatest hope is that they, too, will pay it forward. I have been blessed with incredible mentors and coaches who have guided me to where I am today, and I want to continue that cycle of growth and empowerment. If those I mentor take what they've learned and, in turn, guide and uplift others, the ripple effect of positive change will extend far beyond what I can do alone.

## The Challenge of Shifting Mindsets

One of the greatest challenges I've faced as a mentor is helping aspiring entrepreneurs shift from an employee mindset to an entrepreneurial one. Many people dream of starting their own business, but they struggle to break free from the security-driven mindset they've been conditioned to follow. They expect clear instructions, immediate results, and a safety net—but entrepreneurship requires risk-taking, self-motivation, and resilience in the face of uncertainty.

The shift from employee to entrepreneur is not just about starting a business—it's about rewiring how you think. It requires prioritizing long-term vision over short-term security, embracing failure as a natural part of the journey, and developing the discipline to execute effectively without external pressure. No one can make this shift for you; it is a decision you must make for yourself.

## The Legacy of Servant Leadership

My "why" and deep purpose for coaching and mentoring stem from my greatest mentor and coach, **Lady Amb. Dr. Robbie Motter, (h.c.)** She ignited my passion for leadership, fueled my desire to empower others, and, most importantly, led by example. Even at 89 years old, she continues to dedicate her life to serving others, embodying the true essence of a servant leader.

A **servant leader** does not seek leadership for personal gain, recognition, or power. Instead, their purpose is rooted in uplifting and empowering others. In a world where leadership is often measured by the number of followers one has, the titles they hold, or the accolades they receive, servant leadership challenges that notion. True leadership is not about standing in the spotlight—it is about using that light to illuminate the path for others. It is not about the size of one's audience but the depth of one's impact. Servant leaders measure success not by their own achievements but by the number of people they help rise, by the confidence they instill in others, and by the empowerment they provide.

The most profound leaders do not create a culture of dependency where people constantly seek guidance; instead, they build **self-reliant, strong, and confident individuals** who can navigate challenges independently. They equip people with the mindset, skills, and confidence to step forward and make a difference, not just in their own lives, but in the lives of others. A servant leader sees the potential in someone before they see it in themselves and nurtures that growth until they no longer need guidance—they stand strong on their own. This ripple effect creates a cycle of empowerment where those who have been lifted go on to uplift others.

Lady Amb. Dr. Robbie Motter exemplifies this philosophy in everything she does. She does not seek recognition for herself; instead, she dedicates her time to finding and elevating those who deserve recognition but may lack the confidence to step forward. She has built a lifetime legacy of helping others rise— ensuring that their work, achievements, and contributions are acknowledged. She understands that true influence does not come from accumulating awards or being in the limelight; it comes from the number of lives you change, the number of people you empower, and **the number of individuals who walk away stronger and more self-assured because of your leadership**.

In today's society, many leaders focus on competition—on getting ahead, surpassing others, and securing their own position. Servant leadership challenges this mindset and asks us to shift our focus from personal success to collective success. It is about lifting others as we rise, using our influence to create opportunities for those who need them most, and leading with purpose rather than ego. Servant leadership is not about creating followers; it is about creating more leaders. The most extraordinary impact a leader can have is not in how many people listen to them but in how many people they inspire to take action and step into their own greatness.

This is the kind of leadership that has left a lasting mark on my life. It is the kind of leadership I strive to embody every day. Inspired by Lady Amb. Dr. Robbie Motter, guided by the wisdom of my parents, has helped me understand that **true leadership is not about power**; it is about responsibility. It is about having the courage to serve, the humility to listen, and the commitment to invest in others' growth. The legacy of a servant leader is not written in trophies, titles, or applause—it is written in the lives they have changed, in the confidence they have instilled in others, and in the leaders they have helped create.

## Conclusion: My Ongoing Journey

This is why I continue to be a mentor and coach. This is my "why." I am a work in progress — always learning, always growing — and I embrace this journey with humility and gratitude. Leadership is not about perfection; it's about purpose, presence, and the impact we leave behind.

As you finish reading my story, I encourage you to reflect on your own journey. What challenges have shaped you? What strengths lie within you, waiting to be shared? And most importantly, what is your "why"?

Your journey is not just your own; it's part of a larger purpose. When you live your "why," you don't just change your life — you inspire others to discover theirs.

"Your journey shapes your purpose — and every challenge becomes a steppingstone toward who you are meant to be."

## About Dr. Angeline Benjamin (h.c.)

Dr. Angeline Benjamin (h.c.) is a global Motivational Speaker, Author, and Action Coach known for delivering powerful messages on personal development, cultural diversity, confidence building, and strategic goal setting. With a heart for mentoring and inspiring others, Angeline is committed to helping individuals transform their lives and achieve meaningful success.

She is the author of "Life Lessons Leading to Success" and a contributing author to multiple impactful books, including "It's All About Showing Up and the Power Is in the Asking," "Voices of Peace," and four other collaborative works.

Angeline has been honored globally for her leadership and humanitarian work. Her numerous accolades include:

- "The Most Inspirational People of the World Award" (2022)
- "Global Award for Influential Women – Reaching Beyond Boundaries" (2022)
- Perpetual Award: "SIMA Global Wall Street Robbie Motter Award" (2022)
- Honorary Doctorate in Humanitarianism Degree (2022)
- "Ambassador of Happiness" (2023)
- Honorary Humanitarian Certificate of recognition from the California State Assembly and Congress (2024)
- "International Peace Ambassador," "International Peace Leader," and "Coach of the Year" (2024)
- "Legacy of Excellence Award" (2025)
- She currently serves as a **Board Member and Director** of the Virtual Thursday Network for GSFE (Global Society for Female Entrepreneurs).
- Dr. Angeline Benjamin is available for **public speaking, one-on-one coaching, and group coaching sessions.** Her mission is clear: Show up, take action, and make a difference.

## Contact Information

Amb Dr. Angeline Benjamin (h.c.)

Action Coach with Results

Director - GSFE Virtual Thursday Network

Email: albenjamin.bb27@gmail.com

LinkedIn: www.linkedIn.com/in/angelinebenjamin

Facebook: www.facebook.com/angelinebenjamin.1

# WHY? YOU CAN'T' DIE WITH THE MUSIC INSIDE YOU!!!

*By Angeline Joji*

*A series of WHY questions opened the doors of possibilities leading to self-development, enriching, and transforming the lives of others, seeing beauty in the dark, thrusting into conscious living and a purpose driven life, and finally realizing the meaning of Life to meet with the Ultimate and the Infinite.*

*Joji*

## MISS WHY

Ever since I could remember, I have always been asking questions that start with Why. As a matter of fact, at 4 years old I was called "Miss WHY" because I always liked to talk to grown up adults and ask questions such as. "Why can't the sun shine in the evening." My caretaker vividly remembered all my questions, "Why is it that the stars are far away?" "Why did God plan and design it that way?" It was never ending because the first question turned into another WHY question, and then another, and then another. I am forever grateful for my caretaker who was very patient with me and always encouraged me to do my very best, to be the best version I could be and to excel in all that I did. She always helped me to reach my goals confidently.

## WHY TAKE PIANO LESSONS?

When I was 7 years old, I was sent to piano lessons. I asked my mother why I have to take piano lessons. She answered, "So you can learn how to play the piano, it will also teach you discipline!" I asked the question, "What is discipline and why do I have to learn discipline?" My educator Mom gave me a million reasons and eventually in a graceful but authoritarian voice said, "Just do what I say because I said so!" With encouragement from my big sister who was already playing advanced music, and inspiration from my two hobbyist pianist aunts from both sides of the family, I took piano lessons from Grade 1, non-stop, all the way to senior high school. I was reluctant and rebellious, but I did it anyway.

I had some learning challenges because of the multiple languages and alphabets I was learning at the same time. My father used bribery or carrot dangling along with the German Benedictine Nuns' stick, which certainly did the trick. I received many awards and recognition at school for my success. Like all parents, they took pride in my accomplishments while I was being trained to be disciplined, determined, dedicated, resilient and even to dream big!

## WHY DID I TAKE PSYCHOLOGY?

After I graduated High school, I was shoveled to the University to take up Psychology. After two summers and two semesters of Psychology studies, a traumatic incident led me to question my career path. I had to fulfill a requirement in our Abnormal Psychology class by visiting a mental hospital. I was greeted by a good-looking guy who said, "Hello, I am Jesus Christ, what's your name?" With consternation and a scared mind, I asked, "Why am I here and why am I taking this course?" I went straight to church, and I prayed hard on how to tell my parents that psychology was not for me. I knew I had to finish a degree because that was their requirement, whether I liked it or not, the same as taking piano lessons like my other sisters.

## WHY AND HOW "JESUS CHRIST" PUSHED ME?

A few days after the horrifying incident at the mental hospital, I heard the Fate Symphony playing in the background and it was as if my prayers were answered. I was informed that a Music Scholarship in a prestigious school was being offered to students with a high scholastic background and who had advanced piano performance level skills. I facetiously took the three-day Scholarship Exam, Interview and Audition with no expectations. I took it for the heck of it and tested if my brain was still working after having been traumatized by "Jesus Christ." To my great shock, I was notified that I got the full scholarship. Yes, God has a good sense of humor!

## WHY ME?

I was baffled by why I was chosen among all the other hundreds of students from all over the country who vied for it. Somehow I knew I was an extraordinary kid because I always did extra and was diligent with my studies. I became extraordinary! Thanks to Dad's Bribery Scheme.

Things happened for a reason. This particular stage was actually a preparation and was steering my way towards my life's purpose: to play a specific role in God's Orchestral Symphony for a more beautiful world. I was being called to nurture young children's brains, hearts, and souls through music!

## WHY CROSS THE HIGH SEAS AND EXPAND?

Fate Symphony was still playing and even louder. I was given an opportunity to teach in a school in Brisbane, Australia while pursuing Advanced Piano Performance Studies and Specializing in Piano Pedagogy at the Music Conservatory. I hit a jackpot as

I was mentored by a professor who was one degree away from one of the top pianists in the world of the 20th century and was known to have produced students who won at International Piano Competitions.

Finally, my erroneous technique and bad habits were corrected, and it resulted in me performing at a World Event. My prayer and desire to teach better and touch children's lives through music was answered when I met an iconic figure in the Music Education world, and I was impressed and convinced to specialize in the Mother Tongue Approach Pedagogy under the initial tutelage of the co-founder and co-author of the Methodology. This resulted in a high rate of success in my music teaching. As a matter of fact, my students were winning in piano competitions, getting honors in Music Exams, and even performing in a World event.

## WHY THINGS HAPPENED?

Amid a personal crisis, I was invited by my Aunt and Uncle, whom I considered my second parents, to join them on a tour of the USA. Coincidentally, I was already scheduled to be in the USA to attend a seminar. Right after that I was planning to extend my stay for my own personal vacation. Perfect timing! Somehow, someone out there arranged this whole event because it was perfect timing to meet and join my relatives. We had a wonderful time visiting different states, sightseeing, and participating in other tourist escapades.

## WHY FLORIDA?

Our last stop in our USA tour was Florida. I was already scheduled to leave the USA, but by chance, at a music store, I crossed paths with a Music Director looking for an Accompanist and Pianist for a Professional Ballet Company headed by an ex-Russian Ballet Master and Premier Dancer from a world-famous European Ballet company. I was invited for an audition. Just for fun! Against all odds, I was given this incredible opportunity. I got the job! They offered me the position and sponsored my work in the USA.

## WHY I QUIT THE POSITION AS ACCOMPANIST AND PIANIST?

At the beginning, the seemingly glamorous but grueling position as the pianist for the Ballet was fun, enjoyable, and challenging. It expanded my experience as a musician and helped me grow in my practice and discipline. However, after a while, I felt unnurtured and was simply feeling a melodic metronome. I knew it was time to move on and go back to my love for teaching young children wherein I felt joy and fulfillment with the innocents. I was being called to fulfill my purpose, my deepest WHY.

## WHY CREATE?

Every artist, every woman has the desire to create something to call their own. Since I don't have a child, I have a longing to create something for myself and my own satisfaction. I put together a Music Education program to introduce children to music in a natural, fun, playful and creative way with cute musical animal characters that they could identify with and learn from. This creation came to me at various times in my life and I knew I had to do it. It was part of my purpose, part of my deeper WHY: to nurture young children's brains, hearts, and souls through music!

# WHY REACH OUT TO THE BUSINESS WORLD?

As a child, I struggled to learn music. I had no joy in just learning to identify the notes on the lines and spaces and interpret it with my fingers twinkling on the keys. I had greater success with my own students with the program I had created. I wanted to learn how to put my materials together and be marketable to other teachers and parents around the country and even around the world so that they could avail themselves of what my students were enjoying. Hence, I attended a Business Forum and Training put together by an exclusive Entrepreneurs Club. I learned the business aspect of the program I had created such as intellectual property protection, capital raising, implementation, marketing etc.

At the Forum, I met the Founder and Chairman of the Business Entrepreneur's Club. After hearing my original music composition and seeing the Music Program, the distinguished gentleman in a three-piece suit with salt and pepper hair and piercing blue eyes looked at me and said in a determinative voice, "YOU CAN'T DIE WITH THE MUSIC INSIDE YOU!" After this encounter, I went to the lecture room for his Super Teaching Technology and Classroom wherein his message was reinforced. There was something about what he said and how he said it that touched my soul, deeply and profoundly. Those words would stay with me and guide me for the rest of my life.

# WHY I GOT INTO AN ACCIDENT?

Accidents happen for a reason. Amidst putting together my music program, I got into a hit and run car accident where I was thrown in a projectile fashion onto a slope as I was coming off from a high bridge. My car triple flipped, hit the tree, the tree fell down, and my sports car was totaled. As I was being rescued, I heard a panicking voice, "Is she still alive?" Once again, I heard the voice of that distinguished gentleman who said, "YOU CAN'T DIE WITH THE MUSIC INSIDE YOU!" Miraculously, I survived with minor bruises and fractures.

## WHY MOVE TO CALIFORNIA?

It is said that Southern California is where dreams come true. I had the opportunity to move, and house sit a newly retired executive friend's mansion while they were on a globe-trotting adventure. I took this opportunity to be in a place where I could work on my program and put what I learned at the Entrepreneurs Club into practice. I would take the time I needed to house sit and get my music program ready for the world market.

## WHY HEALTH CHALLENGES?

While working to get my Music Program completed and ready for the market, I was brought to a screeching halt  by a disease I never expected to have nor suspected I had. I was diagnosed with an advanced stage of ovarian cancer. I had major surgery for ten hours and was hospitalized for over a month. I had radiation and chemotherapy for six months and then my doctor still wanted me to have twelve more months of chemo. The side effects of the toxic chemicals made me forget how to read musical notes, blurred my brain, and made me so sick to vomit up there and down there. My chemo friends and buddies were dying one by one. I knew if I stayed this course, I would be one of the casualties as well.

I had no choice but to try to escape and figure out a different route for healing. The  conventional medicine strategy was not working for me. I signed that medical waiver with earth shaking knees, the most difficult document I ever had to sign. Yes, I kept on hearing the voice, "YOU CAN'T DIE WITH THE MUSIC INSIDE YOU! YOU ARE NOT DONE!" like a broken record. I kept on hearing it until it hurt my ears! "YOU CAN'T DIE WITH THE MUSIC INSIDE YOU! YOU ARE NOT DONE!"

## WHY EXPERIENCE DARKNESS?

It was in the darkest and coldest nights of my soul that I discovered who my real friends were. I did not have a lot of friends, but the few friends I had were there for me. I experienced the compassionate beauty of friends and strangers who would become friends. Yes, the real ones glow in the dark! I began really appreciating more about the meaning of life, and my purpose here on earth, and my deepest WHY. As one gets stripped and robbed of everything, it becomes a very humbling experience. Having relinquished all material things makes one focus and realize what is really important in life or what matters the most. Because in order to survive the darkest and coldest night of the soul, you have to have a reason, a purpose, a deep WHY.

## WHY SURVIVE?

Once again, I heard the full symphonic sound, "YOU ARE NOT DONE YET. YOU CAN'T DIE WITH THE MUSIC INSIDE YOU!" And this I knew was my deepest WHY...I had music inside of me that could not die, I had passion inside of me that had to be released, I had a deeper purpose that needed to be fulfilled.

## CONCLUSION

Each and every one of us has a purpose and has a place in this divine Creation of Things. Just like the Great Music Master's Symphonic work, each one of us has an assigned instrument to play and role for the Great Symphonic Work of Creation.

**YOU CAN'T DIE WITH THE MUSIC INSIDE YOU** may be taken literally or figuratively. The Music inside our souls are the Dreams with which we all are gifted. Those gifts are connected to our talents and abilities that are especially given for a Purpose and a Reason to display God's beauty. It is revealed so it can be shared with others: to be enjoyed, to propel human development and evolution, to make a difference in the lives of many. And one can't help but be put to awe and wonder of the magnificence of God's existence as we live out our deepest WHY!

## Angeline Joji

Angeline Joji is my stage name in honor of my mother's assistant in taking good care of me for years while I was growing up who used to call me "My Little Angel" despite that I was a little devil. I owe a lot of my accomplishments from her loving and nurturing energies. My parents picked Joji from Filipina Prima Ballerina named Joji Felix. I was sent to Piano lessons at 7 years old all the way till finishing high school. Ironically, I became the Pianist and Accompanist for Sarasota Ballet in Florida.

Deep inside me I am a Music Educator, a nurturer of the young and impressionable innocents. As a youngster, I had tyrant piano teachers and it challenged me to figure out how to teach music in a natural, fun, easy and enjoyable way. After college, I studied multifarious music education approaches, methodologies and philosophy but finally impressed and specialized in the Mother Tongue Approach pedagogy designed and authored by Dr. Shinichi Suzuki and Dr. Haruko Kataoka, wherein the latter had initially mentored me among some other notable world class teachers.

My success as a Classical Pianist and Music Educator had been paled when juxtaposed to surviving advanced stage ovarian cancer, as one of the 2% survivors in this type and stage of cancer and only survivor among my chemo buddies. I think my accomplishment as a musician had been jaded because as a musician, I was mentored and guided by experts with well-structured methodology, whereas, the other achievement - I was alone facing the lonely cancer battlefield. It was my own initiative. picking ideas from alternative practitioners of Ayurveda, Chinese, Korean and other natural therapies and embracing the Hippocratic philosophy on "Let food be thy medicine and medicine be thy food."

I knew that my Life Purpose has something to do with music, and children since Music Conservatory days. With the cancer episode, I used my musicianship skills to help fundraise for a women Cancer group as a pay forward.

My fascination with music education extended to studying with Dr. Masaru Emoto whose breakthrough discovery on water crystal phenomena has a lot to do with vibrations including music.

With decades of music teaching, I have developed a Music Education Program that is designed to introduce music the way I ideally envisioned it to be - natural and playful at the same time introducing my original compositions into the children's music world applying my knowledge in psychology and neuroscience.

It is a blessing, great honor, privilege, and pleasure to continue my Life Mission in making a difference to the world by nurturing young children's brains, hearts, and souls through music, hence I will be releasing my music CDs and children's books next year. With full conviction, I could say Music Education is not merely an enrichment and entertainment program but can be viewed as a tool and companion in children's life journeys. No doubt it has the potential to create pathways that go beyond music as proven by my former piano students who are now practicing professionals in various fields such as in medicine, education, law, accountancy, engineering, film, architecture, acting etc.

It is my dream to see a more wonderful world inhabited by people who know how to communicate and truly appreciate the beautiful language of their souls- MUSIC!

**Contact information:**

website: Jojiangeline.com

Email: jojipianist@yahoo.com Phone:(1) 626-375-5336

Facebook: Angeline Joji LinkedIn: Angeline Joji

# Understanding Why I've Made Some of The Choices and Decisions I've Made in my Life.

*By Barbara A. Berg, L.C.S.W.*

I wasn't going to write a chapter for this book, "What is My Why?," because I was telling myself and others, I am too busy to write right now. (The truth is this is actually a very important book for me to participate in; and frankly, along with all the other books put out through GSFE and Havana Book Group, LLC, an important opportunity to dig further inside.) I do believe that gives me a deeper understanding of myself and how I tick. And hopefully, some of what is written here will also be useful to others.

Until last night, before I went to bed, my conscious mind was all "set-up" to stick with my decision to not write a chapter here. However, my dear inside "friend" and part of my real Self I believe, "Madam Honest Babs," came through with flying colors to not let me miss an important experience my life was supposed to have. So, she gave me two very eye opening and direct dreams that made me jump up in bed early in the morning and immediately start writing. And so, I did.

Interestingly, I found myself beginning this chapter by mentioning that this week, I came up to Lake Tahoe, for what initially felt like the millionth time, with my husband. Now I generally enjoy going away with him, especially when we are traveling to new places or are doing something that is truly fun and unusual.

And I generally have a great time coming up to the mountains and enjoying Lake Tahoe. However, this time we weren't skiing like we usually do, and while I loved taking gaggles of pictures of trees, amazing clouds, and the Lake, something was missing inside, and that I was truly (dare I say it?) BORED!

But oddly enough, I didn't put my finger on it until I woke up from those two dreams I just mentioned, and realized it was as if those dreams had kicked me in the teeth and said, "WAKE UP BARBARA! You're whiling your life away, when you know you need to keep writing and doing more things that follow your true inner passion and truly matter to you! So, I got to work and began writing. And then, the trip to Lake Tahoe this time began to get a lot better!

And interestingly, from recognizing the powerful difference it is making in my life already in terms of whether or not I will actually write this particular chapter in this book, it is becoming more and more clear to me that, whether we realize it or not, EVERY TIME we say "Yes" or "No" to something, we are actually determining in some way, how our lives will go in the long run in some way. And this is especially true when you or I make the same sort of choice or decision over and over again.

In fact, which is so whether we are choosing to drink a sugary soft drink on a regular basis or water. And it is so when you or I may be considering how far we will go in our education, whether or not we will stay in a job we don't like, or whether or not to become entrepreneurs. It's not just "the big" Landmark moments that count, but it is everything that goes on in the course of a day or an hour. Every move you make either takes you away from your true Self or it brings you closer. Moment to moment.

And, to add to the interesting part of it all, even before you or I even make a move to say "Yes" or "No" to the outside world, we are actually conducting inner negotiations between different parts of ourselves before we even say or do anything to another person or conduct some action in our lives. So, when someone makes the decree to "Be true to yourself," how aware are we of what intricate parts are actually inside us at any given time, which contribute to this "Self" phenomenon we supposedly have? What if, after all is said and done, WHO we actually ARE is ultimately an accumulation of what we have said "Yes" to and what we have said "No" to over the course of an entire lifetime?

While I have always sort of known this to some degree, it wasn't until I began to read "You are The One You've Been Waiting For" by Richard C. Schwartz, that I came to see part of the reason I have come to make some  choices and decisions in my life that didn't always turn out to go very well or go very easily at some stage of the game, was that a number of my various parts inside me conflicted with other parts of mine to the degree that if I did something that would satisfy one part of me, another part of me would be thrown off or be put into fear about what I had done. So, on my next move, on the "game board of life," I would then feel compelled to counteract that last action and pull back and go in another direction.

Looking back, I do vividly remember hearing my wonderful agent at the time, who got my second book, "How to Escape The No-Win Trap" published by McGraw-Hill in 2004, say during a phone call to me in a very nice and caring voice, "Sometimes you're with us Barbara, and sometimes you're not." I now get that while I feel pleased overall with what I have accomplished in my life thus far, and who I am for the most part, I could have made my life a lot smoother for myself and others if I better understood the "mechanism"  of what turned on the light for me to move ahead at times in my life, and what seemed to hold me back. I do believe some of the insights I'm receiving so far writing this chapter have helped me already in being more aware of when I seem to be approaching some inner conflict and when life feels like "smooth sailing ahead."

Interestingly, Richard C. Schwartz, the author of the above-mentioned book I just started reading, was the developer of the concept of Internal Family Systems SM, (IFS), which has influenced a lot of the psychotherapy world since the 1980's. His work points out quite realistically how different parts of our personalities are developed and shaped by how we learned to engage in our early life interactions and onward. These early interactions directly influence how we operate in our lives as adults.

Almost the second I started reading this book, (which I happened to choose to take on this particular trip to Lake Tahoe), I could truly identify and feel inside myself how some of my own ongoing conflict in my life has been so greatly run by at least two conflicting parts inside myself. They could sometimes get along but could also run into each other depending on the situation as if a war were happening. In fact, at times it has felt as if there was no way they could happily co-exist for any real length of time.

The first part (and actually my favorite) is that side of me who loves and greatly enjoys just "throwing myself out into throngs of people" to speak and perform and interact in real and genuinely fun, close, and insightful ways. Thankfully, being a member of GSFE (Global Society for Female Entrepreneurs) with our amazing Leader and Founder, Lady Dr. Robbie Motter (h.c.) at the helm, has given me just that! I have thoroughly enjoyed each and every gathering, meeting, and event whether I was the one standing up and expressing myself in some way, or another member or entertainer was.)

On the other hand, is another part of me who has (at least up until now), been afraid of feeling "over-exposed" and being put in some horrifically compromising position if I shared too much

about myself and went overboard in some way.

And then, just as I noticed two parts of me that can be at odds with one another, a third piece of what has appeared to be a part of me popped into my head. I do know this has at times interfered with my making choices and decisions and taking actions that were really right for me.

 However, I had never really fully taken it in until right now. It felt as if it was projected into me through my mother, Marie Ina Mackay Cowan, born in Brooklyn, New York in 1916.

She had graduated from Julliard, the renowned school of music in New York City, had an amazing music career, directed a number of well-developed choirs at The Brick Church, and was working on her Ph.D. at Union Seminary which is now part of Columbia University in NYC- when.... she met the man who would become my father two years later. Enter- Milton Howard Cowan, Full professor at Rutgers University School of Agriculture, Middlesex County Agent of Agriculture, "Back Door Man" in New Jersey politics, and "Man of The People" (according to him), with a beloved radio show about growing plants in your backyard that played the song, "I Beg Your Pardon, I never Promised You a Rose Garden" right before he came on the air every week.(I did like the radio part the best.)

To hear my mother tell the story, she was already 36 years old at the time they met. They married soon after, and she was convinced she had reached "the ripe old age" where she'd do better to be under some "safe" man's roof than "stay out on a limb on her own." And- (that's right folks), she gave up her wonderful and glowing career which demonstrated even  greater promise in the future- to become what she later had referred to herself as "My Husband's 'Sit Beside Me Woman'". Marie got pregnant one year later-AND....had me.

Now you might be wondering why I'm carrying on about all this. But I do promise it will begin to make sense when I tell you HOW that third part of my personality seemed to have come into being, which I mentioned earlier and has greatly affected how I have come to make some choices and decisions that have not reflected the "best me" I could be.

So, with no further ado, and moving right along with this treatise, I will get to the next part.

Right about the time I had become somewhere between the ages of 2 and 3 years old, it apparently became quite clear to both my parents that within the hubbub of meeting, marrying, moving to a new home, and having a baby; after stepping out of the seductive fumes of quickly going along the path of the growing "Post Second World War American Dream", both Milton and Marie must have gotten out of bed one day and realized this whole thing they had put together was at least somewhat of a sham. It was more a marriage between two resumes than a budding family with their first child together, oooohing and aaaahing over their dear baby girl.

My father went on to further engage in his first love - his career, and my mother was left alone to her own devises, to contend with a screaming child she had no real use for, (me), and most likely cried all day long, missing her beloved New York City and multiple choirs.

However, not to be stopped in her tracks for long, my ingenious mother still had hope. She got ahold of an aging upright Knabe piano, and had some gracious neighborhood boy help her get it into the musty basement of the "new home" my father had recently bought for $18,000.

The idea I got about it all was that if my mother could direct children before, she could direct her own daughter even better now- all the way to becoming some sort of piano playing maestro by the age of 11 years old. So, with no further ado, and no understanding about the developmental needs of a budding 3-year-old girl, hyper-focused mommy had me playing for what seemed like 8 hours a day. Never mind the fact that I couldn't sit still very long, and my mother would tell me I was "Shpilkes," which is Yiddish for "you have ants in your pants!"

However, my mother was determined for me to keep going! And at some stage of the game, she had me take lessons right after school, (she did let me go there ),from some professor of music at Douglass College, (the Women's College of Rutgers University), and where I later attended as a college student.)

Now, this all might have gone along to my mother's heart's content just fine. Except for one thing. I HATED EVERY SECOND OF IT. And the only way I got through all this was when I got tired of practicing the piano ad nauseam, I pulled out this board game called Carrom, that my mother picked up at a thrift store, and flicked some red and green little wooden circles into the corner pockets to my heart's content.

In fact, I enjoyed it so much that by the time I was ten, I demanded to play less and less piano, and went across the street to play Monopoly with the neighbor kids. By the time I was 11 years old, I quit playing piano altogether! While this didn't go well, to say the least, with my overwrought mother, I finally felt some freedom for what felt like the first time in my life, (except for the times I could attend Girl Scouts and did go to Camp Sacajawea one week a year).

Now, what all this "being stuck in a basement playing piano all day long at too early an age did for that ornery third part of my personality, was that it set me up later in life to be constantly on the lookout for whether or not I could become entrapped in a situation in some way and not be able to escape! Even if an opportunity were the best thing for me, if I thought it would present obstacles to overcome or lower options I thought might come along on the horizon, there have been times when I have bowed out of some things I had wished I had looked into further.

However, at this point, I can see more clearly, to be more aware of this and not be so quick to say "No" or cut something short without taking a really good look at something. But I must say, overall looking back at my life, there have been times when it really seemed like Angels have been right nearby, and said "Barbara, this opportunity really is a good one for you, and we're going to create a situation where you will get involved with this and come to know this was meant just for you!- However, going forward, I'll stop' look, and listen more- and take more time going inside to see if something is right or wrong for me!

Rockefeller Center
New York
20

May 22, 1945

Dear Miss Mackay:

Mrs. Rockefeller and I attended the Brick Church in its new location for the first time on Sunday, May 13th. We heard the youth choir sing the anthem which you had written and which you conducted. The words of this anthem are as beautiful as the music. The children sang it as I have never heard a children's choir sing, with a volume, a variety of expression and a maturity of execution such as I would not have thought possible with a group of that age.

I write to tell you how greatly Mrs. Rockefeller and I enjoyed this anthem and how warmly we congratulate you as its composer and also as the Director of this unusual choir.

If the anthem has been published, I would be glad to know where it can be bought for I would like to send copies of it to several churches which we attend in various parts of the country where there are youth choirs. I cannot speak too warmly of this lovely anthem and of what you have done with your choir.

Very sincerely,

John D. Rockefeller Jr.

Miss Marie Lee Mackay, Director
Youth and Young People's Choirs
The Brick Church
Park Avenue & 91st Street, New York City

*Reflecting on a heartfelt letter from John D. Rockefeller Jr. to my mother in 1945, praising an anthem she composed at just 29 years old for her incredible children's choir. He inquired if it was published, but it wasn't until her seventy's that she gathered the courage to pursue it. Sadly, the publisher deemed it 'too sophisticated' for today's children's choirs. I can't help but think that if she had the support of an organization like GSFE, her extraordinary anthem might have found its place in the world much sooner!*

# Barbara A. Berg, L.C.S.W.

Barbara A. Berg is a licensed Clinical Social Worker. She has conducted psychotherapy for over 30 years, serving individuals, couples, children, and families across Southern California. Inspired by her early life experiences within a family of brilliant but emotionally complex individuals, she developed a deep passion for helping others navigate emotional and psychological challenges.

Barbara earned her License in Social Work in the State of California, got her Masters Degree in Social Work at Virginia Commonwealth University, and built a distinguished career as a psychotherapist with Haven Psychological Associates. There, she worked from 1992 until 2020. During her tenure there, along with psychotherapy services, she was also a critical resource during times of crisis, including robberies, shootings, and workplace related serious incidents. She conducted over 1,000 Critical Incident Stress Debriefings for those affected by traumatic events. Since July of 2020, Ms. Berg has continued these activities while in her own practice in Claremont.

Throughout her career, Barbara's compassionate and empathetic approach made her a trusted guide for clients seeking healing and personal growth. Her work has been marked by her ability to support others through complex emotional issues with understanding, professionalism, and care. She has written 4 Self Help books of her own, conducted over seven hundred workshops and Keynote speeches, and has been a guest on over 700 TV, radio, and Internet shows in addition to collaborating on a number of anthologies produced through GSFE and the Havana Book Group LLC.

Today, Barbara continues to inspire others through her commitment to mental health advocacy, resilience, and her belief in the power of early intervention and compassionate support.

# Natural Self-Discovery and
# The Road to Finding Your Why
*By Belinda Foster*

Life is a process of self-discovery every single day. Every single moment. Just as flowers blossom from a bud, so do we blossom in our engagement with one another. Our social interactions are not superficial in nature. As we interact in society in our relationships with one another, there is a unique strategy of why we interact and give as we do.

Have you ever asked yourself, why do I do all that I do? You don't say it aloud. Rather, the answer stays in the position of an internal thought that fuels our daily choices. It may be a scenario of you sitting in a movie theater watching a film that you don't like but doing so because you want to be a good friend. A selfless act of kindness. Another scenario is a man walking down Hollywood Boulevard in the daytime hoping that a TV producer will discover him as an actor. Even simple things like writing a text to a friend. We engage in actions for distinct reasons whether we are aware of it or not. There is always a purpose that motivates us to do what we do. And that purpose is what we are here to discover and manifest.

I recently had lunch with a friend of mine who introduced me to a friend of hers who had flown into LAX from Brussels, Germany. The woman had a very thick accent and spoke no English. Even though we were not able to communicate with the English language, we found ourselves having a conversation with each other through the use of photos and visuals.

While waiting for a table sitting in the lobby, she picked up a magazine in the waiting area and started from the back turning the pages left to right. She was looking puzzled. I showed her the front of the magazine, and she smiled. She realized then the magazine read from right to left.

There was a nice bouquet of flowers on the table where we were seated. I noticed how she smiled at them. I knew from that moment that she loved white roses as much as I did.

The waiter brought two bottles of apple juice in glass bottles and fruit punch in two other bottles. The waiter came back and sat on the table tall drinking glasses filled with cubes of ice. In that moment, the nice lady smiled. She held up her hand as to say, "Wait a moment." She poured in each glass a little apple juice, then a little fruit punch until each glass was filled. Cinnamon sticks were provided .We followed her lead by stirring the beverage with a cinnamon stick. We tasted it and it was simply delicious. She nodded and said Kinderpunsch. Thinking about that day and the experience that we all had, I am so happy I made the choice to go to that restaurant on that day and at that time. We can learn so much about other cultures by being kind and open to what others enjoy and love. It is in our engagement that we find that we are all connected.

Everything happens like it is supposed to. You have to see it. You have to know it. You got to believe it. What you do has a purpose because you have a purpose as a unique flower in the garden of humanity. As we reflect and choose our paths, there is always something new to discover. We have what we need to get where we are going. We will be provided with what we need as we move along through new mentors along the way. Life is full of new discoveries that go beyond what we plan. Our why is the reason for the choices we make. It is a factor that shapes our inner identity and purpose.

Some years ago, I found myself filling out an application to attend college. I was hopeful. At the same time, I was not sure how it was going to go. A few months went by, and I received a letter in the mail from the college. I sat and stared at it for some time. I just couldn't open it right away. My dad came into the dining room where I sat and asked why I looked nervous. I showed him the envelope. He looked at me and said, "Either way, I love you and you are going to be just fine."

In that moment of hearing him speak those words to me, I found the anchor of strength to open that envelope. I opened the letter and saw the word "Congratulations, you've been accepted." I jumped up and down. I cried. I hugged my dad. I ran to my mom. We all hugged like we had won a Super Bowl championship.

There were a lot of choices that we as a family made that helped us as a family achieve that moment. I say us as a family because if it hadn't been for my parents working to support me as a child and providing every aspect of support to my educational journey, I would not have arrived at that moment. Their support and love gave me hope that a shy girl like me could one day grow up to become a writer, a teacher, an advocate for other kids and pay it forward.

Even though I was now accepted into college, there was a new challenge. I didn't' know what direction I wanted to go in as far as a major is concerned.

Up until that point, basic academic courses were designed as the uniform curriculum of the public school system from kindergarten through twelfth grade. Suddenly, there is an all-you-can-eat buffet of majors available to choose from. Each major carries with it a series of courses that we are to study over a period of four years to arrive at a level of expertise in education. Which one do I choose? I liked several and simply did not have a clue or know for sure which one to choose.

This is where the search for my identity began in a deep dive. What is my why? Why do I want to go to college in the first place? After all, I enjoy cooking, hairstyling and doing nails for friends and family. I could have just focused on these trades and opened up my own business. This would have consisted of networking with other businesses, passing out my business cards at events and conferences. That would have been a nice road, but it did not stand out as my true path.

I had a conversation with my father on one occasion who said he had a dream that I was going to become a writer, speaker, educator, and leader in advocacy for literacy. He believed that I was going to author books one day. I chuckled and thanked him for sharing his dream. I didn't see it at the time. Sometime later, I reflected back on his insight into what he saw in me. I realized that it's important to listen to the people we love. Self-discovery takes reflection, time, and a willingness to listen to those who care about us as well.

Being accepted in a college is nice. Not knowing what to study is like sitting at a crossroads. It is like entering a movie theater with a paid ticket and not recognizing any of the movies on the marquee. The one thing you do know is that you can get popcorn and a soda. That is familiar, a cushion in a moment of indecision.

In cases like this, indecision is a good thing. It is truly about giving yourself permission to find your identity and passion in your journey.

One day I drove to the college to take a walk throughout the campus to learn my way around. I made an appointment with a guidance counselor in the admissions building. As I was walking out of the building, I met a gentleman with a suit walking by. He said, "Good Afternoon." I replied with the same greeting. He gave me his card and said I can stop by anytime this week between

the hours of 10am and 2pm. Office hours. I took him up on it and visited him about an hour later. I explained to him my quandary of being at the crossroads as a new student who simply didn't know which way to go.

He smiled and said, " Welcome to your new journey.

So began a wonderful beginning of a mentorship relationship with my first educational mentor in college. I often stopped by his office where he shared more about his journey and how he too did not know his choice of course of studies until several years down the road. The one thing he shared is that you should not push yourself. You will naturally walk into your self-discovery through recognizing the moment when you know exactly who you are, your purpose, and what you are enthusiastic about most. He said just like it takes time for grapes to ferment into wine, we are each a work in progress.

Suddenly the pressure of wanting to excel and make the right decision fell off of me. It was a relief. College was no longer a challenge. In that moment, college became an experience. A part of my journey that would be defined and shaped with time.

I took a few general education classes the first semester to ease my way into the college experience. It was different than public school. For one thing, it was much easier as a teenager to go to a public high school. All the classes were on a small campus and many times in the same building. Now, in college, I discovered that you could take one class in one building and your second class for the day is a block away in another building. I got a decent work out walking from one building to the next. It soon became second nature. I did not need to go to the gym anymore. Walking to class was my daily workout.

In my journey of taking classes, I began to change. I began to learn and grow. I became more socially active in attending networking events and mixers. There I began to meet with students from other countries around the world. Suddenly the world was a lot smaller than it seemed before. The world was accessible on campus in that way. Through this process of learning and meeting new students from around the world, I realized I enjoyed being social. We all gathered in our dorms and would cook specialty meals to share our favorite cuisines. Suddenly we all began to build solid friendships of camaraderie on a mission to work hard in school while dreaming of changing the world to make it a better place.

Why did I continue to go to college for the first two years without knowing my direction? I began to find strength in the uncertainty of it. I found strength from the accomplishments of the teachers who I met. The faculty who became close friends and mentors. The students who I studied with and bonded with as friends. A second home now. It was okay not to know what I wanted for myself. I found joy in listening, bonding, and building friendships. My why became even more clear. My passion is helping others. My passion is learning and growing in my educational process...and taking the knowledge that I learn to give back to others....This was a revelation so clear to me after my second year of school. I became a major in international relations and continued the journey toward that goal.

What is the essence of our why? Why represents our motivation as to the reason we do what we do. Some people are motivated based on their desire to be recognized with a personal achievement or seeking accolades from others such as trophies and awards. This is the Self-Recognition Why.

Then there is the Humanitarian Why. This is reflected in making choices that are purposed to help enrich the lives of other people in the world, such as creating music, art, literature, and other creative projects that inspire the world.

It is true that no person is an island. We are all connected. We are all human. Yet, we each have a different path to travel. It's simply fine to not know. It doesn't mean you are behind. It means you are in touch with where you are in the moment and where you need to be right now. Your purpose is in motion each day. When we learn to accept moments like that, we give ourselves permission to simply be who we are and embrace it. It is when we are patient with ourselves in this way that self-discovery and the road to our purpose become possible.

The most important thing in life is living each moment with a sense of hope and knowing that there are people who we will meet along the way who will help us, guide us, encourage us... People who we don't know. Life will send them our way.

 From entering college to entering a new career or even a new relationship, these experiences provide dynamics that shift our environment of what we are accustomed to into new environments where we must adapt to learn and grow.

I hope that my writing gives your insight into the power of hope. You are unique and different; your life journey is truly going to be magnificent. To find that space of ultimate joy, it starts with getting to know your why, and that your why reflects your identity. What do you love to do and why do you  love to do it? Sometimes it takes a number of walks at the beach with friends while taking moments to reflect upon what you have inside of you to share with others.

You will be surprised by all the remarkable things that you have inside of you. Just know that there are certain people who will understand each gift along the way. They are your mentors in your journey that continues. Embrace those moments.

I woke up one day and realized the major that reflects my motivation and passion. Humanities. I embrace it as a source of intellectual insight and as a tool that I can use in my work in humanitarianism.

There is a joy unspeakable from knowing that you can contribute to helping others. Meeting people where they are and helping them overcome their challenges through hope and kindness.

When your motivation is founded upon finding ways to make the world a better place, that is the true catalyst for true happiness. Happiness is the effect of giving for the purpose of helping others. You are magnificent and there is no one else like you in the world. You have a purpose. Walk in your path and your destiny will unfold in the spirit of hope and trust the process through your kindness. The kindness inside of you.

## Belinda Foster

Belinda Foster is the founder of  AWJ Platinum PR, a Los Angeles-based full-service marketing and multimedia firm.

As a seasoned expert in Public Relations and Marketing, she is best known for engaging and strategizing major campaigns in the entertainment industry for both indie and major projects across the television, literary, film, fashion, sports, and music to name a few.

She also works with private sector businesses in PR and marketing with respect to consumer engagement for business development.

In addition, Belinda Foster is a professional writer, radio host, and producer. Her clientele list includes Morris Day, Parish Smith, and Dr. Cherilyn Lee, who has appeared on CNN, the CBS Early Show, FOX National news, and other major outlets.

www.awjplatnum.com

# Creativity With a Purpose
*By Bella Castillo*

## Prologue

A radiant light, alive with shifting hues of blue, purple, red, green, orange, and gold, broke through the night, illuminating the vast expanse around me. The world shimmered, filled with an unearthly glow as if the very canvas of existence had been painted with the colors of creation. It evoked a profound sense of connection with something greater than me. I knew I was in the divine presence of our Creator.

I walked alone, yet I was not alone. The white stone beneath me stretched endlessly and felt smooth, untouched by the passage of time. And beside me—although unseen —I felt the presence of our Creator. Not through sight or sound but through the quiet knowing in my heart. A presence so familiar and infinite that it filled me with a profound sense of peace and awe. The air carried the scents of Jasmine and Roses, and it was neither hot nor cold but the perfect temperature. I took in my surroundings, mesmerized by the beauty of the place, both foreign and deeply familiar; time did not exist here, only the journey.

After what felt like forever, yet no time at all, I spoke, not with my lips, but with my heart.

**"¿Puedo despertarme ahora?"**

Can I wake up now?

The Creator answered, though not with sound but with something more profound. Something I felt deep within my soul.

**"No, sigue caminando."**

No, keep walking.

And so, I did. At five years old, I obeyed without question, without fear, moving forward with unconditional trust, love, and faith—embraced by the mystery of something far more significant than myself.

Time passed, or maybe it didn't. Then, I asked again.

**"¿Puedo despertarme ahora?"**

This time, the answer was different.

"Sí, puedes despertar."

Yes, you can wake up.

And I did. My eyes opened. I found myself in my familiar, warm bed, in the world I had left behind. Was it a dream? A memory? A glimpse into something beyond? Can one dream change the journey of a life? I didn't know. All I knew was that it was real—real in a way that dreams are not.

And now, looking back, I wonder why I ever wished to wake up at all.

My journey began in the vibrant and ancient lands of Mesoamerica, Guatemala, in the late 1970s—a place where history whispers through the ruins and forest, where the earth pulses with ancestral Mayan stories, and where the sky stretches endlessly, holding dreams, struggles, and ancestral sacrifices.

Between 1960 and 1996, Guatemala and El Salvador were engulfed in civil unrest, with various rebel groups rising against military dictators like Carlos Castillo Armas. The air was thick with uncertainty, and the streets echoed with the weight of political assassinations and human rights violations. My Mayan ancestors faced genocide at the hands of the Guatemalan government as longstanding struggles over land and natural resources fueled oppression.

In the 1970s, Carlos Manuel Arana Osorio rose to power through electoral fraud, further tightening the government's grip on the impoverished population. The military even sought to impose a dress code, forcing the impoverished to wear only white cotton shirts and pants in an attempt to distinguish them from the wealthy. During the conflict, an estimated 140,000 to 200,000 people were killed or forcibly disappeared, including 40,000 to 50,000 who vanished without a trace. Survival became a calling, a need for survival, and courage was a necessity, not a luxury.

By the 1980s, the Guatemalan military had reached the height of its power, ruling with near-absolute control for five long years. Amidst this turmoil, my single mother and I embarked on a journey to the unknown—one that was not merely a passage across borders, but a journey carried by little more than faith, hope, resilience, and love, which bound us together.

Fear shadowed my mother's every step, the haunting thought that she might not one day return home from work, that I might be left an orphan beneath a sky heavy with loss. We carried little—just a tiny, worn cloth bag filled with bare essentials. But in our hearts, we carried everything: an unwavering love for one another, an unshaken belief in a better future, and the silent prayers of our ancestors.

The path was neither easy nor kind. It was paved with fear and sacrifice, and there were moments when the "el norte," the north, seemed impossibly far. Yet, despite the unknown, we pressed on, guided by an unrelenting hope that somewhere ahead lay the promise of something greater within us.

My mother and I were genuinely blessed even after leaving our homeland, culture, language, and our only family. When we arrived in Los Angeles, it was Christmas. I felt like I was living a dream again. We lived in a tiny studio, but I didn't care because we were together. After some time, the Swank Family, for which my mother was working, embraced us both as a family. So, we moved in with them to Seal Beach, California. The Swanks were a married couple. He was a lawyer, and she was a surgeon. They had a little boy who was about two years old. They treated me like their daughter. They showed us so much love and kindness. We now had a new family that would love us and protect us.

Living with the Swank family opened my eyes to a world I had never known—a world of stability, giving rather than taking, and the quiet rhythm of a home filled with warmth, joy, and love. For the first time, I glimpsed the possibility that I, too, could carve a future in this land called the United States of America.

According to "A Nation at Risk: The Imperative for Educational Reform" (1983), a report by the United States National Commission on Excellence in Education, our youth at that time faced numerous challenges that could negatively impact their educational progress and hinder their ability to reach their full potential in society. These risk factors included:

1- Growing up in a family that receives government assistance, including welfare, food stamps, SSI, and General Relief.

2- Speaking a primary language at home other than English.

3- Being raised in a single-parent household.

4- Having a mother with less than a high school education.

5- Living in a community with high rates of teen pregnancy and teen births.

6- Being a first- or second-generation immigrant.

7- Exposure to substance abuse and violence within the community.

I have personally experienced four out of the seven risk factors above, along with my learning disability—dyslexia. However, the kindness of the Swank family, woven with my ancestors' dreams and my mother's unwavering strength, ignited a fire within me. I pursued my education with a relentless hunger, each lesson a step toward honoring those who came before me. And through that journey, I did not just earn a degree—I claimed a destiny once thought impossible, earning both my bachelor's and master's degrees in business administration through perseverance and resilience, or "ganas" as we say in Spanish.

Moreover, life has granted me many titles—daughter, Goddaughter, friend, student, sister, lover, wife, professional, leader, manager, mentor, and advocate. Still, none of these titles defines me as profoundly as the "relentless seeker." For over 15 years, I have walked the path of a Human Resources professional, serving as both a bridge and a guide for those navigating the complexities of careers, workplaces, and personal growth. I have dedicated myself to excellence, earning certifications that validate my knowledge and continually striving for more; yet knowledge alone has never been enough.

I have created policies, shaped cultures, and sat at tables where decisions shaped lives, where I was often the only Latina. I have witnessed ambition bloom, dreams shatter, and people fight to be seen, to be heard, to matter, for a chance to be given an opportunity.

Like brushstrokes on a canvas, I have endeavored to make my HR decisions contribute to the broader picture of growth, belonging, and purpose. Art has taught me to see beyond structure, embrace the human spirit, and weave creativity into leadership, building not just policies but possibilities. However, as an HR professional, I influenced how employees should be treated, encouraged, and promoted for advancement.

And through it all, I have often asked myself:

"Is this my purpose? Is this what sets my soul on fire?"

For years, I followed the script of success, the story sold to me by American society and our educational system. Each accomplishment, each degree, each certification, and each promotion was—"para adelante," a step forward, a testament to perseverance. And yet, some mornings, I felt the quiet weight and ache of something missing within me, the feeling that I was existing, not truly living.

I now understand that my soul comes alive when I am creating. Creativity is my oxygen, my water.

Whether through art, ideas, or poetry, I am most alive when I bring something into existence that did not exist before. In these moments, with brush or pen in hand, my mind unraveling ideas, my soul in motion—I feel connected to something vast and eternal. When I am creating, whether it's an oil painting or a poem, it feels like it's not me doing it. I am just a vessel.

Perhaps this is what it means to contribute to the world—not merely through work, but through passion, not just through duty, but through joy.

I have spent years helping others build their futures and dreams. But now, I ask myself: What am I building for myself? What now?

In my search for my 'why,' for something greater than my achievements, I yearn for reassurance. Just like in my dream, I was reminded that I was not alone on this journey. And in a quiet moment, I heard a voice, a presence whispering to me...

## Never, Alone
by Bella Castillo

Alone? You are never alone.
I am with you—
I am the woven fabric of every day.

I am the gentle breeze,
that whispers, "I love you,"
and cradles your inner child.

I am the smile.
and the laughter in a stranger's eyes.
I am the painted ribbon-
that stretches across the blue sky.

I am the resilient healer-
who mends the universe.
I am the trembling earthquake-
beneath your feet,
urging you to dance once more.

I am the persevering river,
that quenches your deepest thirst.
and the breath inside your heart.

I am all these things—
and infinitely more,
for I am the maker of time,
igniting the unearthly stars.

I am the beginning,
I am the end,
and the time in between,
which is the unfailing love
You have always been looking for.

Always with you,
*Your Father, God*

These words came to me like a whisper in the wind. However, some emotions cannot be fully captured in words alone; they require color, form, and movement. So, I picked up my brush and let my soul speak in strokes and shadows. Just as my words sought to capture presence and reassurance, my hands sought to capture the face of a man who embodied both—my grandfather. His furrowed brow, unwavering gaze, and the weight of his wisdom are forever preserved in this piece—a tribute to the strength and resilience that shaped my mother and me.

Life is a fleeting breath, a whisper in time, a story written on the winds of existence. We are here for only a moment, and in that moment, we must choose to conform or to create, to exist merely or to truly live and experience life through this body that has been given to us.

I have chosen to bloom, reach down for strength, and reach up to the light for inspiration.

Like a wildflower pushing through the cracks of a hardened world, I reach down and up. Shaped by my past, yet reaching for the light, for all the hues of that unearthly glow. I have learned that fulfillment is not found in titles, degrees, achievements, material success, or the "American Dream," but in the courage to embrace one's true essence. And my essence is creation.

In a world that often measures worth by productivity, efficiency, and contribution rather than artistry, creative expression through music, art, poetry, and joy is a powerful force that unites us as humans. Through my travels worldwide, I have come to understand that we, as a species, share far more in common than we do differences—whether it be our color, gender, culture, or even political affiliation.

With this understanding, I have chosen to lead with my heart, build with imagination, and serve purposefully. My mission is not only to contribute to my community through knowledge and leadership but also to express the depths of my soul through art.

Perhaps the meaning of life is not in the pursuit of success but in the pursuit of meaning itself, and to hear my Creator say to me, "You have done well in sharing the gifts I gave you, my child!"

This is my why: to create, inspire, and leave behind something that will outlive me that whispers— "¡Estuve aquí!" *I was here!*

**Bella Castillo** is a creative artist, poet, author, Human Resources professional, community organizer, and entrepreneur. She creates works of art to support social justice activists worldwide and helps organizations generate revenue through art auctions. Motivated by the global lack of access to affordable, culturally relevant art, Bella is committed to introducing our youth to the arts and creating professional development opportunities for emerging artists.

As a proud Guatemalan immigrant, Bella was raised by her courageous single mother. She became the first in her family to earn a Bachelor of Science degree from the University of Southern California (USC) and an MBA from Pepperdine University.

In addition to her professional endeavors, Bella is deeply committed to community service. She volunteered with the Boys and Girls Club and Big Brothers Big Sisters. She has participated in humanitarian trips to Ecuador and Cuba, spreading love and delivering medical supplies to underserved communities.

La Opinión newspaper, Wells Fargo, the National Latina Business Women Association (NLBWA), TELACU, the United States Congress, and the California Legislature have recognized Bella's contributions and inspired others to follow her example.

You can connect with Bella Castillo at:

- Website: www.BellaCastillo.art
- LinkedIn: linkedin.com/in/bella-c-6a3bb8173
- Facebook: facebook.com/ArtistBella01
- Email: Bella@letscallHR.com

# My Why: A Life of Purpose, Power, and Global Impact
### By Professor Caroline Makaka, PhD

I was born with a dream that didn't have a name yet—a calling that would only make sense after I walked through fire, loss, triumph, and purpose. Today, I know that dream is my "why." My purpose in this world is to unite cultures, empower the most vulnerable, and inspire people everywhere to rise from adversity and become agents of global change. My name is Professor Caroline Makaka, Founder and President of Leaders of All Nations International (LOANI), creator of the We Are the Change World Movement, and most importantly, a mother of two, a survivor, and a voice for the voiceless.

## A Journey Born from Pain

My journey began with a devastating loss—one that carved a permanent space in my heart but also planted seeds of strength. I was orphaned at a tender age, losing both of my parents far too soon. No pain compares to that kind of loss—the raw confusion, the silence that echoes through every part of your being, the disorientation of having your world ripped from beneath you. My parents were everything to me. They were my pillars, my encouragers, my protectors. Suddenly, I was left to face a world that didn't care about my sorrow. But somehow, in that void, I found purpose.

It wasn't just the loss that shaped me—it was the will to survive, to protect my younger siblings, to keep our family's light alive. My younger brother became my strength. Every time I looked into his eyes, I was reminded that I had no choice but to push forward. Giving up would have meant the end of his hope, too.

I promised myself I would build a life that honored our parents, one that stood for everything they had dreamed for us. That was my first encounter with purpose. My "why" was born in the ashes of loss.

## From Survivor to Global Changemaker

I didn't want my story to be one of tragedy. I wanted it to be one of transformation. From a young age, I understood the power of resilience. I became a voice for those who could not speak an advocate for those who had no platforms. My lived experiences taught me to lead with empathy, to embrace people from all walks of life, and to dedicate myself to creating pathways for those who had been left behind by society.

This passion would eventually lead me to create Leaders of All Nations International (LOANI)—a global platform built on the belief that unity transcends difference. LOANI is not just an organization; it's a movement, a legacy, and a revolution of compassion. It brings together cultures, ideas, and visions from every continent under one unified purpose: empowering the most vulnerable and creating sustainable change.

## Empowering the Marginalized

Throughout my journey, I've encountered thousands of women and children who have been silenced by poverty, war, oppression, and systemic inequality. I've looked into the eyes of young girls who had no access to education, of widows forgotten by society, and of youth lost in systems that did not see their potential. In every one of them, I saw myself.

My "why" is rooted in empowerment. It is about giving voice, visibility, and value to those who've been overlooked. It's about showing women that they are not defined by the trauma they've endured but by the greatness they possess. It's about transforming survivors into leaders.

As the creator of the We Are the Change World Movement, I've launched initiatives that have trained and mentored women and youth across the globe—offering tools in leadership, entrepreneurship, education, and social responsibility. I have stood on platforms across Africa, Europe, Asia, and the Americas championing diversity, cultural understanding, peacebuilding, and sustainable development.

## Why I Created the Beautiful Survivors Initiative

Beautiful Survivors was born from my own journey—a path marked by pain, loss, resilience, and ultimately, purpose. It is a movement I created to shine a light on survivors from all walks of life, honoring their courage and grace not despite their scars, but because of them.

As part of my why, I wanted to create a space where those who have faced life's greatest challenges could be seen, heard, and celebrated. A platform that uplifts stories of perseverance and transformation, while restoring dignity, beauty, and strength to every soul that has endured.

Over the years, we have honored more than 500 survivors from around the world—each one a living testament to the power of the human spirit. Through their stories, we witness the radiance of resilience and the brilliance that can rise from brokenness.

This year, we mark a powerful milestone in that mission: Celebrating courage, grace, and transformation.

Our 2025 theme, "Rooted. Resilient. Radiant.," symbolizes strong foundations, emotional strength, and the inner light that shines from within each survivor. It reminds us that no matter what we've been through, we can rise—not just to survive, but to lead, to heal, and to inspire.

At its core, Beautiful Survivors is a call for unity.

Against all odds. Across all borders. For every voice.

Because all means all.

We are building a global community where every person is valued, heard, and belongs.

A world that embraces inclusion, dignity, and hope.

A future where healing turns into purpose, and pain gives birth to power.

There is beauty in surviving. There is power in rising. And together, we create a world where all means all.

## A Global Legacy of Leadership

As a Professor of Global Leadership, I view education not as a privilege but as a human right. My goal is to democratize access to leadership and development—especially for underserved communities. I believe education is the foundation upon which we build peaceful, inclusive, and progressive societies. Through LOANI and our global partners, we have facilitated workshops, conferences, and cultural exchange programs aimed at developing transformational leaders—leaders who will prioritize people over power.

My leadership philosophy is centered around servant leadership. I don't lead from above—I lead from among. I lead by example, by vulnerability, and by listening deeply. True leadership is not about titles or accolades; it's about action, humility, and impact.

## Recognition and Purpose Beyond Awards

Over the years, I've been honored with some of the world's most prestigious accolades. From the Nelson Mandela International Award to being featured on the billboard in New York's Times Square, these recognitions are humbling. I've been celebrated as

one of the Top 100 Most Influential Women in the World, the Global Chairperson of the Year, and even received recognition at the UK House of Parliament.

But these titles are not my legacy. My real legacy is the child who goes to school because of a LOANI scholarship. It's the woman who starts her first business because she attended one of our empowerment summits. It's the cultural barriers broken when nations come together for a shared purpose. These are my real trophies.

## My Family, My Foundation

Amidst all my global travels and initiatives, I am first and foremost a mother. My two children are my heartbeat. They are the reminder of why I do what I do. I want them to grow up in a world where kindness leads, where diversity is celebrated, and where their generation has the courage to fix what ours could not. Every lesson I teach them is rooted in compassion, leadership, and responsibility. And every success I achieve is dedicated to them and to the memory of my parents, whose dreams still live through me.

## Living a Heart-Centered Life

My life's mission has always been to live from the heart. This doesn't mean a life without boundaries or structure—it means a life led by values, empathy, and purpose. I don't want to just build programs—I want to build people. I don't want to just raise funds—I want to raise hope. And I don't want to just gather accolades—I want to gather stories of transformation that will be told for generations.

Living a heart-centered life also means confronting injustice wherever it exists. It means using my platform to challenge inequality, gender discrimination, and cultural division. It means using my voice not for noise but for impact.

## Uniting the World Through Humanity

LOANI's mission is to bring the world together under the umbrella of humanity. In a time when the world feels increasingly divided, we have chosen unity as our most powerful tool. We believe that when people from different cultures, faiths, and nations come together, transformation happens. Borders fade, biases dissolve, and something truly beautiful emerges—shared purpose.

We have built bridges between communities in Africa, Asia, Europe, and the Americas. We have launched humanitarian campaigns that deliver not only food and healthcare but also dignity. We have created platforms for collaboration, innovation, and global citizenship. Our ethos is simple: All Means All. Everyone matters. Everyone belongs.

## My Vision for the Future

As we look toward the future, my dream is to expand LOANI's impact to every corner of the world. We are already working on innovative models for global centers that will focus on education, sustainability, and enterprise. I envision a world where every woman and child, no matter where they're born, has access to the tools they need to thrive. I see a world where unity is not just an ideal—it's a lived reality.

This is the world I want to leave for my children. This is the legacy I want to build in honor of my parents. This is my "why."

## My Message to the World

If you've ever lost someone you loved, if you've ever felt invisible, broken, or silenced, I want you to know this: your pain can be the birthplace of your purpose. Your suffering can become your

strength. You don't have to wait for the world to notice you. You don't need permission to rise. Begin now. Begin where you are. Begin as you are.

This is part of my why—to stand in unity with those who have faced unimaginable odds and still dared to dream, to love, to rebuild, and to rise. Against all odds, you are still here. You are not alone.

We believe in a world where all means all—where no voice is too small, no story too broken, no soul too lost. A world where every person is valued, heard, seen, and belongs. Where unity is not just a dream, but a daily mission.

This is not just a message. This is a movement.

A mission to unite every person, every community, and every nation.

Because when we lead with love, when we stand in unity, and when we remember that all means all—we don't just change lives. We change the world.

Let us rise as one—across borders, beyond labels, above fear— with courage, compassion, and conviction. Together, we can co-create a future that is inclusive, sustainable, safe, and rooted in love and dignity.

I am on a mission to unite each person, every country, and every nation under one truth.

*Let your story be your power. Let your heart be your guide. And let your why lead you into a life of meaning.*

**Professor Caroline Makaka, PhD**

Contact Information

Professor Caroline Makaka, PhD

Founder/President, Leaders of All Nations International

Creator, We Are the Change World Movement

www.leaders-of-all-nations.org | info@leaders-of-all-nations.org

loaniafrica.loaninet.net

+447478281693

# From Surviving to Soaring: Why I Became a Holistic Prosperity Navigator
*By Amb. Charles Hai Nguyen*

*Power Quote: "Your self-worth is not your net worth.*
*YOU are your wealth!"*

## Personal Intention:

My story is a testament that no matter where you begin or how far you fall, you can rise into your purpose, prosperity, and power. This chapter is for every soul who has known hardship and is ready to remember their inner wealth. You are not your bank balance or your broken past. You are your wealth.

Curled in bed one night, I asked a question no one ever wants to ask: "What's the point of living?"

I had lost nearly everything—my family, my job, my finances, and most painfully, my sense of self-worth. With just $20 in my account and a heart full of regret, I questioned everything I thought I knew about success.

But even in that darkness, something within me refused to die. I remembered: I've always been a fighter.

I was born prematurely on June 9, 1969, in Can Tho, Vietnam, weighing under four pounds. My mother didn't see me for the first week as I fought for life in an incubator. Survival wasn't new to me—it was the beginning of my story.

By age six, during the final days of the Vietnam War in 1975, my family lived in fear of bombings and raids. We slept on the bottom floor, unsure if each night might be our last. At eight, we tried to flee by boat. We were captured, and I spent two months in a communist prison—witnessing horrors no child should witness.

Still, we didn't give up.

On our second escape attempt, we spent seven days lost at sea—starving, chased by Thai pirates—before a German oil tanker rescued us. We lived in Indonesian refugee camps for over a year before finally arriving in America in 1980.

That night in bed, I realized something: If I survived all that, I could survive this. And not just survive—but rise again, with purpose.

America was a promise—a chance to build something better.

My father came to this country with no English and no formal education, yet through sheer will and business savvy, he became a multimillionaire. Watching him rise from nothing, I believed that education and effort were the keys to success. So, I pursued a degree in Business Finance, determined to follow his path.

But life had different lessons for me.

Despite my education, I found myself overwhelmed by financial missteps. At just twenty-one, I had my car repossessed and was forced to file for bankruptcy. I felt humiliated, confused, and frustrated. I had done everything I thought I was supposed to do—but success still eluded me. That confusion sparked something powerful in me: a relentless hunger to learn the truth about wealth.

I became a student of financial literacy—not just theory, but real-world mastery. I read every book I could find, attended seminars, and sought out mentors who had built wealth from the ground up. Through hard work and divine guidance, I built a multi-income career in real estate and insurance. My family had a home. My business was growing. For the first time, I tasted

what I thought was the American Dream.

Then, in 2008, the economy collapsed—and so did my world.

My business partner passed away suddenly. Our company, already under pressure from the recession, couldn't survive the loss. I lost my business. I lost my home to foreclosure. And most painfully, I almost lost my family under the weight of financial strain.

In that moment of despair, I dropped to my knees and prayed.

By God's grace, I got my home back, eliminated over $400,000 in debt, and gained $130,000 in equity. It was nothing short of a miracle.

I started over—again.

I returned to help my father's spice manufacturing company, which was on the brink of collapse due to lawsuits, tax issues, and economic downturns. Applying everything I'd learned, I helped bring the company back from survival mode to profitability. At the same time, I was building a financial literacy company to help others do the same.

I thought I was back on track—stronger, wiser, finally gaining momentum.

But in 2019, everything came crashing down again. I was going through a divorce. I lost my job. The pandemic hit, freezing the world. My father—the same man whose company I had helped save—locked me out and withheld my share of our investment. My children didn't want to speak to me. My bank account had just $20 left.

I had once managed seven-figure accounts. Now, I was broke. Alone. Devastated.

But even in that darkness, something stirred.

I remembered the movie It's a Wonderful Life—a story of a man on the brink, saved by the revelation that his life had meaning far beyond what he could see. I realized I had lost sight of all the lives I had touched, all the people I had helped. I had forgotten who I was.

In a moment of deep prayer and meditation, I cried out to God for guidance.

And I heard a whisper from within:

"Your self-worth is not your net worth. I never left you. Why are you seeking your value from what you've lost, when your true wealth lives inside you?"

Tears streamed down my face. I felt seen—not by the world, but by something greater. That moment was not just emotional—it was transformational. It was the beginning of my true rebirth. That moment changed everything. It became my turning point. I realized I had been measuring my value with the wrong yardstick. I wasn't broken—I was being rebuilt. I wasn't lost—I was being redirected. I wasn't unworthy—I was being refined.

I stopped judging myself by my failures. I stopped chasing external validation. I began healing from within—emotionally, spiritually, and financially. I faced my pain, forgave my past, and found peace in my present.

And that's when my why became crystal clear.

I realized that I wasn't meant to just help people with money. I was meant to help people reclaim their power. To remember their worth. To rise into the fullness of who they are—not just financially, but holistically.

## Why I Became a Holistic Prosperity Navigator

I didn't become a Holistic Prosperity Navigator because I had all the answers.

I became one because I've lived through the questions.

I know what it feels like to lose everything—your home, your business, your marriage, your sense of self—and still rise. I've battled shame, guilt, betrayal, and heartbreak. I've questioned my worth. I've been the dreamer, the provider, the fallen, and the forgiven.

And that's what qualifies me.

Not just my credentials—but my compassion.

Not just my success—but my scars.

My journey spans refugee camps, bankruptcy courts, boardrooms, ballrooms, and spiritual awakenings. I've held real estate and insurance licenses, led financial workshops, built businesses, coached entrepreneurs, and spoken on national stages. But none of these roles defined me. What defined me was my resilience, my redemption, and the realization that true wealth isn't just about money.

**Wealth is wholeness. Wealth is meaning. Wealth is alignment.**

Over the past 30 years, I've worked across every financial lane—real estate, insurance, tax, credit, debt, and investments. But the missing ingredient in most financial coaching?

**Humanity.**

People don't just need spreadsheets. They need healing.

They need someone who sees beyond their debt and into their destiny.

Someone who understands that financial chaos often stems from emotional wounds.

That's why I created the **Master My Money System**—a financial empowerment program that teaches not just how to manage money, but how to align it with your values, purpose, and power.

That's why I'm writing my transformational book, The Cinderella Effect: **Embrace the Personal, Professional, and Financial Prosperity Through a Timeless Tale**—a modern retelling of a classic story for women who feel overlooked, overworked, and underestimated. It's a guide to reclaiming your voice, value, and vision.

That's why I speak, coach, and mentor for organizations like **Woman of Achievement, Global Society Female Entrepreneurs (GSFEUS.com), and AssistNA.org.** In 2014, I joined Woman of Achievement as a board advisor, helping women and teens prepare for pageants and platforms—filming, judging, and annually speaking on "Claiming Your Queendom."

From 2023 onward, I've served as Ambassador to GSFE—supporting women's leadership, visibility, and vision. And Chairperson of ASSISTNA.org—supporting a diverse cultural community in providing financial literacy & housing counseling.

**Why women?**

Because I watched my ex-wife juggle two jobs to care for our children while I felt powerless to help.

Because 90% of women will manage their finances alone at some point in life, yet most aren't prepared.

Because when you empower a woman, you uplift a family, a community, a generation.

Helping women is not just about money.

It's about impact.

It's about healing.

It's about breaking cycles of poverty, pain, and silence.

This is soul work. And I am here for it.

---

## My Mission, My Message, and My Movement

Today, I'm building something bigger than me.

I'm developing coaching programs like the **Holistic Prosperity Breakthrough, Financial Freedom System, and Money for College**—to guide people from survival to sustainability to soaring and to guide our children to be debt free students.

My mission is to help people—especially women—heal their money wounds, align their finances with their dreams, and build lasting wealth in every area of life.

My message is simple:

**True wealth includes emotional healing, spiritual connection, and purposeful living.**

And my movement is rooted in education, transformation, and legacy creation.

I help clients:

- Heal financial trauma and limiting beliefs!
- Master budgeting, credit, and cash flow
- Build multiple streams of income!
- Align money with meaning!
- Break generational cycles!
- Step into their power and purpose!

Through private coaching, group programs, workshops, and keynotes—I walk beside people at every stage of their journey, offering practical tools, emotional intelligence, and spiritual insight. I offer a new lens to see money not as stress, but as a sacred tool to support your highest calling.

## What I Believe

I believe everyone has a dream—and every dream has a price.

Not just in money, but in discipline, belief, clarity, and courage.

People often live in one of three stages:

- **Surviving** – Just getting by, stuck in fear or debt.
- **Sustaining** – Stable but unfulfilled, living paycheck to paycheck.
- **Soaring** – Living in alignment with purpose, prosperity, and peace

My purpose is to help people ascend through these stages—not just financially, but holistically.

Because true prosperity is not about how much you earn.

It's about who you become.

It's about living a life where you don't need a vacation from—one of freedom, fulfillment, and faith.

That's the life I fought for.

That's the life I now help others create.

That's why I became a Holistic Prosperity Navigator.

## Queen's Code to Prosperity: 10 Steps to Reclaim Your Crown

These are more than financial strategies—they're invitations to remember who you are, to heal what's been wounded, and to build a life that reflects your wholeness. Use them not just to prosper, but to rise in every area of your life.

## 1. Remember Your Worth

You are not your past. You are not your pain.

You are a child of God, already worthy, already whole. Begin each day by standing in your truth: "I am enough. I am valuable. I am my greatest asset."

## 2. Dream Without Limits

Allow yourself to imagine a life beyond survival.

What does freedom feel like? What does joy look like? Describe your ideal life in vivid color—this vision is your compass, not a fantasy.

## 3. Heal the Money Story

Behind every financial struggle is a deeper story.

What did you learn about money growing up? What beliefs are holding you back? Name them. Face them. And begin to rewrite the script.

## 4. Align with Your Purpose

Wealth is not just numbers—it's alignment.

Let your spending, saving, and earning reflect what matters most to you. Create systems that support your soul, not just your bills.

## 5. Reconnect to Your Source

You are never alone. God, Spirit, Source—whatever name you use—lives within you.

Return to that connection daily through prayer, silence, nature, or worship. Your answers are waiting in the stillness.

## 6. Set Your Past Free

You cannot soar while dragging chains.

Forgive what hurt you. Release the shame. Give yourself the grace to be human. Healing is your birthright—not a reward for perfection.

## 7. Surround Yourself with Light

Your environment shapes your elevation.

Choose relationships that uplift, challenge, and believe in you. Let go of what dims your light and move toward those who fan your flame.

## 8. Speak the Language of Prosperity

Learn the tools—budgeting, credit, investing, debt management.

But also learn the energy—gratitude, generosity, abundance, trust. Mastering both mind and money creates unstoppable momentum.

## 9. Celebrate Every Victory

Whether it's paying off a bill or setting a boundary—acknowledge it.

Celebration reinforces your progress and trains your mind to expect success.

## 10. Live As the Future You

Stop waiting. Start becoming.

Speak, walk, and act like the empowered version of you who already exists. Your dreams manifest when you embody them.


## Final Reflection

I've walked through the fire.

I've lost homes, businesses, relationships—and at times, even hope. I've felt the crushing weight of shame, failure, and isolation. I've questioned my worth, doubted my purpose, and wondered if I could rise again.

But I did.

Not because I had it all figured out—but because I chose not to give up.

Because I dared to believe that my past didn't define me, and that my pain had a purpose.

Today, I no longer measure wealth by dollar signs alone. I measure it by peace, by purpose, by how deeply I love, and by how fully I serve.

I now walk with clarity, compassion, and conviction—because I've been where many are now. And I'm here not to save anyone, but to shine a light forward... so that others can find their way back to themselves.

To every woman, every dreamer, every soul on the edge of breakthrough—

You are not broken.

You are being rebuilt.

And you are not behind.

You are being prepared.

Rise.

Your Queendom is waiting.

# Amb. Charles Hai Nguyen

*About the Author*

Charles Hai Nguyen is not your traditional financial expert—he is a survivor, a spiritual seeker, and a soul-led strategist who transforms financial literacy into holistic liberation.

As a Holistic Prosperity Navigator and founder of the Rever Enterprises LLC, Charles brings over 30 years of experience in real estate, insurance, and finance. But more importantly, he brings the wisdom earned from walking through war, poverty, bankruptcy, betrayal, and redemption.

From Vietnamese refugee to American entrepreneur, Charles has spoken on national stages, served on nonprofit boards, and coached countless women to rise from financial confusion to confidence and clarity. His teachings go beyond money; they touch the heart, restore dignity, and awaken purpose.

He is the author of the upcoming book, **The Cinderella Effect: Embrace the Personal, Professional, and Financial Prosperity Through a Timeless Tale,** and creator of the **Master My Money System**—empowering women and families to rewrite their stories and reclaim their dreams.

When Charles helps someone heal their finances, he's not just fixing numbers—he's helping them find their voice, their vision, and their power.

www.CharlesHaiNguyen360.com

# Driven by Love: My Journey to Finding My Why
*by Ambassador Dr. Charmaine Summers (h.c.)*

As I stand on the driving range beside a young girl gripping a golf club almost as tall as she is, I see a bit of myself in her eager eyes. She swings with all her might, the ball soars high and far, and her face lights up in astonished joy. In that moment, my heart swells with a familiar warmth and I am reminded exactly why I do what I do. This is my why: to empower others to believe in themselves and to share the joy that comes from hard work, passion, and a little bit of courage. But to understand how I found this purpose, I have to start at the beginning of my journey.

## A Childhood of Love and Lessons

I was born and raised in sunny Southern California, the middle child of three. My father, Patrick, had immigrated from Canada with big dreams and a bigger heart, and my mother, Lucy, was a California native with warmth and strength to spare. Together, they created a loving and encouraging home where each of us was made to feel uniquely special. Being the middle child can sometimes mean getting lost in the shuffle, but not in our family – my parents made sure we each knew our worth. I still remember how Mom would tape our crayon drawings on the fridge as if they were masterpieces, and how Dad would cheer at all our school events with equal enthusiasm, whether it was a science fair or a little league game.

In our household, love went hand-in-hand with high expectations. My parents believed that success was built on hard work, integrity, and the courage to pursue your passions.

From a young age, I was taught that if I truly wanted something, I had to be willing to work for it. That lesson became real to me when I discovered a new love: horses. As a girl, I dreamed of spending every afternoon at the stables, brushing horses, and galloping under the California sun. My father agreed to support my passion – but with one important condition. "We'll pay for your riding lessons and horse stabling for now," he told me kindly, "but you need to take responsibility too. Find a way to contribute."

At first, I was taken aback – I was barely a teenager, and the idea of working to pay for my own hobby seemed daunting. But I understood what Dad was trying to teach me. So, at 14, I marched into Tustin Lanes, our local bowling alley, and asked if they had any jobs for a kid who was eager to work. To my delight, they hired me to run the snack bar and help keep the place tidy. After school and on weekends, I'd serve burgers and sodas to league bowlers and carefully save my earnings. Every paycheck went straight into a "horse fund" jar on my dresser.

Working at Tustin Lanes taught me more than how to make a mean chili dog or reset a rack of pins – it taught me responsibility and pride. I learned to show up on time, to handle money, and to deal politely with customers even when I was tired. Even on nights I came home exhausted, seeing the pride in my father's eyes when I handed over the cash I'd saved made it all worth it. "I knew you could do it," he would say, giving me a hug. In those moments, I realized that the confidence and work ethic my parents instilled in me were gifts that would guide me throughout my life.

That early experience of earning my way not only paid for the horses I loved but also laid a foundation for my future. I understood that with determination and effort, I could achieve my goals – and that my family would be cheering me on every step of the way. Little did I know, the strong swing I'd developed hefting bowling balls would soon open the door to another passion I never expected.

## From Softball to the Fairway

True to my parents' philosophy, one opportunity often led to another. In my teenage years, when I wasn't at the bowling alley or the horse stable, I was on the softball field. I loved softball – the camaraderie of the team and the thrill of sending a ball sailing into the outfield. I had a surprisingly powerful swing for my size; a strength honed perhaps by hefting bowling balls and bales of hay. One afternoon during a high school game, I smashed a pitch clear over the left fielder's head. As I rounded the bases amid cheers, I noticed a gentleman by the fence watching intently. After the game, he approached me with a friendly smile and a question that would change my life: "Have you ever thought about playing golf?"

At first, I almost laughed. Golf? To me, golf seemed slow and quiet, nothing like the fast-paced excitement of softball. But the man introduced himself as a local golf coach who saw potential in my swing and invited me to a driving range to give it a try. With curiosity (and a hint of skepticism), I agreed to one lesson – and that one lesson was all it took. As soon as I felt the driver connect with the ball, sending it arcing high into the blue sky, I was hooked. There was something magical in the challenge of golf – just me, the club, and the ball. The raw power and focus it required were different from softball, yet everything I'd learned on the field transferred naturally.

My parents, ever supportive, encouraged me to pursue this new passion. My dad started waking up early on Saturdays to drive me to junior golf tournaments across Southern California. I practiced relentlessly, trading afternoons at the horse barn for evenings on the driving range. Before long, I was competing in – and winning – junior golf tournaments. The rush I once felt sliding into home plate, I now found in sinking a long putt or hitting a drive straight and true down the fairway.

Golf opened doors I never anticipated. I earned a college scholarship thanks to my performance on the golf team. After graduation, I decided to turn professional and test my mettle on the competitive circuit. Those early years as a pro were both exhilarating and tough. I traveled around the country playing on beautiful courses I'd only dreamed of. I'll never forget my first tee shot in a big tournament – my heart pounding and palms sweating as I tried to steady my hands. Some tournaments I shone and made the leaderboards; other times I struggled to make the cut. Through every high and low, I leaned on the work ethic and optimism my family had instilled in me. Each day on the course was a chance to prove to myself what I was capable of.

As much as I loved competing, I discovered another calling along the way: teaching and mentoring. During the off-season, I volunteered at local schools and youth programs to introduce kids – especially young girls – to golf. I saw myself in their unsure stances and hopeful faces. Guiding them, watching their confidence bloom with each swing, gave me a satisfaction unlike any trophy ever could.

Eventually, I channeled this passion for teaching into something bigger. I opened three junior golf academies in Orange County, dedicated to nurturing young talent. These academies weren't just about perfecting a swing – they were about instilling the same values of integrity, perseverance, and respect that my parents taught me. On Saturday mornings I'd often be out on the practice green with a gaggle of kids, turning drills into games, and ending summer camp days with high-fives, popsicles, and pep talks. Seeing a shy child transform into a self-assured golfer or a hesitant teen become a mentor to younger kids – those moments became some of the most rewarding of my life.

By my early thirties, I had worn many hats: professional golfer, coach, entrepreneur, and mentor. I was living my dream and making a difference in the lives of others. I didn't know it yet, but a profound loss was about to change my course – and ultimately bring my evolving "why" into even sharper focus.

## A New Beginning After Loss

Then life threw me an unexpected curveball: my beloved father – my biggest champion and moral compass – passed away. Losing Dad felt like the ground had dropped from under me. In the weeks and months that followed, I went through the motions of running my golf academies, but inside I felt a profound emptiness. Why pour so much energy into work? What was I really accomplishing? Without my dad's daily encouragement, I began to question everything.

I realized I needed a change of scenery to heal. Everywhere I looked in Orange County reminded me of him – the golf courses we'd strolled together, the bowling alley where my journey began. I craved a quieter place where I could hear my own thoughts and figure out how to move forward without my father. That's what led me to move to Menifee, California – a smaller, slower town not too far away, but far enough that I could start fresh.

At first, moving to Menifee was liberating yet intimidating. I left behind the comfort of lifelong friends and a community that knew my name. In this new town, I wasn't the "golf pro" or the successful entrepreneur – I was just Charmaine. I spent a lot of time alone, writing in my journal and taking long walks, trying to make peace with my loss and decide what came next.

But I am my father's daughter, and even in the depths of grief I could hear his gentle encouragement: "Keep going, sweetheart. Keep giving it your all." I knew he wouldn't want me to stay withdrawn and isolated. I still had so much life left to live – and so much left to give. So slowly, I opened myself up again, looking for new connections in my community and a renewed sense of purpose.

## Reigniting My Passion to Serve

In time, I discovered the Global Society for Female Entrepreneurs (GSFE), a network of women devoted to supporting each other and giving back. It sounded like exactly what I needed, so with a hopeful heart I attended their next meeting.

Walking into that GSFE gathering, I was immediately embraced by a group of warm, dynamic women who made me feel at home. The guest speaker was Lady Ambassador Dr. h.c. Robbie Motter, GSFE's founder – a powerhouse of positivity and purpose. She spoke passionately about the importance of "showing up" for yourself and for others, about turning pain into purpose and using your talents to uplift your community. Her words resonated deeply, reigniting a spark in my soul that I thought I had lost.

After the meeting, I shared a bit of my journey with Robbie. She looked me in the eye and told me something I'll never forget: "Charmaine, everything you've done and been through has prepared you for what's next. We need women like you to lead and inspire others. Don't ever doubt that." In that moment, I felt seen and valued in a way I hadn't since my father's passing. It was as if this group of women, led by Robbie, had thrown me a lifeline of renewed purpose.

Energized, I jumped into GSFE activities with both feet. Before long, I was helping organize events, mentoring newer members, and even speaking at meetings to share my experiences. I dusted off my golf clubs to host a charity ladies' golf clinic, raising funds for scholarships for young female entrepreneurs. The more involved I became, the more alive I felt. In helping other women find confidence and clarity in their journeys, I was rediscovering my own.

Within a year, Robbie asked me to become the Director of a new GSFE network in Lake Arrowhead. Though it was a couple of hours away in the mountains, I embraced the challenge. Soon I found myself driving up winding roads to host networking meetings and workshops in that community, bringing together women of all ages to learn, share, and empower one another. I even opened our meetings with an uplifting song – a little touch from my performer side that everyone enjoyed.

Through GSFE, I gained an extended family. These fellow entrepreneurs, leaders, and dreamers became my sisters in success. We celebrated each other's milestones and rallied around each other in tough times. With their encouragement lighting my path, I felt brave enough to pursue all facets of my passions again. My love for serving others, which had always been inside me, was now burning brightly, guiding me forward.

## Living My Why

Today, my life is as full as it has ever been – not with the frenzy of chasing accolades, but with the steady rhythm of purpose.

I spend my days doing what I love: teaching golf, volunteering in my community, and cherishing time with family. In a typical week, you might find me coaching a group of girls at the local driving range, their laughter ringing out as they conquer their fears and learn to believe in themselves. Another day, I might organize a holiday parade through a senior center, decorating golf carts as "sleighs" and serenading our elders with their favorite carols. Seeing their faces light up as we deliver gift baskets and songs is a joy beyond measure. Those smiles remind me that simply showing up and caring can ripple out and touch hearts.

In between these community endeavors, I make time to care for my mother, Lucy, who is now in her golden years. Looking after Mom is a precious gift – a chance to return a fraction of the love she has always given me. Three generations often gather in my home: Mom at the kitchen table sharing old stories, me stirring a pot of her favorite soup, while my children and grandchildren fill the house with laughter. The warmth and sense of belonging in these moments are all part of the legacy of love my parents began.

Reflecting on my journey, I realize that everything I've done – from swinging a bat on the softball field to leading a parade for seniors – has been driven by the values my parents instilled in me. I believe in kindness, in the power of showing up for others, and in lifting people up so they can achieve their dreams. These beliefs are the compass that guides me every day. My "why" is clear now: it's to spread love, encouragement, and hope wherever I go. Whether I'm coaching a swing, planning an event, or singing a song, I know I am living my purpose when I see others shine. And I know my father is smiling down, proud that I've embraced the calling to serve – the very calling he quietly prepared me for all along.

## Ambassador Dr. Charmaine Summers

Ambassador Dr. Charmaine Summers is an LPG Golf Pro and Golf Instructor, a singer/performer, an event planner, an award-winning author, and the Director of the Lake Arrowhead GSFE Network. She built a professional golf career playing in major tournaments and went on to open three junior golf academies in Orange County, California, sharing her expertise and passion with the next generation. With over 30 years of experience in the golf industry, Charmaine has dedicated herself to coaching and inspiring others on and off the course. As the Director of the Lake Arrowhead chapter of the Global Society for Female Entrepreneurs (GSFE), she leads and mentors women entrepreneurs, reflecting her deep commitment to empowerment and community service. She also pours her event planning talents into organizing charitable fundraisers and community events that bring people together – from golf clinics for a cause to festive holiday parades for seniors. An accomplished singer and performer, Charmaine often lends her voice to entertain and inspire at community gatherings and GSFE events. Her writing has been featured in inspirational anthologies, earning her recognition as an award-winning author.

Charmaine's life mission is centered on kindness, leadership, and lifting others up. Her contributions to business, sports, and community have earned her an honorary doctorate Dr. (h.c.) and the distinguished title of "Ambassador" in recognition of her positive impact. She remains passionate about mentoring the next generation and fostering a culture of positivity wherever she goes. Charmaine and her husband Fred Trujillo reside in Southern California, where they enjoy a multigenerational family life rich with love and laughter. Through every role she holds, Charmaine continues to inspire those around her to pursue their own "why" with confidence and compassion. She is also a Wife, Mother to her daughter Crystal Ward and Grandmother to Charlotte age 9 and Bobby age 4.

Email: orangecountygolfuntygolf@yahoo.com
Phone: 714-350-3626

# The Fabric of Unity: Ochea's Journey
*By Amb. Dr. (h.c.) Chebra "Ochea" Dorsey*

In a world defined by constant transformation, Chebra Dorsey—better known by her artistic name, "Ochea" stood at the intersection of fashion and spirituality. Sunlight poured through the tall windows of her design studio in Southern California, casting a warm glow over the spools of fabric that adorned the space. Each thread held a story, a memory forged in textiles, destined to wrap around someone's essence and make them feel beautiful. For Ochea, fashion was not merely a profession; it was her profound calling—her 'why.'

Ochea is a #1 International and US award-winning author with her thought-provoking book, "What Are You Wearing: The Spiritual Side of Fashion." In it, she outlines her belief that clothing is more than a mere necessity; it is a powerful language that speaks volumes about identity, culture, and aspiration. She believed that every garment has the power to uplift the soul, whether it be an extravagant designer gown or a simple everyday outfit. Her mission is clear: to make people of all shapes, sizes, and ages embrace their unique beauty.

At the heart of her story was her childhood in California, where she lost her mother at an early age and where dreams felt like fragile butterflies, always just out of reach. Born to a creative mother and a pastor father, Ochea spent her early years in a home filled with creativity. Fabric scraps littered the floor like confetti, remnants of her tireless work. Ochea would often find herself lost in a reverie, her small hands running over the silky surfaces, imagining the lives and stories they could tell.

It was in her sewing room where the seeds of her passion were sown. She watched as she transformed dull fabric into jubilant skirts, chic blouses, and extravagant gowns for local celebrations. Yet, what fascinated Ochea most was not just the transformation of fabric but the happiness radiating from her customers when they donned her creations. Each garment made the wearer feel cherished, beautiful, and unique. Ochea recognized that beauty is not confined to a singular image; it is a spectrum, showcasing the diversity of humanity.

As she grew older, Ochea ventured beyond her town, yearning to witness the bustling world of fashion.

Every city she visited unfurled new layers of culture and expression before her. One of her customers wore one of her designs in Paris, and another at the White House in Washington, D.C. and she marveled at the haute couture shows, an explosion of color and creativity. In other countries, the fashion embraced technology and superstition in a fluid dialogue. Yet, amidst the glamour and high stakes, Ochea felt a yearning for something deeper, something profound that transcended trends—the spiritual connection that fashion could evoke.

This search led her to the heart of Beverly Hills, where she sought to realize her dream of becoming a bigger celebrity designer—a beacon of hope and beauty amidst the glitz and chaos. Yet, it was in this delicate landscape that she faced her greatest challenge. Despite her undeniable talent and burgeoning reputation, Ochea found the industry relentlessly dictated by conventional beauty standards. The pressure to conform to a singular narrative—the thin, glamorous ideal—was suffocating and disheartening.

One evening, overwhelmed by feelings of inadequacy, Ochea found herself wandering the streets, contemplating her next move. It was during this contemplative stroll that she stumbled upon a small gallery hosting an exhibition called "The Beauty Within." The show featured portraits of women of all ages, shapes, and backgrounds, their eyes sparkling with resilience and grace. As she absorbed the stories behind each image, Ochea felt a surge of inspiration wash over her.

Determined to shift the narrative, she returned to her studio, the fire within her reignited. Ochea began to create a new collection she named "Ochea Sachi Collection," emblematic of her belief that every individual is deserving of beauty. Each design celebrated different body types, while colors and textures were selected for their emotional resonance. She sought to empower her clients, urging them to wear their stories proudly without the weight of societal judgement holding them back.

Ochea's creations quickly gained traction. Her garments filled with vibrant patterns and designs began to grace the bodies of individuals from all walks of life, including actresses, models, and everyday heroes. In her designs, women alike overcame their insecurities, realizing that the fabric adorning them was an affirmation of self-worth. Spurred by this success, she was invited to showcase her collection at many prestigious gatherings.

The night at one of the runway shows, Ochea's heart raced with a mixture of exhilaration and nerves. The venue was abuzz with the elite of the fashion world, and Ochea stood backstage, surrounded by her models clothed in her creations. As the lights dimmed and the music pulsed to life, Ochea inhaled deeply, reminding herself that this was a celebration of uniqueness—an affirmation of love for every individual.

One by one, the models stepped onto the runway. The audience, initially shrouded in silence, erupted into applause with each passing figure. Each model, showcasing the raw beauty of their bodies, radiated confidence and grace. Ochea watched with tears in her eyes as the crowd began to rise to their feet, paying tribute to the intricate tapestry of humanity she sought to celebrate.

Moments later, the show culminated in a standing ovation, and Ochea was invited onstage. With a microphone in hand, she gazed out at the radiant faces in the crowd, letting their energy fuel her words.

"Fashion has the power to tell our stories," She began. "It is a universal art form that transcends beyond age, size, or culture. Tonight is not just about what you see on the runway; it's about embracing who we are as individuals. We each bring a unique thread to the fabric of this world—so let's weave a masterpiece together!"

The thunderous applause that followed felt like a harmony of countless hearts united in a shared purpose. In that moment, Ochea knew she had found her 'why.' It was no longer just about clothing—it was about connection, unity, and harnessing the transformative power of self-love.

With her journey gaining momentum, Ochea embraced the opportunities that came her way. She turned her focus to writing and sharing her experiences, culminating in the birth of her acclaimed book, "What Are You Wearing: The Inspirational Spiritual Side of Fashion." It became a heartwarming exploration of identity through the lens of style, encouraging readers to look beyond the surface and acknowledge the spiritual significance of what they choose to wear.

The book became a catalyst for open conversations about body positivity and self-acceptance in the fashion industry. Readers resonated with her words, sharing their stories of struggles, triumphs, and the transformational moments that occurred when they embraced their true selves. Ochea knew her mission was evolving, and through her writing, she ignited a movement

aimed at redefining the narrative of beauty in today's world.

In her quest to make beauty inclusive, Ochea established workshops and programs aimed at varied audiences, from teenagers grappling with self-identity to elderly communities finding empowerment in self-expression. Each session was a safe haven where individuals could explore their personal stories through fashion. They stitched together their self-portraits using fabric, guiding them through the cathartic process of expressing their journeys, transcending insecurities, and recognizing the inherent beauty within.

Throughout this journey, Ochea encountered countless individuals whose lives she touched. One young girl, Sophia, arrived at her workshop with apprehension etched across her face. Burdened by societal expectations and the pressure of fitting a specific mold, she reluctantly participated, unsure of her path. As they progressed through discussions and projects, Sophia began to shed her inhibitions, ultimately crafting a dress that symbolized her journey of self-acceptance—each detail crafted with her love and resilience. On the final day, when Sophia wore her creation before the group, tears of joy filled Ochea's eyes, witnessing a young girl reclaim her narrative.

Days turned into years, and the ripple effect of Ochea's vision transformed lives, prompting a cultural shift within the industry. She understood that the work was just beginning. The heart of her mission lay in the abundance of diverse voices ready to share their narratives—a symbiotic relationship between fashion, identity, and spirituality.

Ochea's continued journey led to her involvement in various non-profit organizations aimed at uplifting marginalized communities. She often traveled to remote locations, inspiring future generations and cultivating a sense of unity through fashion outreach programs. Her heart swelled with pride as she witnessed individuals embodying their beauty, transcending borders, and celebrating their culturally nuanced identities.

"Fashion is a language," she would often say in her workshops, "a medium that speaks the stories we yearn to share." As students adorned their creations with intricate patterns that reflected their backgrounds, they recognized the shared experiences that knotted their hearts together.

Ochea's mission, once rooted in her desire for self-expression, evolved into a legacy of empowerment. The eclectic tapestry of her journey painted a vivid portrait of humanity—the struggles, the victories, and the unwavering commitment to honor the beauty that exists within every single person.

As the years turned, Ochea realized that what started as a personal quest transformed into a movement—a heartfelt mission to redefine beauty into something that is inclusive and everlasting. In this world that constantly changes around us, her message remained grounded in acceptance, mindfulness, and love—the fabrics that entwined them all together.

And so, the story of Ochea continued, an ongoing journey sewn intricately and irreplaceably into the vast narrative of humanity—a beautiful reminder that, indeed, fashion is not just what you wear; it's an exploration of your essence, and the validation of your spirit woven through every garment you embrace.

Through her journey, Chebra Dorsey (Ochea) sought not only to elevate the fashion world, but to transform it into a nurturing space where every individual could wear their stories with pride, celebrating diversity in color, size, and soul. As the spotlight shone upon her, her heart whispered, "This is my why," reminding her that each thread woven with love constructs a more compassionate world, forever celebrating the artistry of being authentically oneself. Over the years she has received hundreds of awards honoring her including from three US Presidents. She has also graced the cover of three magazines.

### Amb. Dr. (h.c.) Chebra "Ochea" Dorsey

Chebra Dorsey, is a distinguished award-winning celebrity designer who has been designing for about 15 years, her passion is to make her clients feel beautiful. Her boutique Ochea Fashion Boutique the House of Ochea is in Lemon Grove, CA 7951 Broadway, Lemon Grove, CA 91945 she can be reached at 619-985-3804 or 619-736-0645 or email ocheafashion1@gmail.com. Her Facebook is chebradorsey or ocheafashionproduction or ocheafashionboutique.

Her Instagram is Ocheafashion and TikTok chebradorsey721. She is live on Facebook every Tuesday for her special sales.

# The Unfolding of my Why:
# Embracing Purpose in Every Step of the Journey
*By Amb. Dr. Cherilyn Lee, PhD, PA, CHNP*

As I reflect on my life, the question of "What is my why?" echoes through the corridors of my mind. It takes me back to my childhood, a period marked by an overwhelming sense of isolation. Hospital walls were my constant companions, the sterile smell of antiseptic a reminder of my struggles. While other children laughed and played, I endured countless hours in quiet rooms, my only friends the nurses and doctors who tended to my needs. In the solitude of those moments, I often wondered why I was forsaken. Why did suffering seem to be my constant companion?

As an adult, I've come to understand that those early experiences were not simply about suffering; they were about shaping me. They instilled in me a resilience that I carry to this day. Spiritual teachings often remind us that our pain has purpose, that every trial is a lesson designed to lead us toward our true selves. In reflecting on my childhood, I realize that my why was not solely about the pain; it was about the strength I gained from it. I learned to find solace in my own company, fostering a deep sense of self-reliance and inner peace.

Scripture reminds us in Isaiah 41:10, "Fear not, for I am with you; be not dismayed, for I am your God; I will strengthen you, I will help you, I will uphold you with my righteous right hand." This promise of God's unwavering presence has become a cornerstone of my faith. Even in my darkest moments, I learned that I was never truly alone; He was there, guiding me, nurturing my spirit.

Yet, as I transitioned into adulthood, new questions emerged. Why wasn't I more prosperous in my career? Why did I marry a man who didn't value me as I deserved? Why, despite my efforts, did my daughters sometimes struggle to love one another? Each of these questions has its roots in my past, and each has led me to deeper spiritual insights.

The struggles I faced in my relationships highlighted the importance of self-worth. I married seeking love yet found myself in a partnership that mirrored the abandonment of my childhood. Through the lens of spirituality, I learned that we attract what we believe we deserve. My journey involved recognizing my intrinsic value, understanding that I was worthy of love and respect. It was a powerful realization, one that transformed my perspective and paved the way for healthier relationships and a more fulfilling life.

With my daughters, I often ponder the dynamics of sibling love. Why do they sometimes drift apart? I've come to see that their relationships, like mine, are shaped by our experiences and perceptions. Spiritual teachings emphasize the importance of communication and empathy. By fostering an environment of love and understanding, I can guide them toward nurturing their bond. My why now includes a commitment to instilling values of compassion and unity within our family, ensuring that my daughters grow to be each other's greatest supporters.

Today, I stand on the brink of a wonderful multimillion-dollar journey—one that transcends financial gain. This journey, driven by divine grace, is an opportunity to impact the world positively. I am filled with excitement for what lies ahead, recognizing that my past, with all its trials, has equipped me to undertake this mission. As Jeremiah 29:11 reminds me, "For I know the plans I have for you, declares the Lord, plans to prosper you and not to

harm you, plans to give you hope and a future."

As I navigate my spiritual journey, I understand that my why is not a single answer but rather a tapestry woven from threads of experience, pain, growth, and love. Each question leads me to a deeper understanding of myself and my purpose. It's a journey of continuous discovery, where I seek to transform my past struggles into a source of strength and guidance for the future.

In embracing my why, I acknowledge that suffering has been a part of my story, but it does not define me. My experiences have taught me resilience, compassion, and the importance of connection. Ultimately, my why is about seeking growth, embracing love, and fostering unity in my life and the lives of those I cherish. I am excited about the unknowns that God has planned for my life, for I know that His love for me surpasses all understanding, even when I struggled to love myself. Through this journey, I am not only finding my purpose but also inspiring others to explore their own whys, encouraging them to see the beauty in their struggles and the potential for profound growth.

## Ambassador Dr. Cherilyn Lee, PhD, PA, CHNP

Dr. Cherilyn Lee, PhD, PA, CHNP is a speaker, author, and wellness expert. Dr. Lee is a certified Natural Healthcare Practitioner and Functional Nutrition Specialist. Dr. Lee is known for her work in pioneering integrative approaches for optimum wellness. She also holds a Doctorate in Theology and Divinity Studies. In 1980, she studied and graduated from the Charles R. Drew University of Medicine and Science.

Dr. Lee is now expanding her outreach serving as Ambassador for the Women's Federation for World Peace, Dr. Lee's advocacy for global harmony is rooted in her daily work ethic. Her humanitarian initiatives have garnered widespread recognition. She has received prestigious recognitions that include four United States Presidential Lifetime Achievement Awards—awarded under the administrations of President Barack Obama, President Donald Trump, and President Joe Biden—in honor of her lifelong service to humanity. In addition to her presidential accolades. Dr. Lee has been recognized by the Los Angeles City Council, among others, for her profound impact across communities.

She was instrumental in the California Senate recognizing October 3,2018 as Inflammatory Breast Cancer Awareness Day.

Dr. Cherilyn Lee embraces community outreach to empower individuals and transform lives through education and advocacy as an internationally sought out holistic practitioner.


Contact:

Dr. Cherilyn Lee

Email:drlee@nuwellnesshealthcare.com

Phone: 310-929-2408

# Shifting Seasons of Purpose

*By Reverend Amb. Dr. Christine Park, DD (h.c)*

In the grand journey of life, our purpose, our "why", often emerges as a series of questions, guiding us through the ebbs and flows of experience. As a daughter, a mother, a grandmother, and even a great-grandmother, I've learned that our reasons for being aren't fixed; they shift and adapt, reflecting the different seasons of our lives and the ever-changing experiences that shape us.

Looking back on my childhood, I remember being a small girl filled with an insatiable curiosity. I would bombard my mother with countless questions: Why is the sky blue? What makes the leaves dance in the wind? Each inquiry was not merely an attempt to gather information but a longing to understand the world around me and my place in it. These early questions laid the groundwork for understanding life's deeper mysteries.

My first understanding of "why" in this season was centered around a simple yet powerful motivation: to make my parents happy. I sought their approval and validation, believing that my worth was intricately tied to their perceptions. As I navigated the complexities of childhood, I began to sense that my purpose was also geared towards creating joy and harmony at home. With every accomplishment—no matter how small—I would strive to see the pride in my parents' eyes, which created a cycle of love and affirmation.

As I grew older, I witnessed my mother embody resilience and love. Her ability to navigate life's challenges with grace taught me the value of empathy and kindness. During difficult times, she became the guiding light of strength, and it was here that

I realized my purpose had started to diverge. No longer was it only about making my parents proud; it blossomed into a desire to cultivate strong relationships not only within my family but also across our community.

In my teenage years, my "why" expanded. I sought to make my parents and teachers proud while also helping my peers navigate the turbulent waters of adolescence. As I volunteered in community service and engaged in school activities, I discovered another layer of fulfillment: the joy of giving back. I learned that my purpose could also extend beyond my immediate family to embrace those around me. It became evident that our interconnectedness is a vital part of our existence, a lesson that would echo through the years.

Entering motherhood marked a profound transformation in my purpose. Suddenly, I was faced with the delightful yet daunting task of nurturing a new life. My focus shifted as I sought to guide my children through the maze of childhood and adolescence. I aspired not only to teach them foundational values but also to equip them with the tools they needed to face the world with courage and integrity.

I became acutely aware of how my actions and choices would shape their understanding of love, compassion, and resilience. Each day became an opportunity for teaching and learning—both for them and for me. In their laughter, I found solace; in their tears, I discovered the depths of my empathy. Every milestone we shared was a reminder of the incredible responsibility entrusted to me. Yet, it brought me immense joy and a renewed sense of purpose. My "why" in this season crystallized into a commitment to be the best mother I could be, drawing upon the strengths I had cultivated throughout my life so far.

As time marched on, my role expanded once more. Becoming a grandmother added another chapter to my purpose. I started to appreciate the beauty of connections that span generations. There was something profoundly fulfilling about sharing stories and wisdom with my grandchildren, a chance to nurture their hearts and minds. I sought to impart not just memories but the invaluable lessons that could only be obtained through experience.

During family gatherings, I often found myself surrounded by the chatter and laughter of multiple generations. These moments became an opportunity to ignite curiosity in my grandchildren as I introduced them to the traditions and values that have been cherished in our family. I wanted them to understand their roots, to feel the richness of our history, and to embark on their own journeys with purpose.

This sense of purpose continued unabated until I reached my fifties, and it was in that moment of reflection that I realized my "why" had predominantly been about someone else. I had spent decades focusing on being someone's daughter, sister, wife, mother, grandmother, teacher, employee, and boss. Somewhere along the way, I lost sight of myself. I became adept at fulfilling roles defined by others, to the point where my own identity felt obscured.

However, entering into this new chapter of my life prompted a profound shift in my perspective. During this season, I began to reclaim my "why," and it became centered around my own wants, needs, desires, and expectations. This newfound focus might seem self-centered, and perhaps it was. But I recognized that sometimes you need that seemingly selfish push to begin evolving into the best possible version of yourself. It's easy to lose track of who we are amidst the myriads of responsibilities of life, but asserting my voice in this new way became an act of reclaiming my purpose.

If I reflect deeply, though, I realize that my drive to share wisdom goes beyond mere family obligation. There is something inherently spiritual about passing down knowledge. It feels like a divine calling to engage with the younger generation in a way that honors our shared lineage, fostering a sense of identity and community that is vital in today's fast-paced world.

As I embraced my role as a great-grandmother, another evolution began. This season is characterized by wisdom and acceptance. Here, I've come to appreciate the transient nature of life. It is marked by the understanding that simplicity can be just as powerful as action. Sometimes, the most significant contribution we can make lies in our ability to be present, to listen, and to support. I often find solace in reflecting upon the everyday miracles—sunrise, a child's laughter, shared meals—reminders of God's grace at work in our lives.

Recently, when asked what is my why; I replied, "because God woke me up today and the devil yelled, 'Oh no, she's awake!'" This humorous awareness serves as a daily reminder of the power within me—the power to choose how I engage with the world and the people in it. Even in times of struggle and doubt, there lies a profound strength in simply being. I recognize that every morning presents a new opportunity for growth and exploration, both for myself and those around me.

As an ordained minister, I increasingly find that my mission is one of teaching rather than preaching. I don' t aim to deliver heavy-handed doctrine; rather, I wish to spark curiosity and genuine exploration of faith. I approach my ministry as a dialogue, creating spaces where questions can be voiced without fear of judgment. In my journey, I have discovered that faith is not meant to be rigid but flexible—an ongoing quest for understanding and connection.

Through my blog, Random and Spiritual Reflections, I share my thoughts on various life experiences, spirituality, and wisdom gathered over the years. Each post becomes an opportunity for connection and learning—not only for my readers but for me as well. Writing serves as a means of processing my thoughts and deepening my understanding of our shared human experiences. I strive to explore the various ways we can find purpose in life, whether through joy or in moments of quiet reflection.

As we navigate life's complexities, we may find that our purpose—our "why"—is constantly changing. Each phase of life offers new questions that compel us to grow. What drives us forward? What ignites our passions? What is our true purpose?

As you consider these questions, it becomes essential to engage with yourself honestly. What prompts you to get out of bed in the morning? Whether it's the laughter of loved ones, the pursuit of a dream, or even the yearning to make a difference in your community, allow those motivations the space to flourish.

Take a moment to reflect on your current season of life. Are there elements that resonate deeply with you? In these quiet moments of introspection, you may uncover layers of purpose that have been waiting to be recognized. Understand that it's okay for your "why" to change, just as the seasons do. Embrace this evolution, for it signifies growth and the lessons you are meant to learn.

This journey of self-discovery often involves surrendering to the wisdom gained from past experiences. As I've moved through different roles and challenges, I've found that each phase has brought valuable lessons that contribute to my understanding of purpose. Recognizing this interconnectedness allows me to navigate the uncertainties of life with a deeper sense of clarity and hope.

In closing, I encourage you to reflect on once again: What is your purpose? What is your "why"? Let the answers flow freely as you engage with your heart and soul. Life is a rich exploration, one that welcomes introspection, inquiry, and commitment to growth. Each phase offers a chance to uncover more about yourself and your higher calling.

Remember that your journey is ongoing, marked by multiple seasons. As you travel through the landscapes of your existence, remain mindful of the power within you—the ability to shape your life through choices grounded in love, service, and authenticity. When you embrace your purpose, you allow the divine spark within you to illuminate the path not only for yourself but for those who walk alongside you.

## Reverend Amb. Dr. Christine Park, DD (h.c)

Christine Park is a US and International #1 Best-selling author, Blogger, speaker, pastor, singer, Director of the GSFE Menifee Network, teacher, retired entrepreneur, and proud matriarch of a loving family. She shares her reflections on life, spirituality, and intergenerational wisdom through her blog, Random and Spiritual Reflections. With a deep passion for nurturing connections, she helps others find clarity in their lives.

To read more of her reflections, visit:

https://www.randomandspiritualreflections.com

For inquiries, reach out via email at: random.and.spiritual.reflections@gmail.com

or menifeegsfe@gmail.com

# Seemingly Simple Encounters

*By Cynthia Wilson Pleasant*

Have you ever felt that gentle nudge, that quiet inner knowing that you're destined for something more? That's your "why" softly calling.

My own understanding of this inner compass was powerfully affirmed through an unexpected detour – an undiagnosed illness that led to a seemingly ordinary encounter with a phlebotomist. What initially felt like frustrating medical delays blossomed into a divinely orchestrated moment, a simple act of kindness that illuminated my core belief: we are all intentionally created to uplift one another and reflect something greater than ourselves. It's often in these moments, both big and small, that our purpose reveals itself. My life verse, 1 Peter 2:9, reminds me that we are chosen to declare how light breaks through darkness. This very journey of life, with its unexpected turns, became a potent reminder of my "why." And it's this very principle I want to share with you: discovering your "why" holds the transformative power to change your life and the lives of those around you by making you aware of how simple encounters can have a life-altering impacts.

## Rekindled Purpose – The Journey Home

The summer I returned to California felt like a true homecoming—a move years in the making, driven by an undeniable pull of the heart. Five trips back in the prior year made it crystal clear: this was where I belonged. Now, the decision itself came easily, but navigating the housing market was a different story. It was a year-long test in resilience; full of shifting strategies and unexpected turns, before I finally landed in the right place. Once here, I was surrounded by a supportive community and a shared faith, I felt an immediate and deep sense of belonging. I embraced this new chapter with open arms and a surge of renewed energy.

Excitement and motivation fueled a period of incredible productivity. I launched my life coaching business - VIP Coaching and Consulting, joined the Global Society of Female Entrepreneurs, took on a new senior manager role in my primary career, and reconnected with family and friends. I was rebuilding and redefining my Cali lifestyle with intention and heart. I accomplished more in six months than I had in the previous six years. I even pursued a lifelong dream of writing, contributing to two anthologies. It all felt divinely orchestrated. It was a season of clarity and purpose, finally sharing the insights and strategies I'd learned through the years. I now felt ready and even compelled to share what I'd learned—so others could rise, too.

The new year dawned with a renewed sense of purpose, a personal challenge to step outside my comfort zone and embrace new opportunities. I boldly branched out, attending conferences, exploring new business ventures, and meeting new people. While I don't make New Year's resolutions, I was energized by my ambitious goals and overflowing checklist.

Then, days into this vibrant start of the new year, after a week of fruitful networking, a subtle scratchiness in my throat appeared. I thought, 'perhaps it's just allergies.' Unfortunately, none of the usual remedies offered relief. That minor irritation quickly escalated into a constant runny nose, a persistent cough, and a fatigue that would cling to me for weeks. This was the kind of cough that jolted you awake in the dead of night, made your head pound and your stomach ache.

Without an established primary care physician, two virtual visits led to a referral to urgent care for an in-person visit. There with closing time looming, the examination felt rushed, a quick listen to my chest being the extent of it. Despite mentioning the brown mucus I'd been experiencing; I walked out with a prescription for antibiotics for pneumonia – a diagnosis that felt more like a guess. The very next morning, a truly alarming symptom appeared: I started coughing up not brown, but distinctly bloody mucus. Still, trusting the doctor's orders, I continued the antibiotics. A week later, my gut telling me something was still wrong, I went to a clinic and the nurse there took my concerns seriously and sent me for a chest x-ray at the ER. The result? Clear. No pneumonia. To top it off, nausea had now joined the growing list of symptoms, yet I finished the entire course of antibiotics, still searching for what was really going on.

During this period of profound weakness, the ability to work from home was a blessing. Pajamas became my uniform and sleep my immediate reward. Simple tasks felt monumental. Delivery services became my lifeline for nourishment, my appetite waned. I distinctly remember showering before my visits to urgent care and the ER, convinced that it would necessitate admission. But each time, I went alone and was sent home feeling defeated. So, I turned to what I knew best: prayer. My primary plea was for energy, followed by healing, and ultimately for God's will to be done. I supplemented with vitamins and natural remedies, hoping for any sign of improvement.

Without a clear diagnosis, the prevailing thought was that it was viral, and after five days, there was nothing more the providers could offer. A dangerous thought began to creep in: was I just being lazy and unmotivated? It's scary to admit, but I actually started researching ways to boost my motivation. Frustrated, but always the fighter, I pressed on, pushing through the fatigue and the relentless cough, convinced I simply needed more willpower. I believe now that my body was fighting something significant internally, and my strategy was to work until exhaustion claimed me, sleep as long as possible, and then begin the next day with the same slow, dragging determination to achieve my goals.

## Divine orchestration of the ordinary

The previous year, I had planned a birthday cruise – a promised opportunity for rest and rejuvenation, a break from the whirlwind of my new life. Now, the need for respite from this mysterious illness was even more urgent. The daunting question arose: would I even have the energy? It was during the lead-up to this trip that a seemingly insignificant event became a powerful turning point.

A long-awaited new patient appointment with my PCP began with the symptoms I had been battling all month. I shared my frustrating journey, and as a precaution, the provider ordered lab work – this was now three days before my cruise. I debated putting it off but ultimately decided to take care of it before I left and headed to the lab on Friday, the day before my cruise.

The waiting room was standing room only. After an hour, a staff member announced walk-in wait times could be up to five hours due to the volume of patients. She suggested we make appointments online. I waited a few minutes then decided preparing for my cruise was a more pressing matter. I left, grabbed breakfast, and headed home. Shortly after arriving home, my phone rang. "Ms. Pleasant?" the voice on the other end inquired. Confirming it was me; she explained that my name had been called in the waiting room, and they wondered if I was nearby. I explained the earlier announcement about the long wait and that I was only ten minutes away but had already eaten. "No worries," she replied, "it will take another twenty minutes for any food or drink to show up in your blood work. Please come back now." Perplexed but compliant, I immediately returned. The incredibly busy yet kind phlebotomist called me back right away and drew my blood. As she prepared the samples, she mentioned what had prompted her to call. "We share demographics," she explained, "and I wanted to take care of you." I was shocked by this unexpected random act of concern. I had only encountered one other provider who seemed to take a genuine interest in helping me. I was grateful and thanked her and her colleague for their kindness and swift action then headed home, tired but now with a small boost of energy. I rushed to pack, gathered my documents, and headed to my friends to be closer to the port.

The next morning, about an hour before we were scheduled to leave for the port, an unknown number flashed on my phone. I rarely answer such calls, but for some inexplicable reason (a divine nudge, I now believe), I picked up. The pleasant woman on the other end identified herself as a nurse from my doctor's office. My immediate thought was, "Why are they calling me?" She informed me that my lab results were in, and my white blood cell count was critically low. The doctor needed to see me immediately and wanted to schedule an appointment for Monday. I explained that I was literally about to leave for a cruise. "When?" she asked. "Today, in an hour," I replied. Her response was firm: "No, you're not." "What do you mean?" I asked, bewildered.

She continued, "You can't go on your cruise; people are nasty." I laughed, but the reality of her words slowly sank in. "The cruise leaves today!" I exclaimed. She repeated, "You can't go." She offered to write a doctor's note for the cruise line and proceeded to give me strict instructions: avoid crowds (wear a mask if necessary), wash hands frequently, drink plenty of fluids, and rest. If my temperature rose above one hundred degrees or I felt lightheaded or dizzy, I was to head to the ER immediately. She explained that my body's ability to fight off infections was severely compromised, and any exposure could potentially lead to sepsis. I understood it all.

Completely stunned, I shared my email and cruise line details, sent a cryptic "I can't go" text to my friend and sister, and immediately began mentally searching for connections between low white blood cell counts, neutropenia, infection, and my father's battle with leukemia came to mind. I remembered neutropenia (low WBC's) was a common consequence of chemotherapy. However, I hadn't undergone chemo. A quick consultation with my trusted friend Google confirmed my fears: this could be cancer. Tears welled up and gently streamed down my face. True to my nature, I prayed. "God," I whispered, "so many wonderful things are happening in my life right now. I feel like I'm just getting started, like you still have plans for me, like I'm meant to positively impact your people. But if this is your will, Lord, please take me quickly. I don't want to linger." There was no anger, just an acceptance of life's uncertainties, especially without a clear diagnosis. I was afraid, but I just kept tapping into my faith. So, I prayed again: "Lord, help me reflect you in everything I do and everything I go through. May your glory shine through my life."

Soon after, I shared the news with my friend; my neutrophil count was 374, significantly lower than the normal range of 2500 or more. We talked, and the overwhelming emotion brought another wave of tears.

Returning to the lab for follow-up tests, I had the awesome opportunity to thank the remarkable woman whose seemingly ordinary act became a pivotal moment in my journey. Sharing the impact of her decision, I recognized it as more than professional courtesy – it was divine intervention. What touched me deeply was her response: she, too, was a believer but didn't feel God spoke to her directly. It was a privilege to affirm her experience, I shared, **"He spoke to you for me! You were His instrument."**

We talked about her relationship with God and the uncertainty she felt when she prayed. I asked if I could pray with her, and she allowed me to pray over her. Overwhelmed with emotion, I asked if I could hug her. She readily agreed, and we embraced like sisters—now bonded over this life-altering moment. A powerful connection was forged, a living testament to the truth that God often moves through everyday people, using the smallest gestures to accomplish the most meaningful work.

Henry Blackaby wisely wrote, "God is always at work around you." This encounter—and my entire journey through illness— underscored that truth in ways I never expected. The frustrating search for answers, the medical bills, the weariness from countless appointments—each detail was a divine thread in a larger tapestry. It wasn't about superstardom, social media influence, or fleeting material gain. It was about purpose unfolding in real time, in the kindness of a phlebotomist, in the unwavering support of friends, in God's divine orchestration of the ordinary.

## My Legacy

Entering my fifties ushered in a deep reflection on legacy. Without biological children, I feel an even stronger pull to leave something lasting—a piece of my heart, my mind, my spirit. My legacy is not confined to DNA; it's the ripple effect of encouragement, the wisdom shared, the lives touched, the inspiration sparked. It's about that peculiar me God crafted—used daily to uplift, guide, and remind others that their unique brilliance has a divine assignment. This is my why.

It's about helping others uncover their own "why," their own sacred calling. My joy is rooted in helping others tap into their potential—to live on purpose and with purpose. I truly want to see you win.

So, I ask you:

**What ignites your soul?**

**What makes your heart beat a little faster?**

**What gifts, experiences, and perspectives do you carry that were tailor-made to bless others?**

Your why is not some elusive mystery—it's the divine spark within, waiting to be awakened. My journey—with its detours, delays, and divine encounters—serves as a living reminder that even our greatest challenges can be the soil where purpose blooms.

As a certified life coach with decades of corporate experience, and degrees in psychobiology and healthcare management, I bring a unique blend of insight, strategy, and spiritual depth to guide you. I'm here to encourage, equip, and empower you to uncover your own God-given purpose—and to walk boldly in it.

**Let's journey together. Your purpose is calling. And I'm here to help you answer.**

VIP Access to Vision, Intention & Purpose
Not just a code – It's a Calling!

### Cynthia Wilson Pleasant

Meet Cynthia Wilson Pleasant: Owner and founder of VIP Coaching and Consulting. A visionary hailing from the vibrant city of San Diego, CA. She has 2+ decades of experience in training, development, and management where she orchestrated a symphony of IT enhancements and solutions for users throughout the enterprise, all while dancing to the rhythm of her own beat – from the comfort of her home office.

Cynthia is no ordinary manager; she's a trailblazer with a heart of gold. Fueled by an unshakable faith and an unyielding pursuit of excellence, she thrives on connecting with people on a profound level. While her role might involve millions of dollars saved and projects managed, her true triumphs lie in nurturing talents, guiding colleagues towards their dreams, and igniting the spark that leads to personal achievement.

From a pioneering first-generation college graduate at the University of California, Riverside, where she mastered the intricacies of Psychobiology, to earning an MBA in Healthcare Management from the University of Phoenix, Cynthia's journey is an embodiment of relentless dedication.

Cynthia's world is painted with diverse strokes. An entrepreneur at heart, she's not just about numbers and projects. With a coaching certification in her pocket and a passion for massage that runs deep, was the mastermind behind Heavenly Cynsations for over two decades – a testament to her dynamic spirit.

Life isn't just about business for Cynthia – balance is the key. Her heart finds joy in exploring new horizons, chasing thrilling adventures, and tracing uncharted motorcycle routes. Every twist and turn in her journey is a testament to her zest for life.

So, if you're ready to turn your life around, to rewrite your story with Cynthia's strategic guidance, you're in for an exhilarating ride. Let her unique blend of professional prowess and personal passion light up your path to success. After all, Cynthia Pleasant isn't just a coach; she's the architect ready to help you build your extraordinary tomorrow.

VIP Access to Vision, Intention & Purpose

Not just a code – It's a Calling!

# What's My Why?
# Self-Defense (From A Woman's Point Of View)
*By Debbie Love*

It has now been 37 years since my life was changed. I went from a life where I was simply sailing through - to a life with purpose.

After my cousin, Julie Love, was murdered in 1988 in Atlanta, I began going to self-defense classes. The moves made no sense to me, they were impossible to do; I wasn't big enough nor were my limbs long enough, frankly, it all seemed overly complicated. I wasn't learning anything useful. Even if I managed to successfully mimic a technique once, there was absolutely no way I was going to be able to do it again. This happened time after time, in class after class. Then it all made sense; every self-defense instructor was a man, and nine times out of ten, a very large man. How could a large man ever know what it's like to be so small and defend yourself against someone so big? This was of huge importance, Julie and I were practically identical in size – both under five feet and less than 100 lbs. Teaching those techniques to women made no sense. Because women do not talk openly in the presence of a man, I have no idea what the other women thought, but I was thinking what are you teaching and why teach those techniques to women. What I truly thought was WHERE ARE THE WOMEN?

In 2020, the COVID pandemic as well as a presidential election left many women indoors and in abject fear of their partner for exacerbated domestic violence cases and abuse. More victims were trapped at home with their abusers with no excuses to get out. Abusers maintained practically complete control of the women and their households. Everything was going online.

Abused women were once again stuck and invisible with no way to escape.

I'm not sure people can see how much our world has changed since 1988, when Julie Love was still here. I'm not sure she would recognize the place. One of the rights women lost and are experiencing the consequences of is the overturning Roe v. Wade.

When I first read the following paragraph from the book Survivor Justice, by Kylie Cheung, I thought I was reading something out of the 1800's, but I was actually reading geographer, Leslie Kern's words from her 2020 book Feminist City:

A woman alone is presumed always available to other men. It links back to notions of women as men's property. If a woman out in public isn't clearly marked as property by the presence of another man … then she is fair game. Women instinctively know that the quickest way to deter a man's unwanted advances is to tell him you have a boyfriend or husband. Men will respect another man's property rights more readily than they'll respect a woman's simple "NO."

The consequences of overturning Roe v Wade took women back generations. Sometimes I have to wonder; did they arrest these women because they usually don't put up a fight and are easier to handle. Please note paragraph B below.

A. In 2019 Brook R. of Ohio, an 18-year-old high school student, was charged with aggravated murder, involuntary manslaughter, child endangerment and gross abuse of a corpse after giving birth to a stillborn fetus and burying it in her yard. After a trial, she was acquitted in Sept. 2019

B. In 2019, Marshae J. faced manslaughter charges in Alabama after being shot in the stomach and had a miscarriage. Police pressed charges because Jones had allegedly started the fight that led to her injuries, which is yet another example of how victims of violence and abuse can potentially be punished for self-defense, especially if they are pregnant.

C. In 2021, Jennie M. of Idaho, a mom of three who had her first child at 14, was arrested for terminating her pregnancy with an abortion pill she purchased online. She was charged under a 1973 state law in Idaho which treats self-managed abortion as a felony punishable by up to 5 years in prison.

D. In 2016, Katherine D., a 26-year-old Virginia woman was convicted and jailed after experiencing a stillbirth.

E. Amber A., in 2017, Amber, an 18-year-old, was criminally charged for "procuring a miscarriage."

There were many, many more horrible stories which I chose not to include.

## An Example of a Kid's Intuition:

Take notice: If your kid makes a comment about someone and, in his or her way, is talking differently. Let's say a family friend comes over (your kid's loves this person) but out of the blue he says he doesn't like this person and how he sees this person has totally changed, e.g., someone who is visiting leaves your home and your kid makes a comment about someone who makes him or her feel uncomfortable or says he doesn't like it when that certain person is around. Her mood may suddenly change. Please take note and listen to what your kid says. This person could be a neighbor, family friend, relative, coach, teacher, friend of a sibling, clergy, babysitter (or her boyfriend). LISTEN TO YOUR CHILD AND WHAT HE or SHE SAYS! No kid, or adult for that matter, would suspect someone at church would use grooming techniques on your kid. If you dismiss your kid because you've known the 'groomer' for years and your first response is 'there's no way,' this sends the wrong signal to the kid. The kid must have it wrong. If the kid is shut down, there's a good chance the kid won't bring it up again, ever. Remember, this is someone who has some authority over the child, someone older, in school or church, on the playground, at soccer or other practice. No matter what the age of the child, once the kid finds the courage to bring it up but is then shut down by a parent or guardian not believing it's possible, the kid may shut down and never bring it up again. Never leave your kid alone with this person, not in a room, not in a car, not in a studio, not in a dojo, not in a rink, not in a pool, not in the back yard or the front or ever permit this person be alone with your kid in a car or other environment. Never ever!! This leads to all kinds of problems. Even if you don't understand it or can't define it, it's not easy to talk about. The kid is simply uncomfortable when this person is around and she's trying to tell you. Maybe it's the way the person looks at her or always picks her up and squeezes her to his chest. If the kid can't explain what it is, that's normal. Don't refuse to believe it because this guy is your brother, best friend, clergy, boss, partner, etc. and he'd never do anything to hurt your kid. Anyone with authority over your child might not have your child's best interest in mind. They are masters at manipulating vulnerable kids.

If mom and dad are not in the kid's corner, who will be? If someone makes your child uncomfortable, take note that your child's intuition is working. Don't ignore what he or she says! Don't second guess what is said! Feel free to ask questions because often a predator will insist that "this is our little secret – don't tell anyone – not even mom and dad."

If your girl says she saw Coach today and says it in a sad way, don't leave it at that, ask questions.

1. What did you and the coach talk about? Then ask follow up questions.

2. Where did you see him? What did you talk about and where?

3. What else happened?

Being a Female Martial Artist and Self-Defense Instructor.

As a woman, I bring a different style of training and philosophy to self-defense. My focus uses the same basic principles of self-defense; I simply teach them differently and in a way women will understand and thereby be able to do.

## AWARENESS + INTUITION + MOVEMENT

## AWARENESS

This is #1 for a reason. Be aware of who and what is around you. If you do the same thing every day, take the same route every day, usual place for coffee, lunch at the same place most days (tip: get to know one of the women who work there or a friend who shares a love for the place and know them by name) She knows your secret too. If you gesture tilting or moving your eyes in his direction, she is tipped off and possibly moves you to safety.

## INTUITION

If someone makes you feel uneasy, or unsafe, but you don't know why. Maybe it's the way he looks at you, but it's a little scary – meet Intuition. Intuition is real. When it speaks, listen. Like, 'something's not right here .' That feeling when something is off, but you don't know why. Trouble can start if you wind up alone. If you feel something in your gut ... it's Intuition! Don't dismiss it.

## MOVEMENT

When you think of defensive movements as dance steps, they are easy to remember. When we dance we engage our hips for flair. Defensively, the hips create your power. The more flair-the more power! Chai

I work with your strengths, so you are working with your best and strongest parts. If a downward elbow is your go-to #1 best strike, that's what we work on first. Then go from there. Having a go to move–knowing where you are strongest builds confidence. I explain exactly what you're doing and why – woman to woman. It makes a huge difference.

A female instructor understands coercion, intimidation, and fear. Why? Because every woman has been there.

The movements are simple. It's a matter of being in the best position possible for the best result. Be balanced and in a solid position. If you're off-balance or out of position for what you want to do–stop! It could backfire.

Reduce intimidation and fear by knowing what to say and do if a line is crossed.

1. If possible, keep your distance.

2. Either don't get in a position where harm may find you, or

3. Know what to do if it does.

A female instructor will see where your strengths are and make them stronger. She will show you how to use what you've got and not waste time on things you'll never need or use. The best position for your strengths. And, that every situation is unique.

Why should girls learn from a female instructor?

What works for a man may not work for a woman. Women must be clever in what they do; being clever is something the opposition never sees coming. Fighting is not top of mind for girls because it never was. Even knowing what to do, girls don't have the experience of rough play as boys do. Boys wrestle; girls do not. But we are changing that.

Men and women do not think the same. They aren't raised the same. They don't compete in the same sports. Men are bigger and stronger. If he wants it, he can take it and he can take it by force if he has to. What she thinks doesn't matter once he has made the decision. He has a plan that she isn't aware of.

It's time for women to be in charge ... to say what is and what's not ... to set priorities ... to say what is legal and what is not ... no longer are we passengers on this train ... we always have been the quiet engine ... now we are loud!!!

At first, my story was about Julie Love and the details of a horrible night that changed my life and many others. I understand the gamble she took that night because I had done it dozens of times. I didn't want to think this could have been avoided by filling her gas tank.

## Dr. Debbie Love

Debbie Love is a 4th Degree Black Belt and Certified Instructor in Karate and Kobudo. With over 30 years of martial arts training focused on self-defense, she's all about empowering the ones who might feel like easy targets. Standing at 4'11" and 95 lbs., Debbie found that traditional self-defense classes didn't quite fit—literally. So, she decided to reinvent the game. With her vast experience, Debbie is a powerhouse advocate for safety and empowerment. She uniquely blends smarts, instincts, and some seriously cool moves into a seamless groove of protection and awareness. She's on a mission to show that self-defense isn't just about muscle—it's about wits, wisdom, and maybe having a little fun along the way.

Contact: Dr. (h.c.) Debbie Love Warrior Women Workshops

Phone: 760-455-8562 or Email: lovedebbi@gmail.com

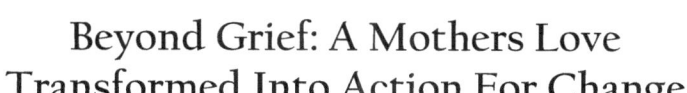

# Beyond Grief: A Mothers Love Transformed Into Action For Change

*By Amb. Dr. (h.c.) Dorothy Wolons*

## In memory of Jordan Donny Hughes
## July 20, 1996 - December 31, 2023

Why? Losing a child is one of the most profound and painful experiences one can face, and I can only begin to share the depth of MY grief. While I can provide some words and thoughts that may resonate with you, please know that your journey through grief is uniquely your own. Most importantly don't let anyone tell you the difference.

## What is My Why?

In the quiet moments of the morning, when the world is still wrapped in a soft blanket of dawn and here comes the sun, I often find myself struggling with a question that feels both heavy and puzzling: What is my why? Why do I wake up each day when the very essence of my joy, my son, is no longer here? The pain is apparent, a constant ache that shadows every thought and memory. Yet, deep within this sorrow, I feel the stirrings of purpose—an unyielding desire to honor my son's memory, to create meaning from the tragedy, and to help others who find themselves in the depths of desperation, misery, pain, and sorrow.

## The Weight of Grief

Grief is a complex and multifaceted journey. For me, it comes and goes, sometimes crashing over me like a tidal wave, other times allowing me brief moments of relief, ease, forgiveness, laughter, and many times a breather. Each day is a reminder of what I have lost: his laughter, his knowledge of unexpected things, his kindness, the dreams I had for his future, everything we will not have as a family. There are moments when the weight of his absence feels unbearable, where the thought of moving forward seems impossible. Every shower I take is a release of pain, tears, and an occasional laugh of my memories of my son Jordan. Yet, in those moments of darkness, I often reflect on the love we shared, him as a child, teen and adult, the conversations we had, the struggles he felt—the love a mother and son share, that transcends even the most profound loss.

**A Journey of Memories**

When I think of my son Jordan, I am flooded with memories. I recall the way his face lit up with joy during family gatherings, his infectious laughter echoing in the room. He had this remarkable ability to bring people together, to find joy in the simplest things—a shared joke, music trivia, historic facts, a funny story, a quiet moment of connection. I remember the dreams he spoke of the plans he made, and the limitless potential he had. He had gotten a truck, had a paycheck, a job, got an apartment lease, been clean for six months, going to get his smog license, becoming a certified mechanic, an entirely new set of friends that gave him purpose and hope for new beginnings.

And then, in a heartbeat, it was taken away. One moment, one hit of fentanyl, and everything changed. My heart aches not just for the loss of his life, but for all the moments he will never experience: the milestones he will miss, the love he will not find, the family moments that will forever remain unfulfilled.

## Finding Purpose in Pain

But as I navigate this overwhelming grief, I am confronted with a choice: to be consumed by my sorrow or to find a way to channel it into something meaningful. This is where the question of "why" becomes essential. What can I do with this pain? How can I honor my son's memory in a way that both acknowledges my grief and seeks to create something positive in the world?

In the wake of his death, I have witnessed firsthand the devastating effects of addiction, not just on the individual, but on families, communities, and society at large. I have seen how stigma often prevents people from seeking help, how the fear of judgment silences those who are struggling. I want to change that. I want to be a voice for those who are suffering, to advocate for awareness, compassion, and understanding surrounding addiction and mental health.

## Becoming an Advocate

My why is becoming an advocate for change. I want to share my son's story, to raise awareness about the dangers of fentanyl and other substances that claim lives too soon. I want to participate in community initiatives that educate families about the signs of addiction, the importance of open conversations, and the resources available for those who need help.

I envision more COMMUNICATION, keeping open discussion amongst family, friends, communities, which provides comfort, and awareness for families affected by addiction. It should not be shamed or kept a family secret if someone is struggling, because it does affect everyone. There are people who offer counseling, resources, and a safe space for those who feel alone in their suffering. Those resources are not just for those dealing with addiction but everyone in their circle. I want to ensure that other families don't have to endure the same heartache that I have. My son's life, though tragically cut short, can serve as a catalyst for change—a beacon of hope for those still fighting their battles. But we need to talk, communicate, and bring out these demons to help slow down this drug moment. Bring awareness to the darkness that surrounds so many families. Communicate and get involved, be a voice, be present and most of all be aware.

## Embracing the Journey of Healing

Healing is breathing, breathing more and more each day. There are days when the weight of my grief is all-consuming, and other days when I can smile at a memory without feeling the sting of loss. I am learning to embrace this journey, to allow myself the space to feel, to grieve, and to heal. I understand that my son would want me to continue to live, to find joy again, to cherish the moments we had while also creating new memories with those who are still here.

I am learning to celebrate his life, to honor him not just in grief, but in love. I think of how he would want me to carry on, to find laughter amidst the tears. My why encompasses not just my grief, but my love for him—a love that will never fade, even in his absence.

## Building a Community

As I embark on this journey of advocacy, I am discovering the power of community. In connecting with others who have faced similar losses, I find solace and strength. We share our stories, our heartaches, and, in doing so, we create a network of understanding and compassion. This community becomes a sanctuary, a place where the weight of grief feels a little lighter because we are not alone in our suffering.

The stories we tell—each one unique yet threaded with common pain—remind us that we are part of something larger than ourselves. We are mothers, fathers, siblings, friends, all navigating the aftermath of loss. Together, we can raise our voices, advocate for change, and foster an environment where open conversations about addiction are not only welcomed but encouraged.

## Honoring My Son's Legacy

As I pursue my why, I am constantly reminded of my son and the legacy he left behind. His spirit—one of kindness, humor, and love—motivates me to keep pushing forward. I want to ensure that his life is remembered not only for the tragedy of his death but for the joy he brought to those around him. I carry his memory with me, a guiding light that propels me toward my mission.

I envision a world where conversations about addiction are met with empathy rather than judgment, where individuals struggling with substance use can find the support they need without fear of stigma. My son's story can be a part of that transformation—a reminder that behind every statistic is a person, a family, a community left to deal with loss.

## A Mother's Memorial

I never thought I would be sitting here, writing about the loss of my precious son. It's a pain that no parent should ever have to endure. Jordan, my beautiful boy, was taken from me too soon, a victim of the drugs that plague our community. During my grief, I knew I had to do something to bring awareness to the devastating impact of drugs in our city. I wanted to honor my son's memory and make sure that his story would not be forgotten. That's when the idea of a memorial bench came to me. I decided that the perfect place for Jordan's memorial would be John V. Denver Park, 28050 Encanto Drive, in the City of Menifee California. It was a place close to his heart, where he used to attend his AA and NA meetings at Unity Hall, just a block or two away. I wanted his memorial to be a source of comfort and support for those struggling with addiction, a reminder that they too can fight this battle. With a sense of determination, I reached out to the city. I had never seen a memorial bench in any other park, but based on a referral from a friend, I called the city and set up a meeting. To my surprise, they mentioned a program they were considering. We saw this as an opportunity to partner together and make Jordan's memorial a reality. Through this partnership, Jordan became the first recipient of one of these benches in the City of Menifee. I am deeply honored that his memorial not only features the serenity prayer but also includes his picture. The city recognized the urgent need to combat the use of fentanyl in our community, and they saw this memorial to raise awareness. The power of asking was evident throughout this process. Sometimes, all it takes is the courage to ask for what you want. In my case, it resulted in a beautiful memorial for my son. Though he will never see it or come home, we now have something tangible to remember him by. And I hope that this bench will also serve as a source of strength for others in the park, reminding them that they too can overcome their battles. Losing a child to drugs is a pain that no parent should ever have to bear. But through this memorial, I hope to bring awareness to the drugs that are tearing apart our community. Let us come together and fight against the devastation caused by addiction. It is time for us to support one another and provide the resources necessary for recovery. In memory of Jordan, let us honor his life by standing up against drugs. Let this bench be a symbol of hope, resilience, and the power of unity. Together, we can make a difference and create a community free from the grip of addiction.

On December 6, 2023, the Menifee City Council recognized Ms. Dorothy Wolons for donating a beautiful bench at John V. Denver Park to honor her son, Jordan Donny Hughes.

Jordan, a long-time Menifee resident, passed away earlier this year. To memorialize his life, Jordan's family and friends raised funds to donate a park bench that includes his photo and a custom engraving of the serenity prayer to the City of Menifee. John V. Denver Park was selected for the memorial bench as Jordan's family and the Denver Family are close friends.

#JordanHughes13

We have witnessed the incredible strength and resilience of a grieving mother who, in the face of unimaginable loss, found the power to ask for change. Through her partnership with the City of Menifee, she successfully brought awareness to the fentanyl crisis and secured a bench in a city park, serving as a powerful symbol of the struggles of addiction that plague our communities. This chapter serves as a reminder that by showing up and asking for help, we can make a difference and bring about positive change in our community.

## The Impact of Awareness

One of the greatest challenges we face in addressing addiction is the stigma that surrounds it. Many people view addiction as a moral failing rather than a complex health issue. By sharing our stories, we can challenge this narrative. We can illuminate the fact that addiction does not discriminate; it affects people from all walks of life, regardless of their background or circumstances.

Through awareness, communicating with friends and family, community workshops, and educational programs, I hope to help others understand the realities of addiction. By providing information about the risks associated with substances like fentanyl, we can empower individuals to make informed choices and seek help when needed. Education is a powerful tool, and in my quest for purpose, If I can save one life, I am successful, if I can relieve some pain of grief, I have honored my son.

## Creating Safe Spaces

In my advocacy journey, I envision encouraging families and friends to come together to share their stories and feelings of dealing with addiction or grief, communicating with each other about how it is affecting them, at a planned family get-together, a support group, community forums, or online platforms where individuals can connect, share resources, and find comfort in knowing they are not alone. By fostering an environment of openness and understanding, we can help break the cycle of silence that often surrounds addiction.

I want to encourage families to have difficult conversations about mental health and substance use. The more we talk about these issues, the less stigma will surround them. By creating a culture of compassion and understanding, we can help those struggling to feel seen and heard, reminding them that they do not have to face their battles alone.

## Embracing the Future

While the future may seem daunting at times, I hold on to the belief that it is also filled with potential. My why extends beyond my grief; it is a call to action, a commitment to make a difference in the lives of others. As I navigate this path, I remind myself to be patient with my healing process. There will be days when the grief feels overwhelming, and that is okay. Each step I take, no matter how small, is a step toward honoring my son and the life he lived.

I find strength in the connection I make with others, and I recognize that my journey is not just about my pain; it is about the collective experience of loss that binds us. I am part of a larger narrative, one that encompasses hope, resilience, and the possibility of healing.

## Continuing the Conversation

As I move forward, I am committed to continuing the conversation about addiction and mental health. I want to engage friends and family, with policymakers, healthcare professionals, and community leaders to advocate for better resources and support systems for those affected by addiction. Together, we can work toward creating a society that prioritizes mental health and provides accessible, compassionate care for individuals in need. But above all is communicating, keep talking about addiction, fentanyl, death you never know who is listening and going through the same, and just needs some help or someone to just listen.

I also plan to continue writing, co-authoring, and using other platforms to share my journey, raise awareness, and connect with others who share similar experiences. The power of storytelling can foster understanding, empathy, and support. By sharing my son's story and the lessons I have learned through grief, I hope to inspire others to find their own why and start the talk.

## Finding Joy Amidst Grief

In the midst of it all, on a daily basis, I am learning to find joy again. I am discovering that it is possible to hold both grief and happiness in the same space. I cherish the moments when I can laugh at a memory, feel the warmth of connection with others, and celebrate the beauty of life despite the pain of loss.

I have begun to engage in activities that bring me joy—whether it be through creative expression, quilting, writing, spending time with loved ones, playing with my grandchildren, or immersing myself in travel. I find solace in the distraction, listening to music, looking at photos, or the rustle of leaves on a breezy day, birds flying by, the warmth of the sun on my face, and the laughter of friends and family. These moments remind me that life continues, and while my son may no longer be physically present, his spirit lives on in the love I carry in my heart.

## The Importance of Self-Care

As I navigate this multifaceted journey of grief. I've come to understand the importance of self-care. Caring for myself is not an act of selfishness; it's a necessity. It allows me to replenish my emotional reserves, to stay grounded as I face the challenges of grieving and the hopes for my family's future.

I've started to incorporate practices that nurture my well-being, such as freedom to cry, express emotion, not suppress my feelings, volunteering, and writing. These tools provide me with the space to reflect on my emotions, to honor my grief, and to celebrate my son's life. Through writing, I can express my thoughts and feelings freely, creating a dialogue that helps me process my experiences and find meaning in them.

## Building Resilience

Through self-care, I am building resilience. I am learning that it's okay to ask for help and to lean on others when I need support. Friends and family have been invaluable during this time, providing love, understanding, and a listening ear. I've found strength in their compassion, and together, we navigate the landscape of grief, learning to hold space for one another.

In moments of despair, I remind myself of the resilience that exists within me. This journey is not just about survival; it's about thriving in the face of adversity. I want to emerge from this experience not only as a mother who has lost her son but as a woman who has learned to channel her grief into purpose. I want to be a testament to the power of love and the capacity for healing, even in the depths of sorrow.

## Sharing My Journey

In sharing my journey, I hope to empower others to find their own voice in the battle against addiction. I want to encourage individuals to speak openly about their struggles and to seek help when needed. By opening the conversation around addiction, we can foster a culture of support and compassion.

I plan to participate in public speaking engagements, sharing my story, and co-authoring by writing. I want to reach those who may be affected by addiction, whether directly or indirectly, and inspire them to take action. It is my hope that through these conversations, we can create a ripple effect that encourages others to share their stories, seek help, and advocate for change.

## The Power of Storytelling

Storytelling will be one of the most powerful tools in our movement. By sharing our experiences, we can break down barriers and challenge the stigma surrounding addiction. Each story is a thread in the larger tapestry of our collective experience, illustrating the diverse realities of addiction/grief and the impact it has on families.

I plan to encourage individuals to share their stories through social media, community events, and networking events. I personally will continue to add my thoughts and stories through books and let my story be published. By amplifying these voices, we can foster understanding and compassion, creating a ripple effect that encourages others to seek help and support.

## Jordan's Legacy of Love

Ultimately, my why is rooted in love—the love I have for my son Jordan and the love I want to share with others. Each step I take in this journey, whether through advocacy, community engagement, or simple acts of kindness, is a tribute to him. I want to honor his memory not just by morning the loss but by celebrating the life he lived and the impact he had on those around him.

The legacy I wish to create is one of hope, compassion, and resilience. I want my son to be remembered not just as a victim of addiction but as a vibrant soul who touched the lives of many. In doing so, I hope to inspire others to view addiction through a lens of empathy and understanding rather than judgment.

## Embracing the Journey Ahead

As I look to the future, I know that the path ahead will not always be easy. Grief is a lifelong journey, and there will be days when the waves of sorrow feel overwhelming. However, I also recognize that amidst the pain, there is the potential for growth, healing, and transformation.

I am committed to continuing to share my story and connecting with others who share the same sorrows. I want to show my support for families affected by addiction, helping them navigate their own journeys and find hope in the face of unimaginable loss.

In the quiet moments of reflection, I remind myself that my son's spirit is woven into the fabric of my soul. His laughter, his kindness, and his dreams are not lost; they live on in our family and the people we touch. Each step I take is infused with Jordan's memory, and I carry him with me as I strive to make a difference in the world.

That is my Why!

## Amb. Dr. h.c. Dorothy Wolons

Amb. Dr. h.c. Dorothy Wolons is a dedicated professional and active community member based in Menifee, California, originally from Detroit, Michigan. She began her career in finance as a Collections Manager after graduating from Wayne State University and transitioned to running a national sales team before starting her own retail businesses. Dorothy served as CEO and Director of the Menifee Valley Chamber of Commerce for 10 years, contributing significantly to the community and volunteering with various organizations, including the Global Society for Female Entrepreneurs. A devoted mother and grandmother, she is also an accomplished international best-selling author and an ordained minister, driven by her faith and desire to help others. Following the tragic loss of her son, Dorothy is passionately advocating against the fentanyl crisis, aiming to create a safe environment for children. Through her advocacy, she works to raise awareness and promote prevention efforts to combat this urgent issue, showcasing her commitment to making a positive impact on society.

Cell: (951) 240-0219

Dorothy.Wolons@yahoo.com

# My Why: A Journey from Mango Trees to Majesty

*By H.R.M. Prof. Dr. Queen Eden Soriano Trinidad*

## Introduction: The Power of Why

What's your why? It's a question that lingers in the air, simple yet heavy with meaning. Why do you rise each morning and choose the path you walk? Why do you pour your heart into the work you do, the relationships you nurture, the dreams you chase? I've asked myself this countless times, and I've come to believe that finding your why is the compass that guides every decision—whether it's choosing a career, a partner, or the quiet intentions you set for your own growth. Without it, we drift. With it, we move with purpose, clarity lighting the way through life's inevitable storms.

My why has carried me from the shade of mango trees in a rural Philippine village to the uncharted sands of a new nation, from the hum of a classroom to the weight of royal titles bestowed by kings across continents. It's a story I never imagined for myself, yet one that feels destined when I trace the threads of my life. This chapter is my invitation to you—to pause, to reflect, and to uncover your own why. Because if a teacher named Eden can become Her Majesty Queen Eden Soriano Trinidad, then your why, too, holds the power to shape a legacy beyond your wildest dreams.

## The Call to Serve: Roots in Education

My journey began with a whisper from God—a call to serve children. I didn't come from wealth or privilege; I came from a heart that swelled with joy at the sight of a child's eyes lighting up with understanding. Teaching wasn't just a profession; it was a sacred mission. I remember the first time I heard a little voice stumble through a nursery rhyme, then recite it with pride days later. I'd watch them trace shaky letters into words, count pebbles into numbers, and I'd feel a thrill that no paycheck could rival. Those moments—watching a child read a Bible verse for the first time or beam as they mastered a simple sum—were my reward.

It started small, as most great things do. In the rural reaches of Zambales, Philippines, I felt that call grow louder. The children there didn't have gleaming classrooms or stacks of textbooks. Many didn't have shoes, let alone access to a school. But I saw their potential, bright and boundless, and I knew I couldn't turn away. That's when I decided to act—not with grand plans or resources, but with faith and a fierce determination to give them what they deserved: an education.

## Building from Nothing: A Pioneer's Spirit

In Zambales, I became more than a teacher—I became a builder. I pioneered an outreach school with nothing but a vision and a heart full of purpose. There was no funding, no brick walls, no desks. I started with preschoolers gathered under mango trees, their laughter mingling with the rustle of leaves overhead. We rigged a canopy from coconut fronds, a flimsy shield against sun and rain, and I taught them there—on the dirt, with sticks for pointers and the earth as our chalkboard. I'd lug a sack of battered books and a few scraps of paper, and we'd begin.

The early days were grueling. Rain turned our classroom to mud, heat sapped our energy, and doubt crept in like a thief. Parents were skeptical—why trust this woman with no building, no credentials flashing on a wall? But I pressed on, driven by the belief that every child, no matter what their circumstance, deserved quality education. Slowly, they came—,Slowly, they came—five students, ten, then twenty, then Forty, and then Eighty. We sang songs, recited rhymes, and learned the alphabet under that canopy. Over time, that seed sprouted into a grade school, built not just with my hands but with the trust of a community that began to see what I saw: possibility.

Those years were my training ground. I learned to create something from nothing, to adapt when plans crumbled, to lead when others hesitated. I'd haul water for the kids, mend torn pages, and pray for strength when exhaustion set in. Each step taught me resilience; each child's smile fueled my resolve. That pioneer spirit—unshakable, restless—became the bedrock of my why.

## The Vision Unfolds: From Classrooms to New Horizons

In 2006, a vision seized me, vivid and unrelenting. For three months, every day, I saw it: endless green fields stretching toward a white path that vanished into the horizon. No end, no boundaries—just a promise of something vast. It flashed before my eyes like a beacon, a whisper of a future I couldn't yet grasp. I didn't know what it meant then, but it lodged in my soul, a quiet fire urging me onward.

That vision began to take shape years later when I launched an e-campus—a university rooted in distance learning. The mango trees had taught me that education didn't need walls; it needed will. With technology, I could reach children and adults far beyond Zambales, breaking barriers of geography and circumstance. It was a natural evolution of my why—extending the foundation I'd laid to a global scale. But even as I climbed that ladder, the white path, and green fields lingered, hinting at a calling yet to unfold. Was there more? Should I chase a new passion? The question simmered, and soon, life would answer.

## Legacy and Leadership: A Global Calling

The teacher who built a school from nothing found herself summoned to build again—this time, a nation. In the unclaimed Bir Tawil land between Sudan and Egypt, a new country emerged: the State of Birland. I was chosen as its Prime Minister, tasked with forging a future from barren sands. It echoed Zambales in uncanny ways—starting from zero, no infrastructure, just a vision and a will to make it real. I dove in, drawing on every lesson those mango trees taught me: adaptability, perseverance, faith. We're crafting a nation step by step, a testament to what's possible when you refuse to give up.

Then came the royal titles, bestowed not by one kingdom but by many—Indigenous and traditional kings across Africa, Indonesia, and Venezuela. Why me? I've asked myself that under countless sleepless nights. The answer lies in the bridges I've built—not of stone, but of trust and purpose. My work with education, my outreach to communities, my unwavering belief in humanity's potential—these earned me the respect of leaders who saw in me a kindred spirit. From a teacher to Her Majesty Queen Eden Soriano Trinidad, my why crystallized: to unite, to uplift, to leave a legacy that spans continents.

## Living My Why: Family, Faith, and Fortitude

What keeps me going? It's a tapestry of forces. I thrive on achieving greatness—not fleeting wins, but enduring impact. My family is my anchor; they cheer every triumph, share every burden. They've never seen my dreams as a wedge between us; I'm the glue binding our love. Faith guides me—God's call still echoes in my choices. And fortitude—that pioneer's grit—carries me when the path grows steep.

I don't plan every detail; life's too wild for that. Sometimes I leap on gut instinct, a pull I can't ignore. Other times, I weigh options with care. Flexibility is my strength—knowing when to act, when to wait. It's served me from classrooms to kingdoms, and it's a lesson I pass to you: trust your why, even when the road bends.

## Conclusion: From Humility to Majesty

The teacher Eden is now Her Majesty Queen Eden Soriano Trinidad—not by chance, but by choice, by countless steps from humility to majesty. My why is a legacy of building—schools, nations, hope. It's a story that began under mango trees and stretches to the horizon, a white path I still chase. What's your why? Let mine inspire you to find it, to live it, to leave your mark. This book will unfold more of my journey, but here, I offer you the heart of it: your why is your power. Claim it.

## H.R.M. Prof. Dr. Queen Eden Soriano Trinidad

She hails from the Philippines and in 2021 became the Prime Minister of the State of Birland‐ a country under establishment in Bir Tawil Africa up to this date.

The extraordinary journey from being an educator and school director in the Philippines to—being chosen and conferred as Queen across multiple kingdoms in Africa and beyond—is a testament to the remarkable path that has unfolded before her. The reflection on the abundance of divine love and the unexpected turns of events in her life resonates with a profound sense of awe and purpose.

The titles conferred, granted, and instilled to her from the International Queen of Ovuorie Kingdom in Nigeria to the Queen of Ohanaeze Kingdom Worldwide in Ghana, the Queen of Embo Kingdom in South Africa, and beyond, reflect a tapestry of recognition that spans continents and cultures. Each conferment—whether by HRM Igwe Chinedu Okafor Ogbu, King Bungane III, or Maharaja lansyah Rechza F.W.—speaks to a unique bond between her and the peoples and traditions she now represents. Her words, echoing the kings' response that it is not their choice alone but a higher calling, beautifully capture the sacred weight of this responsibility.

This, alongside her other distinguished titles, paints a picture of a life transformed by grace and destiny. Her gratitude shines through, illuminating the humility with which she carries these honors.

https://www.edensorianotrinidad.com

www.birland.net

Whatsapp: +639176221977

Email: edensorianotrinidad@gmail.com

# My Why: A Journey of Empowerment through the Arts

*By Emiko Ishii*

My "why" is simple yet profound: to empower individuals through the arts, helping them discover their unique voices and inherent strength. To me, the arts are not just a form of expression; they are a powerful tool that can transform lives. My mission is to inspire others to pursue their passions, break down barriers, and unlock their full potential. In both performance and life, I believe in the words of a powerful Japanese proverb: "Fall seven times, get up eight." This encapsulates the resilience we all possess, reminding us to persist in our dreams, no matter what the challenge is we face.

As a British-born Japanese actress, action performer, choreographer, mentor, and career coach, I have dedicated over 23 years to the arts. Throughout this journey, I established Epika Dance, an internationally award-winning Bollywood fusion dance company based in London. Each rejection I faced was not just a setback; it became a steppingstone that fueled my resilience and drive. I've learned to view challenges as opportunities, allowing me to guide many aspiring artists through their own struggles and help them shine brightly.

From a young age, I harbored dreams of becoming an actress in the US, even when faced with adversity. At just 13 years old, my agency told me there were no roles for Japanese girls and that my eyes were "too small." This first rejection ignited a fire within me, igniting my determination to prove that anything is possible. My petite stature and asthma were also hurdles that some said would hold me back from joining the ULOTC, yet I trained relentlessly, dedicating time to develop my mental endurance and teamwork skills and ultimately earning my place.

Establishing my Bollywood dance company was a significant milestone in my career. However, doubts arose about my ability to teach a cultural dance as a Japanese woman. Despite the skepticism, I successfully taught thousands of students, creating a multitude of opportunities for them. Balancing parental expectations to pursue university studies at King's College, I fully immersed myself in my passion to showcase Asian representation through directing and producing Bollywood and Japanese short films, ultimately earning recognition with a Professional Practice Award.

A turning point in my journey came in 2010 when I embraced the opportunity to star in "Mad About Dance," leading me to the semi-finals of Britain's Got Talent and a chance to contribute to the choreographic team for the London Olympics opening ceremony. I began planning my move to America, receiving support from my family. However, life took a challenging turn when my grandmother fell ill, and I became one of her primary caregivers, working and building Epika Dance, all while striving to inspire future leaders in the arts.

An unexpected injury requiring ACL surgery and navigating profound personal loss tested my resilience. I amazed my doctors by returning to dance within just three months, driven by my determination to chase my dreams in the US. My experiences also led me to work with individuals with disabilities, providing dance therapy and training teachers to work with autistic children, reinforcing my belief that the arts can be a source of healing and empowerment.

In 2019, I took the bold step to move to Los Angeles, ready to embrace the challenges ahead. Amidst the global pandemic and the re-application process for my visa, I didn't lose hope. After four years of dedication and the completion of 380 pages of documentation, I was overjoyed when my O-1 visa was approved, along with a business grant aimed at creating globally recognized qualifications for aspiring Bollywood dance instructors, BollyOn.

In my first six months in LA, opportunities began to manifest. I found myself involved in a wrestling program and action films, breathing life into my dreams. However, life threw more challenges my way with an injury to my other knee leading to surgery and ongoing health issues in the family. Yet, these experiences only solidified my resolve: I will rise again. I am committed to using my strengths and experiences to empower and inspire others.

Through mentorship and coaching, I strive to help individuals build their confidence and strength, preparing them to become leaders in their own right. My journey is one of resilience, and I firmly believe that we all possess the power to rise above adversity. I encourage those around me, saying, "I will rise – just watch me!"

## Emiko Ishii

Emiko Jane Ishii is a dynamic force in performing arts, now based in Los Angeles. A British born Japanese multidisciplinary actress, action performer, choreographer, mentor, and coach with over 23 years of experience.

As the visionary behind Epika Dance, Emiko's innovative fusion of Indian, Japanese, hip hop, and martial arts has captivated audiences worldwide. Her dedication to mentoring and coaching emerging artists underscores her commitment to nurturing future leaders in the arts.

As a passionate educator, Emiko teaches dance intervention in Special Educational Needs (SEN) schools and conducts workshops internationally, inspiring others to follow their dreams and create sustainable careers in the arts.

## Social Media Links

@emikojaneishii @epikadance @bollyondance

IMDB - https://pro.imdb.com/name/nm4316748?s=a8caa98d-be7b-39fd-4b31-593941b7dcbf&site_preference=normal

Contact - emikojaneishii@gmail.com

# My Why: Glorifying God Even Through Life's Deepest Valleys

*By Grace Richardson*

*"What is the chief end of man? Man's chief end is to glorify God, and to enjoy Him forever." – Westminster Shorter Catechism, 1674*

## The Question That Plagued Me

When the world as I knew it collapsed around me in September 2021, one question kept piercing my heart: Why? Why would God allow my beloved husband, Doug, and my precious daughter Joanne to be yanked from me and Ethan? Why was my daughter's life cut short at only 41 years old? Why did my 5-year-old grandson have to lose his mom? Why would I have to fight a legal battle just to see my grandson, whom Doug and I helped raise? And why would my mom have to die under such heartbreaking circumstances in April 2023?

This question haunted me through sleepless nights, endless tears, and moments when breathing felt like too much effort.

I remember standing in front of my bathroom mirror days after their passing, hardly recognizing the woman staring back at me. Thin, fragile, with sunken eyes and a face that seemed to have aged twenty years in a matter of days. Grief had ravaged not just my heart but my physical body too.

But as I stood there, something from my childhood rose within me, the Biblical wisdom my mother had instilled in me that God makes all things work together for our good and His glory. In that moment, through tears and pain, a different question began to form: not just "why did this happen?" but "how can I glorify

God in this?"

That shift became my saving grace—not an immediate healing but a guiding light in the darkest time of my life. It gave me a "why" when everything else was broken into a thousand pieces.

Before the Storm: Preparation I Didn't Know Was Happening

God had been preparing me for this "wilderness" long before I entered it. Looking back, I can see His hand equipping me for what was to come.

The strong spiritual foundation my mother built meant that when crisis hit, I knew where to turn. Even when I couldn't feel Him or see Him, even when my prayers were nothing but sobs, the truth is: He is in the story.

Over the years, I studied natural healing methods, like essential oils and how they affect our emotions and physical wellbeing. I learned about face reflexology and how our bodies process trauma. I explored nutrition and breathing techniques that support healing. They were tools God was placing in my hands for the dark valley ahead.

The relationship with Jesus Christ I nurtured through years of walking with Him gave me a foundation that, though shaken, would not and did not collapse. When everything else was stripped away, that closeness became more intimate.

None of this made the pain disappear. But it gave me a framework to process it. A way to understand that my deepest suffering can indeed glorify God.

## The Valley of the Shadow

The days after losing Doug and Joanne blur together. I remember certain moments with crystal clarity: the flurry of activities

preparing to celebrate their lives, holding Ethan as he expressed these words to me: "Grandma, I'm glad you didn't go to heaven!," after being told his mommy and papa went to heaven.

I remember the physical symptoms of grief; headaches, digestive problems, weakened immunity, perpetual exhaustion, and the inability to sleep.

And then came the second blow: a legal battle just to see and spend time with Ethan, the little boy Doug and I helped raise, who needed his grandmother's love more than ever.

I wish I could tell you I responded with perfect faith. I didn't. There were moments of anger, despair, questioning God's goodness. There were days when I couldn't pray beyond "Help me, Lord." There were nights when all I could do was clutch my Bible and weep.

It was a battle I couldn't win! But God. Ethan's father bad mouth me to everyone who would listen. The court system in California wasn't on the side of truth. I was told by a friend in the system that unless there was blood on the floor, they gave the child to the parents! Here's what I clung to: **"But Jesus looked at** *them* **and said to them, "With men this is impossible, but with God all things are possible.""**

Even then, the question remained: How can this glorify God? I was reminded that pain has a purpose. Nothing is wasted in God's economy. That this "wilderness" could become a place where God's glory is displayed in full view.

## How Do I Glorify God in My Brokenness?

To glorify God meant that even in my brokenness, I could reflect His light and hope onto others. Not that I needed to pretend I wasn't devastated, but that I could grieve with hope, with honesty, with a determination to honor Him through my tears and a heart broken beyond repair.

And to enjoy Him forever? That felt impossible at first. When my heart was shattered? But slowly, I began to understand that enjoying God isn't about constant happiness. It's about finding Him sufficient. It's about experiencing His presence as the One true Comfort when all else is stripped away. It's about the promise of eternity with Him and being reunited with my loved ones, forever!

During one particularly difficult night, I opened my Bible to **Psalm 34:4: "I sought the Lord, and He answered me; He delivered me from all my fears."** I whispered through tears, "Lord, I can't find joy right now. But I'm in Your presence. I'm holding onto You. Joy will be in enjoying You forever."

It's in the most imperfect circumstances that our purpose becomes most clear. Anyone can glorify God when life is good. But to glorify Him from the valley of the shadow of death? That's a testimony that echoes into eternity.

## The Turning Point: From Victim to Victory

I had a choice. I could be a victim, or I could allow God to transform this pain into purpose. I could let grief define me, or let it refine me into someone who could help others get through their grief.

What emerged was what I now call the AromaReflex Healing™ method, a five-step approach addressing the spiritual, emotional, and physical dimensions of grief:

1. **Essential Mindset™**: Cultivating a positive, even a faith-centered perspective through prayer, Scripture, and community support.

2. **Essential Beauty™**: Addressing the physical manifestations of grief through aromatherapy for skin and body.

3. **Essential Stimulation™**: Using face reflexology to promote internal healing and emotional balance.

4. **Essential Breathing and Exercise**: Incorporating proper breathing techniques and gentle movement to oxygenate the brain and recharge the body.

5. **Essential Nutrition/Hydration/Supplement**: Nourishing and hydrating the body properly to support healing.

This wasn't just a method; it was the practical outworking of my deepest why: to glorify God even through life's worst circumstances. Each element regards us as whole beings—body, mind, and spirit.

Essential Mindset™ became the foundation because, without addressing our state of mind, physical and emotional healing remains elusive. Through prayer, Scripture meditation, and faith and secular community, I began to renew my mind daily, **"And do not be conformed to this world, but be transformed by the renewing of your mind, that you may prove what is that good and acceptable and perfect will of God,"** Romans 12:2 I restored my resolve, fired up my resilience, focusing not on circumstances but on God's unchanging character.

Essential Beauty™ emerged from my shocking experience of looking in the mirror and seeing a stranger. Addressing grief's physical toll isn't vanity, it's stewardship of the body God gave us. Specific essential oils didn't just improve my appearance but also affected my brain chemistry, helping balance emotions and reduce stress.

Essential Stimulation™ came through discovering how face reflexology could release physical tension and grief stores in our bodies. By stimulating specific points corresponding to internal systems, I found relief from grief's physical manifestations.

Essential Breathing and Exercise arose from noticing how grief literally takes your breath away. Learning to breathe deeply again, to oxygenate my brain, to move intentionally, these became vital practices in my healing journey. Scripture tells us God breathed life into Adam, **"And the LORD God formed man of the dust of the ground and breathed into his nostrils the breath of life; and man became a living being" Genesis 2:7;** relearning to breathe properly became a reclaiming of that divine gift.

Essential Nutrition/Hydration/Supplements addressed how grief often destroys appetite and disrupts nutrient absorption. Nourishing and hydrating my body properly became an act of stewardship, honoring God with the body He gave me.

Each of these elements worked together in restoring me and not allowing grief to destroy me. Scripture reminds us in 1 Corinthians 3:16-17, **"Do you not know that you are the temple of God and that the Spirit of God dwells in you? If anyone defiles the temple of God, God will destroy him. For the temple of God is holy, which temple you are."** This truth guided my approach to healing and honoring my body as God's temple even in grief. My AromaReflex Healing method became a way for me to glorify God by restoring my whole being with the tools and skills He gifted me. Through this holistic approach, I could fulfill my purpose: to glorify God, to demonstrate that even in devastating loss, He remains faithful to His promise that He **"will never leave you nor forsake you" (Hebrews 13:5).**

## My Grandson's Wisdom

Sometimes God speaks through unexpected voices. In this

instance, it was my grandson, Ethan, who, at just 7 years old, gave me a perfect picture of our journey.

I was trying to explain grief to him when he responded with wisdom beyond his years: "Grandma, I put my grief on one leg and happiness on the other leg!"

Out of the mouth of babes! He captured what I'd been struggling to articulate. Grief doesn't have to consume us. We can acknowledge it while making room for joy. We can glorify God not by denying our pain, but by allowing Him to bring beauty from ashes.

That's when I truly understood, glorifying God isn't about struggling to escape life's valleys. It's about finding Him present in those valleys, understanding that His grace is sufficient. It's about allowing Him to transform the deepest pain into the most powerful purpose.

## Called for Such a Time as This

As my journey continued, I was convinced that God had called me for such a time as this. My pain had a purpose. My testimony was for His glory.

I thought about Esther in the Bible. I was no queen, but I was a woman who had walked through fire and emerged not unscathed, but undefeated. A woman who discovered that even in unimaginable loss, God's purpose remains, and it cannot be thwarted.

That's when I knew I needed to share the AromaReflex Healing™ method. Not just for myself, but as a testimony to God's faithfulness. As a practical guide for others walking through grief. As a way to show how natural remedies, faith practices, and community support, whether faith-based or secular or both can foster healing.

My "why" became crystal clear: to take the worst thing that happened to me and allow God to use it for my good and His glory. To transform pain into purpose. To show others they too could move from victims to victors through His grace.

**Romans 8:28 says, "And we know that all things work together for good to those who love God, to those who are the called according to His purpose."** Not some things—ALL things. Even losing my Doug and Joanne in the same week. Even the harsh and humiliating legal battle for Ethan. Even my mother's death in the hands of her greedy children. Even the loneliness and pain of being alone. ALL can work together for good when surrendered to the God who specializes in redemption.

The Path Forward: Glorifying God Through Every Season

Today, I still miss my loved ones every minute of the day. I miss seeing my Ethan everyday. I miss the hum of activities around me. I miss the smell of food Joanne used to cook. I miss even the sound of sports that I didn't much care for, but Doug loved to watch. The grief hasn't disappeared; it has transformed. I've learned to carry it differently, to weave it into the tapestry of my life rather than letting it consume everything.

Ethan and I hold onto the Blessed Hope, that one day we'll be reunited with his mommy and papa. Until then, I've learned to embrace this unexpected life. It wasn't what I planned, but it's where God has placed me, and I'm determined to glorify Him here.

Each day, as I practice the five steps of the AromaReflex Healing™ method, I'm fulfilling my purpose: to glorify God even in this season I never wanted.

And as I share these tools with others, as I see the light return to eyes that once held only pain, I catch glimpses of joy. Not the carefree happiness I once knew, but something deeper. A joy that comes from walking closely with God through the valley and discovering He is enough.

My "why" is this timeless wisdom lived out in real pain with real hope: to glorify God through everything, even grief, and to discover that in His presence, even in the valley, there is indeed fullness of joy.

As I reflect on what God has done with the circumstances of my life, however heartbreaking or painful, I am grateful and excited to one day hear these words of Jesus: **"His Lord said to him, 'Well done, good and faithful servant; you were faithful over a few things, I will make you ruler over many things. Enter into the joy of your Lord.'"** Mathew 25:21

If you're walking through your valley right now, hold onto this truth: your purpose remains. You were created to glorify God and to enjoy Him forever. Not just in sunshine but in storms. Not just in blessing but in brokenness. Not just on the mountaintop but in the valley. This is not where you saw yourself, but it is where God placed you. Use your testimony of restoration by the grace and mercy of God, the Father, and our Savior and Lord, Jesus Christ.

And somehow, I don't know how, but I believe it with everything in me—as you seek to glorify Him through your tears, you'll discover that joy is not lost forever. It's waiting for you on this path of healing. A different joy, perhaps — a deeper joy, but joy, nonetheless.

# ABOUT THE AUTHOR

## Grace Richardson

With a foundation of unwavering faith instilled by her mother from childhood, she has walked through the valley of unimaginable loss with God as her constant companion. After losing both her husband Doug and daughter Joanne in a single week in September 2021, made worse by the legal fight to see and spend time with her grandson. Followed by her mother's passing in April 2023, she clung to the promise that "all things work together for good to those who love God" (Romans 8:28).

A certified clinical aromatherapist and face reflexology practitioner with decades of experience in natural healing modalities, she uniquely combines Biblical wisdom with evidence-based holistic approaches. This God-given expertise became the foundation for AromaReflex Healing™, her comprehensive recovery and rejuvenation method that addresses mind, body, and spirit. Through her blogs, online courses, speaking, and one-on-one work, she guides fellow grief travelers from darkness to light, sharing the practical tools and spiritual insights that transformed her from victim to victor through Christ's sustaining grace.

Email: gracefulwellnessco@gmail.com

IG: @thriveingriefchat

FB: @thriveingrief

LinkedIn: @agracefulapproach

Website: thriveingrief.com

Blog: gracefulwellnessco.com/blog

YouTube: @agracefulapproach

# Exploring Uncharted Paths
*By Holly Porter*

Through struggle we often discover our true strengths and purposes in life; here's the story of how my encounter with COVID-19 altered my perspective - leading me down an unexpected journey that resulted in ventures aimed at empowering women worldwide.

But more than that, this essay is an invitation for you to see your struggles as part of what will define your legacy.

## Unexpected Descent

My journey started quietly enough at a women's conference--an event filled with laughter and shared stories--but unbeknownst to me was my encounter with COVID-19 Delta variant, known for its increased transmissibility and severity.

"After spending years teaching women how to trust their intuition, here I was dismissing my own subtle fatigue as travel fatigue; an embarrassing reminder that even guides need guidance."

Within days, my symptoms worsened: an ever-soaring fever, profound fatigue and shortness of breath that nearly incapacitated me. Even as his own illness worsened, my husband still insisted on taking me to hospital when my oxygen levels dropped dangerously low (63%).

"Prepare for the worst," the doctor's face conveyed without words. In response to their urgency, I was admitted into ICU before my husband could even return from parking his car. In that moment I wasn't CEO, mother, or leader; rather I was just another fragile human fighting for survival.

At first, it seemed unrelenting; my world shrunk into the ICU with me intubated twice, then a trachea, and tied down to avoid accidental removal of life-sustaining equipment. A ventilator took away my hearing; COVID-19 stripped me of taste and smell. Until finally it all stopped; darkness descended like an onslaught. Then came sepsis, as if I didn't have enough challenges.

Imagine living in a world without hearing your children's voices, smelling rain, or tasting chocolate--where all your memories have vanished like mine did. That was my reality.

To alleviate my suffering, the medical team induced a coma which would last thirty-two of my seventy hospitalization days. Being redheaded made me particularly susceptible to certain medications; those given to me (oxycodone and fentanyl) metabolized rapidly which put me into an unsafe cycle of overdose and withdrawal.

My body had become a battleground: scarred lungs from fibrosis, weak muscles due to atrophy, strained hearts from inflammation. Yet my spirit was just beginning to be awakened.

## Journeys Beyond the Physical Realm

While in a prolonged unconsciousness state, my spirit embarked upon journeys beyond physical reality. Through out-of-body experiences I perceived not just myself traveling as an abstract entity but rather my entire hospital bed transcending physical boundaries to accompany me on these out-of-body trips; oftentimes even other beds joined us along their final voyages.

Are we just passing through, I don't know. What I do know is that when we came together in the ICU I felt relieved of loneliness; suddenly there was a mysterious sense of community among us all.

One powerful near-death experience I had left me in an environment of unparalleled beauty yet an inexplicable sense of confinement, leaving an unsettling paradox behind when I returned to consciousness. Seeking clarity through hypnosis therapy, more layers were revealed within this experience.

When asked by my hypnotist what the tree represented, without thinking I immediately responded "Legacy. It symbolizes how lives intertwine across generations. Now the symbol of my foundation, this tree represents my work I was meant to do."

I witnessed energies converging into rose-colored hearts on the left side of this ethereal plane.

At first it felt arbitrary; now they appear everywhere from sunrises and children's doodles to women leaning in closer when sharing stories. Reminding us all that love is truly worth its weight in gold!

One resonating message of this experience was, "More will be revealed to you when the time is right." This phrase provided immense peace within, as I relinquished any need for immediate understanding. Another guiding principle imparted was "love them where they're at," a mantra which dispersed judgment while encouraging unconditional acceptance.

These mantras weren't mere platitudes--they were survival tools. When my children struggled to reconcile the mother who left with the one who returned, this mantra saved us.


## Emergence From Coma; Lingering Shadows of Long COVID

Recovering from COVID-19 did not mark its end; instead, it marked the start of another struggle - long COVID - characterized by persistent symptoms beyond its acute phase, including pulmonary fibrosis, fibromyalgia, rheumatoid arthritis, sleep apnea, chronic fatigue, and an impaired immune system.

Dressing was no longer a simple task; phone calls took hours of reflection. Now that I had survived death, however, it was up to me to learn how to live again--albeit with limitations.

Yet despite my struggles, I discovered a renewed appreciation for life.

When I tasted strawberries after recovering my senses, I wept. What had once seemed ordinary had become extraordinary. Surviving had become miraculous; my journey became divinely appointed: helping others find purpose within their suffering.

No one could have prepared me for the emotional aftermath, though. For two years after returning home, it became one of the hardest periods of my life; having gone to heaven and come back down, not with celebration but disillusionment.

Every day for two years I cried, often uncontrollably and inconsolably. Each day brought new, excruciating pain--not just physical, but spiritual, emotional, and relational as well. It was harder than my divorces--plural--raising eight children or experiencing financial strain. And it left a greater scar than financial instability or business betrayals through embezzlement--or trust issues within my own circle.

One night, my daughter came in and found me sobbing on the bathroom floor. "Mom," she whispered softly, "you're different now." Her words tore at my heartstrings: how could I explain that the "old me" had died in that hospital bed; or that the new me was quieter, slower, and tender where there once had been calloused places?

My relationships with siblings and children were tested to their limits. Trust had been removed from every aspect of my life; I felt disintegrated, with everything that provided stability suddenly dissolving or breaking apart.

Time has shown me why. To fully grasp why, I needed to experience it all and navigate every shadow before realizing the light I am meant to carry. Though painful, I even acknowledge I may have had to spiritually sacrifice some grandchildren to help other's sons and grandchildren in the future - one of the hardest and most painful truths I ever faced.

But this... this was the moment my purpose came into sharp focus. In those darkest nights, when love wasn't just a virtue but a lifeline, the message 'love them where they're at' sank into my bones. It rescued me from bitterness and gently softened the places where life had left me hardened." And when I feel unprepared or confused by life's mysteries, I return to that whisper from another realm:

"More will be revealed when the time is right" gives me peace, patience, and wonder all at once. It reminds me not to expect instant answers today--I just must show up -with love.

## The Adventure Bucket Wish Foundation: Heart Work

Within three months of leaving the hospital, I filed the paperwork and launched my nonprofit organization. This wasn't just another project - this was an assignment!

"Adventure Bucket and Wish" came to me in a dream: the name represents life as the ultimate adventure while "Wish" stands for every woman having forgotten her dreams due to duty or survival.

## The Miracles That Made This Possible

Miracles were integral in giving me my purpose in life and leading the life that God intended me to lead. They proved my calling with conviction.

## Miracle #1

One of the greatest miracles was when, for the first time in my life, I finally obtained health insurance. Never had it existed in any capacity for me; yet suddenly and just two months before getting sick it miraculously appeared in time to cover a hospital stay that cost over a million dollars - divine timing not luck but provision!

## Miracle #2

An additional miracle was my ability to purchase a hyperbaric chamber for home use, becoming part of my daily healing ritual and saving my lungs in the process. I believe it played an instrumental role in helping restore my ability to breathe - and ultimately live.

Not one but two intubations should have ended my journey here on earth: but my work here had yet to be accomplished.

## Miracle #3

And yet somehow, despite my trauma and missing four months, that year proved to be my most successful real estate year ever! Even more incredible was how only eight months were worked at any one time--something which wouldn't make sense on paper but is evident when living life according to divine providence.

## Miracle #4

Perhaps the greatest miracle of all was my return. After my near-death experience, I emerged with a clear purpose and mission - an underlying reason to live out. Through that experience, I built an extraordinary legacy and will always be grateful for this experience.

This foundation helps women transform pain into power. Our focus is to assist women in rewriting their stories, rebuilding from hardships, and rising into purpose-led leadership positions. Our signature rose-colored hearts represent not just branding; rather they stand as an icon for hope, healing, and heart-led action.

## Why I Matter

I have always seen potential where others perceive obstacles. Perhaps it is because of all the roles I've inhabited: raising eight children, real estate broker, event producer, spiritual seeker, and business strategist. For over 25 years, I've walked alongside women entrepreneurs helping them to build empires, launch ideas and regain their voice.

But nothing, title or role-related, has shaped me more profoundly than when I faced death and emerged different.

Today I am no longer the same woman I was before COVID: then, she knew how to hustle, lead, and perform well.

But this version knows how to give in, listen, and lead from her heart instead of from an Excel spreadsheet.

Retreat RnR was created not just as a business solution, but as an environment to bring more purposeful guidance into people's lives. This sacred container represents everything I've built, survived, and been called to oversee over time.

## Vision Forward: A Global Mission with Soul

What started as survival has since grown into an international movement. Retreat RnR is more than a business; it serves as a portal to healing on an international scale. My dream is for retreat leaders, coaches, and healers worldwide to use my platform for transformational gatherings to take place across mountainsides, ocean shores, forests and town centers every single day because all necessary systems and support systems now exist to make transformational gatherings possible.

Through Retreat RnR, I see a future where I can more actively embrace philanthropy. Success of Retreat RnR will give me freedom to donate towards causes that benefit communities - particularly women and children who have suffered in silence. Our foundation will fund transformational events, scholarship programs, mental wellness resources and legacy experiences to remind women they're not alone and their voice matters.

Scaling Retreat RnR isn't about growing my ego; it's about expanding its impact. The more that Retreat RnR expands its reach, the wider its influence is felt at Adventure Bucket Wish Foundation. Every system I create or piece of software I perfect, serves as a building block towards creating my ideal world--one that embodies restoration, leadership, and legacy.

## Call to Readers:

What If It's You Next? You are reading this for a reason. Perhaps you are experiencing challenges such as health concerns, heartbreak, betrayals, and breakdowns - or are currently going through them. If so, take heart from what has come out so far in this story so far and consider reading further for insight and support from us here at The Awakened Journey Project (TATP).

Let my story serve as both mirror and map for you to follow; your pain could be the perfect soil for finding your WHY, and purpose in life - I didn't expect to survive what I did - yet here I am with a mission that can benefit others like yourself.

Your courage can take you further than ever imagined; all it takes is some action now. And remember just love them where they're at; that will lead you onward to further discovery at just the right moment in time. Just trust it will happen eventually - because it always does!

## Holly Porter
## About The Author

Holly Porter is an internationally acclaimed author, speaker, retreat strategist, SaaS founder, and transformational guide. As CEO of Retreat RnR and founder of Adventure Bucket Wish Foundation, she helps women turn obstacles into opportunities and lead with passion, presence, and purpose. As mother to eight and survivor of near-death experience herself, Holly lives to empower others so they can leave lasting legacies through love and leadership.

Holly Porter International can be found at:

https://www.HollyPorterInternational.com

Adventure Bucket Wish Foundation 501(c)(3)

https://www.AdventureBucketWishFoundation

Instagram: https://www.instagram.com/hollyporterinternational/

Facebook: https://www.facebook.com/HOLLYANNPORTER/

LinkedIn: https://www.linkedin.com/in/hollyporter/

YouTube: https://youtube.com/@retreatrnr

# Honor The Child In Each And Every One Of Us
*By Dr. Iréné Lara, PsyD, Reiki MT, LCSW*

## Welcome

*"Is it true that there is a child in each and every one of us? Yes of course. She is in there, (Note: here I use the female pronoun meaning all) and she is aching to be heard, to play, to be creative, to rest. Your inner younger Self may be mad, happy, restless, and or Joyful! Discover her. Give her space ... to be... her Self." Irene Lara*

## Why did I become a professional in the mental health arena?

Leaving the house, I ran up the hill on the sidewalk en route to the park. By the time I got to the top, I found myself crying, no doubt angry and frustrated, and told myself, "When I am older, I'm going to be a psicóloga." (I say it in Spanish). I'm going to be a psychologist. Obviously at seven years old, I did not know exactly what that meant and yet, I knew enough to claim it. Forty-five plus years later with thirty thousand consultations, and eighteen thousand clients later, and I have been that mental health professional that I said I would become.

I have a doctorate in clinical psychology and licensed as a clinical social worker, a Reiki Master Teacher, a certified Breath-Body-Mind practitioner and trained and practicing EMDR. I am heart-centered in my approach serving children: tweens, teens, young adults, adults, professional women with trauma histories, working with the gay and transgender population on any given day. I am multicultural and multilingual. But why mental health? I knew professionals in this arena helped those in need helping them feel heard and understood. Clinicians listen, understand, and elevate children. We help people solve, reduce, or manage with their problems with the goal of feeling better about themselves, lighter, stronger, more empowered to live their lives of choice. I was a second grader and needed this myself.

My father was not raised with the language of addressing feelings much less expressing difficult ones. My mother herself was raised as the oldest daughter of ten siblings who got some compassion and a handful of play-time growing up - I imagine. She had to be in charge of many and did not receive individualized attention from either of her parents. As an adult, my mother chose an accounting career and had some patience for feelings. We all continue to grow and evolve. People can change and improve often. Some of us need a loving, accepting environment to grow with more grace and power.

I was always one to have big feelings, deeply felt feelings even to this day. Emotions when fully felt, they are exhausting and take time to recover from, as well. It is a workout. Down time in nature is needed to replenish and recuperate energy for daily tasks. Many know this as being an empath. My "why" surely involves connecting with those who do not feel felt or are misunderstood.

As a child three years apart from my older and younger siblings while the others were one year apart from each other, provided an opportunity to hang out and be a part of a triad with my parents, a dyad with my mom or be "alone." My siblings got to have a partner per se - someone else to connect with. Fortunately, I had my Winnie the Pooh stuffed animal, and thumb sucking up until age seven forced to let go of that habit, that resource. On an emotional level, I had to figure out life on my own. Nonetheless, the spiritual connection with the divine was always present, as well as my passion for music and movement - dancing to the beat. I liked school and home overall.

## Resources

Having a relationship with Christ, and being athletic, a dancer have been great gifts throughout my life. A lasting spiritual relationship, the relaxing and invigorating power of nature, as well as playing with stuffed animals (plushies) growing up have been blessings, life-savers in many ways. I use these connections as puissance with the divine to carry me in life and help me as a guide to move forward along my path.

My inner compass is supportive and compassionate, yet the outside world is often less patient. Fourth dimensionality is not understood and is much less appreciated by the "supposed concrete" third dimensional world in which most institutions live. For that reason, I have incorporated eastern principles and spiritual practices like mindfulness, movement, sound, breathwork, Universal Life Force along with the western research and training into my work for the past two decades. I used to refer out for these interventions, yet I now incorporate body-mind-spirit principles into daily living as much as possible. [I still refer out for treatments, as needed.] My work is both heart-centered and grounded in theory and practice.

I have been a dancer at heart all of my life. Although dance classes did not begin until high school, it is such a part of my being, the family parties, my parents' dancing. yet I will say integrating body-mind-spirit made the most sense to me to show up appropriately and authentically to bring my gifts into my service for others through my work.


## Professional Journey

Jumping forward decades later, I knew I wanted to be of service and found the master's in social welfare program. I am blessed that I got accepted and graduated from University of California, Los Angeles. I entered, completed the program, and attained my license to work professionally. I thought it was crazy to have the label "professional" at the beginning when the work was so new to me. So, I knew eventually I would seek out a doctoral degree to further my expertise. I searched for a doctorate program to get better informed. Although it took a while, I finally completed the program in clinical psychology, child/human development.

At some point while working with children, especially their parents, I learned or understood that the inner child remains within each parent. Hence, it required attention for balancing the adult and their roles in life, at work, leader at home, and as a parent. There was so much more healing and education to offer the parents.

Recently, I understand, too, that familial history, our ancestral past is also important. The old inherited patterns co-mingle with new generational demands that want help. The call then is to clear these patterns. My purpose is simple yet complex. I am here to improve as many lives as possible to create a happier, healthier place on this planet. Too big of a task yet possible in smaller chunks.

A mere decade ago, I "discovered" / understood the term empath. Two enlightened souls, lovely women compassionately concerned for me reflected back to me who I am, and most importantly wished me to practice self-care techniques. I quickly started to learn and tried various "cleansing" strategies to clear myself daily after seeing clients, being arounds crowds, and large groups. A big part of my practice now is teaching other empaths who they are and to help them make sense of their needs and how to tend to their sensory needs.

*Are you working on anything exciting lately? What's next on your wish list? If you could have it all, what would you be involved with?*

## The body-mind-spirit connection

So, I did a thing mid-2023, I started to learn a whole new skill: a well-researched and successful intervention: eye movement for desensitization and reprocessing also known as EMDR. It is an advanced system founded by Dr. Francine Shapiro, PhD with an Adaptive Processing of Information. This progressive mindset and intervention was new a long time ago, initially spurring controversy. The mind-body connection was under appreciated then. Yet, with over thirty years of research, it has proven to be 75-100% successful in resolving an extensive variety of traumas in veterans and the civilian population. After my own 30 years of experience as a mental health clinician, I finally chose to be trained in it and am using EMDR with clients. The resourcing and additional supportive skills for clients are quite helpful when used.

## In closing...

Lastly, I want my older parents to be comfortable, strong, cared for, and happy. I love it when they are out and about or simply enjoying themselves. Certainly, I hope to be available to help out when they need it.

I hope you enjoyed reading a bit about my why. There is always more. Reach out to me if you desire a heart-centered approach for mental health support. I can be found on https://www.IreneLara.com. Be well. I wish you peace of mind. And so, it is.

# Dr. Iréné Lara, PsyD, Reiki MT, LCSW

Dr. Irene Lara is a highly experienced professional offering a range of integrative psychotherapies and holistic healing services. With over 30 years of experience, she holds a PsyD in psychology and an MSW in social welfare from UCLA, and Reiki Master-Teacher. Her dissertation focused on integrating yoga into play therapy. Her master's thesis was on the impact of HIV on women in Latino families. Her practice, Quantum Integrative Therapies Pro-Coach is international, often based in California providing body-mind-spirit mental health services such as EMDR, Quantum Healing, Belief and Fear Releases amongst others. Dr. Lara's approach is rooted in the science of interpersonal neurobiology blending Eastern and Western practices to support clients' physical, mental, emotional, and spiritual well-being. She offers both online and in-person appointments emphasizing the possibility of transformation and empowerment through gentle, patient guidance. Her multicultural background, and fluency in Spanish (and some French) enable her to serve a diverse clientele.

Visit her website www.IreneLara.com and request a 20-minute free consultation before scheduling an appointment. Find her on IG and FB @INrPaz. Experience a breath-body-mind Breathwork for balance session on her YouTube channel drirenelara

# Defying Naysayers
## Fueling My Why by Proving Them Wrong
*By Jackie Phillips*

The technician approached my fully cast leg, which supported a pin protruding from either side of my ankle, sporting an electric drill in his hand. I thought, "This is gonna hurt!" But, alas, it did not. Next, he came with a circular saw to cut through and remove the plaster that had encased my leg for over six months. Finally, it was off! I excitedly looked at my leg. I was devastated. What had been a strong, healthy leg was now shriveled. He helped me to my feet as I shakily attempted to stand. I could readily see that my heel was almost two inches shorter than my other leg. The doctor said, "Your leg has healed well, but you will always have a limp. You will never be able to run." From being immobile, my Achilles tendon had atrophied and shrunk. I was only thirty-three years old. Limping for the rest of my life was unacceptable. Until that moment, becoming a runner was something I never considered. Right then and there, I determined I would not limp, and I would run. Due to this doctor's prognosis, I had to fight to get physical therapy. After copious amounts of painful physical therapy and hours in a swimming pool stretching that Achilles tendon, I slowly began to run.

At first, I ran to prove the doctor wrong, but gradually, I loved running. Even today, I still feel the cool breeze on my face early in the morning. For twenty years, I ran recreationally, entering a race here and there. Little did I know that I would, again, be challenged by another naysayer. In my late fifties, I decided that I wanted to run a marathon and started training with a friend.

Properly training for a marathon requires about six months of gradually running more and more miles until, eventually, you can run over twenty-plus miles at one time. Then, about three weeks before the race, you taper and run shorter distances.

Finally, I could run over fifteen miles at once and felt great about my progress. One day, quite unexpectedly, everything changed. On a beautiful summer day, I was water skiing. Cutting outside the wake, I fell and did the splits. The pain was incredible, and it was a challenge even getting me out of the water and back onto the boat. At the emergency room, the diagnosis was a torn hamstring. It was not until years later that I discovered not only had I torn the muscle, but one-third of it was permanently ripped. Once again, I had to fight to get physical therapy approved. I still recall my first physical therapy session. When I told them I wanted to be able to run again so that I could run a marathon, they just laughed and told me to "dream on." Not to be deterred, and through the power of prayer, I searched for a physical therapy business that would work with me so that I could accomplish my dream. A friend referred me to one, but it was an hour away. Not to be denied, I drove back and forth for many months to endure more physical therapy. My faithful friend and running partner stood by me every painful step. At first, I could not even bend my knee and had to relearn to walk. She and I both recall the first time I walked to the end of my driveway, bathed in sweat from the effort.

The physical therapy firm I found had a reputation for helping athletes return to the sport they love. It was a perfect fit for me. God led me to a young physical therapist who was also a marathoner. She understood my dream and worked hard to enable me to accomplish it. She suggested that I change my running program. Rather than run the entire twenty-six miles, you run for a timed amount and then walk for a shorter timed amount. The idea is that when you are running, you are resting your walking muscles, and when walking, you are resting your running muscles. The run/walk is recommended for beginning runners aspiring to run a marathon. Everyone at the clinic, even the therapists who were not directly involved with me, got on board with getting me ready to achieve my dream. One of the guys even took me to the parking lot and patiently helped me change my gait.

Due to other health issues for my running partner and me, it wasn't until August of 2002 that we could begin the arduous training again. We were running twenty-two miles by Christmas, ready for the Carlsbad marathon. On January 1, I was overcome with vomiting, diarrhea, and stomach cramps, requiring a trip to the emergency room. There, I was told that I had appendicitis. When the doctor said to me that I needed to have my appendix removed. I told him I needed to wait until after the marathon, which was only nineteen days away. He told me I might die without the surgery, so that left me no choice. Again, prayers were answered, and my on-call surgeon was a marathoner. What are the odds of that happening on New Year's Day? Did I mention that we had a lot of people praying for us? Rather than discouraging me, he told me how to prepare until my post-operative appointment, which was ten days after my release from the hospital.

The operation left me hospitalized for a few days with a full, four-inch incision in my abdomen. That had to heal first. While hospitalized, I started walking laps around the hospital ward.

The nurses thought I was crazy for hauling my IV stand around the corridor. My dream was not to be denied! For ten days. I was only allowed to walk and not run at all. I was in great shape after the arduous training of the past six months. Furthermore, the Lord blessed me with incredible healing. As prescribed, ten days post-surgery, I ran ten miles and went to the doctor's office for my post-surgery check-up. I saw a different doctor who told me I had healed exceptionally well, but I should not run a marathon. Fed up with another no, I asked to see my original surgeon. He cleared me.

To be able to run, I needed support for my abdomen, so I borrowed a back brace from a friend to exert pressure on my incision and wrapped it around my abdomen, securing a washcloth in place. My running partner and I stood at the start line to begin the long-awaited marathon. Our families and friends were there to encourage and pray for us. For the first half, it was exhilarating, and my partner and I were keeping the pace we had set before my surgery. Despite our challenges, we were on track to finish by the time allotted. Then, at mile twenty-two, I started to wear out. When I get fatigued, I drag my challenged leg and limp. A stranger on the marathon route shouted, "You are looking good. Finish strong!" I knew that I was looking anything but good, but that stranger's encouragement lifted my spirits. We finished those 26.2 miles. Goal accomplished! Check that box! To this day. I am grateful to that stranger who saw my pain, lifted me, and encouraged me.

Completing my next marathon in San Diego six months later was accidental. My running partner, Melissa, wanted to run it, but I was happy just running half marathons. I tried to figure out how best to support her and decided to run half and quit when I got tired. That was not to be. At mile thirteen, Melissa injured her knee and refused to stop. I did not want to leave her. She had been at my side through all my struggles, so we continued and walked the other thirteen miles. You may be thinking, "What's the big deal?" It is not easy when you have only trained for thirteen miles and end up doing twenty-six. Completing it with an injured knee was a Herculean challenge for Melissa.

Fast-forward to 2007. My husband and I were in Athens, Greece. We stood in the magnificent marble 1896 Athens Panathenaic Stadium and took in that breathtaking structure. The five gold rings symbolizing the Olympics were in the curve of the stadium's horseshoe. My forgotten dream of running the Athens Classic Marathon was rekindled that day. I could envision the finish line in that awe-inspiring, iconic stadium with me running across it. I still have a picture of that stadium on my desk.

In the fall of 2008, two friends and I registered for the Athens Classic marathon in the fall of 2009. Before traveling to Greece, I wanted to ascertain that my sixty-five-year-old body could still run a marathon. I ran the Surf City Marathon in February of 2009 as a test run. As I crossed the Surf City finish line, my daughter held up a poster that said, "On to Athens!" Indeed, we were ready to train and head to Athens, Greece, the following fall. Even today, I still feel the thrill of flying over the Aegean Sea at sunset, seeing Athens in the distance, and knowing that my dream was only 26.2 miles from reality.

On the day of the marathon, we woke up to heavy rain. Running in the rain is one of my least favorite times. Your shoes fill with water, and you slosh and slog through every step. It didn't even phase us. We were there to finish the race. The bus took us to the ancient town of Marathon, where the historic first marathon was run, and this one, following that same route, was to begin. We took shelter, waiting for the start. Finally, the gun sounded, and we were off. As the day progressed, the weather cleared. Running through little Greek villages with the church bells tolling was an added treat. Not very many Americans ran this race. The Greek spectators along the way were incredibly warm, welcoming, and encouraging. I learned how to say Good Morning and Thank you in Greek. I had to say Good Afternoon in Greek by the time we finished. At mile eighteen, there is a nasty, steep, upward climb. My husband and daughter had taken a taxi to a spot about halfway up. As I labored to run up, I heard my daughter shout, "After this, it's all downhill, Mom!" As we crested that hill, we could see the city of Athens far off in the distance. Entering the city of Athens, we passed the residence of the president of Greece, complete with guards in colorful costumes pacing back and forth. From there, you pass mile twenty-six. The crowds swelled and became more enthusiastic, cheering the exhausted but thrilled runners. The elite and better runners had finished hours ago, but we trudged on in the back of the pack. The deadline was six hours. After the palace, it's only a short way until you round the corner and see the breathtaking entrance to the majestic Olympic Stadium. The feeling of crossing that finish line is indescribable. Seeing my friends and family in the stands, I was elated. I finished three minutes under the six-hour limit. My time was 5:57.

Since marathon training is arduous and all-consuming, I decided to focus on shorter distances. I ran many races of various distances for the next thirteen years until the summer of 2022. On a daily run, I was not lifting my challenged leg high enough, and my right toe caught on the pavement. Down I went! Once again, I had broken a bone. This time, it was not my leg but a shattered elbow, which required surgery with elbow pins and a plate. After it healed, I was back in physical therapy. Again, my therapist was a runner. Does there seem to be a theme here? All I wanted to do was run again. My arm healed well. A few months later, I was running, and the same thing happened again with my toe catching. This time, I broke the humerus of the same arm. The orthopedic surgeon said I had two choices: 1) remove all the hardware in my arm and rebreak it, or 2) put it in a cast and have a stiff left arm. I picked a stiff arm. Little did I know how stiff that would be. When I came out of the cast, my arm would not straighten. I was back at physical therapy again. To help it be straighter, I wore an apparatus that exerted slight straightening pressure for six months.

Since dragging my leg and possibly falling were my new reality, my family and I decided that my running days were over. What would I do? I am an outdoor person. With balance issues, I feared riding my road bike, and biking has never appealed to me like running did. Before breaking my leg, I had been an avid walker. I decided to go back to walking again. Today, I walk carrying a cane to catch me should that darned toe catch. I continue to walk a lot, and my Fitbit keeps me challenged. Because I still love the atmosphere of a race, I still do 5 K races, not as a runner, but as a walker. There is something about hearing the Star-Spangled Banner, the roar of the starter's gun, and the crowd's push with each runner trying to get in a good position that intoxicates me. I have been the oldest participant in two 5 K races this year. I thank my Lord for still letting me compete.

Even though I am not currently running, I still consider myself a runner. I would love to tell that naysaying doctor, "Thank you for telling me at age thirty-three that I would always have a limp and never run again. Your doubts fueled my desire and gave me a passion for running, something I have enjoyed for almost half a lifetime. By the way, I do not limp. Rather than discouraging me, your doubts just fueled my passion!"

## Jackie Phillips

Jackie Phillips is a highly sought-after inspirational speaker, athlete, wellness expert, and best-selling international author of *Step by Step, 21 Steps to Enhance the Winner in You, An Upward Climb Toward Faith*, plus a contributor in four collaborative books.

At only thirty-three years old, Jackie was told that she would never run after shattering her leg in a skiing accident. She proved experts wrong through sheer determination, proper nutrition, faith, and extensive physical therapy. she has run many races, including four marathons.

Equipped with experience, a bachelor's degree in elementary education from Miami University, and a master's degree in health, physical education, and recreation from Purdue University, Jackie founded *Phillips Wellness Enterprises*. Today, she is active in both her community and her church.

During her downtime, Jackie loves walking, boating, wine tasting, and traveling with her college sweetheart husband, Dick, and their Aussiedoodle. She also dotes on her two grandchildren in their hometown of Riverside, California.

Jackie Phillips, Jackie Jackie-phillips.com

https://www.jackie-phillips.com/

https://www.linkedin.com/in/jackiephillips1/

https://www.facebook.com/4.Jackie.Phillips/

Jackie Phillips

Phillips Wellness Enterprises

(951) 840-7033

https://www.jackie-phillips.com/

# My Why

*By Dr. Jaya Sajnani*

I was born in a small village in Gujarat, India, called Anand. It's a place known more for its milk revolution than for stories like mine. I was one of six siblings in a house that barely had space for our dreams, let alone our bodies. Our house was full of not just of people but of unsaid expectations, economic hardship, and a conservative culture that weighed heavy on the shoulders of girls. Uncles, aunts, cousins all lived together in a shared space where privacy was a luxury and freedom, a fantasy.

We were poor not just financially, but also in the sense of exposure. We didn't know what the world outside our village looked like, and for most girls like me, it didn't matter. The path was already set grow up, reach puberty, and get married. My eldest sister walked that path. As soon as her menstrual cycle began, relatives began whispering that she's ready. She was married off without a question. Then came my turn.

Something in me resisted. I didn't know what it was back then. I couldn't put it into words. But I felt this fire, this itch, this voice whispering, You are meant for more. I didn't want to be a rebel; I just wanted a chance to know who I was before someone else decided who I should be. That chance didn't exist in Anand, and certainly not in my family. So, I had to find a way to escape. But I had to do it silently, respectfully, without dishonoring my parents or clashing with society.

For me, the safest exit was education.

At the age of eighteen, with minimal support and a heart full of fear and hope, I left India for the United Kingdom. I didn't know what awaited me on the other side. All I knew was that I needed to get there. That leap changed my life, but it didn't come without pain.

When I landed in the UK, I felt as if I had landed on another planet. I was alone. The food, the language, the social norms, everything was different. English was my third language. Every interaction felt like a test. I fumbled in supermarkets. I mispronounced words in lectures. I misunderstood conversations. But I survived and then, I learned to thrive.

I stayed. I built it. I married. I became a mother. I became an entrepreneur. Over the next 23 years, I set up multiple successful businesses in logistics, real estate, import-export profit-making ventures that gave me financial independence, stability, and what many people would call "success." I had it all on paper: a beautiful family, a house, companies, a respected role in society.

But something inside me still felt incomplete.

That emptiness, call it a wound, call it a calling, persisted. Every time I visited India, especially after COVID-19, I found myself going back not just physically, but emotionally, spiritually. I visited the same kind of schools I went to. I met young girls whose eyes mirrored the same fear I once had. They were bright. They were curious. But they were trapped by poverty, by expectations, by culture.

When I looked at them, I saw myself. I saw Jaya.

That's when it hit me. No matter how much I earned, no matter how high I rose, there was a part of me that would never rest until I helped free those girls. Until I gave them what I fought so hard for, a chance!

That's why I created Global Talent Solution Hub (GTS). It's not just a non-profit organization. It's my answer to that whisper inside me that said, *You are meant for more* and now I pass on that whisper to every girl we reach.

GTS works with the United Nations' Sustainable Development Goal: **Quality Education for All.** But for me, it's more than a goal, it's a personal mission. We focus on breaking barriers, creating bridges, and building opportunities for girls from underprivileged backgrounds. We started in India, but we are expanding to Africa, Kenya, Nigeria, Ghana because Jaya is not just Indian. Jaya is every girl who wants to break free.

Our scholarships are not just academic. We fund residential costs too because we know the barriers are not just tuition fees. Sometimes, the bigger challenge is where the girl will live, how she will eat, how she will be safe. We create that ecosystem, so girls don't just study abroad, they thrive.

We also organize **free educational seminars in India three times a year**, especially in girls' schools. We introduce them to **STEM education, AI, and data sciences,** fields where even now, girls are underrepresented. We want them to know: You belong here. You have a right to sit at the table. You have a right to make decisions, write policies, and create the next innovation.

We collaborate with **colleges, universities, industry experts**, and we provide this knowledge free of cost. We don't ask what their family earns, we ask what they dream.

As the world becomes one connected village, education must also be borderless. In this new AI-driven economy, where your client could be in the US, your employer in Germany, and your supplier in China, global knowledge isn't a luxury, it's a necessity. If we want our girls to be **financially independent, confident, and capable**, we must equip them with **international education**.

But let me tell you: this journey wasn't smooth for me as an Asian woman.

In the UK, I faced bias, overt and covert. I was too brown, too female, too immigrant. I was underestimated in business meetings. I was questioned in the boardroom. I was expected to settle for less. But every time they lowered the bar for me; I raised it for myself. Because I wasn't just fighting for Jaya, I was fighting for every girl who would come after me.

I've had moments of self-doubt. I've cried in silence. I've wanted to give up. But every time, something deeper pulled me back. A voice that said: Don't stop. She's watching. And by "she," I mean that 13-year-old Jaya in Anand, and that 13-year-old girl in Nigeria, and that 13-year-old in rural Bihar, who just got her first period and was told her life is over. I want to tell her: Your life is just beginning.

**That's my why**.

My why is every time I see a girl pick up a robotics kit for the first time and say, "I want to be an engineer."

My why is when a father from a village calls me and says, "I was wrong. My daughter is shining."

My why is when a girl who didn't speak English two years ago gives a presentation to a UK university board.

My why is healing that pain inside me that never got the chance to speak.

My why is freedom, mine, theirs, ours.

Today, as I sit down to write this, I no longer feel incomplete. I feel awakened. I know now that the money I earned, the businesses I built, those were the how. But this, this mission, is the why.

We are just beginning. GTS is growing. We are forming partnerships with global institutions. We are entering more communities. But more importantly, we are entering more lives. I want this movement to be a revolution. I want every girl to know that her story doesn't have to end in silence. It can begin in strength.

So, if you're reading this and you relate, if you are that girl, or if you once were, know that this chapter is for you.

We are not victims. We are visionaries.

We are not statistics. We are stories.

And this story isn't mine alone—it's ours.

# Dr. Jaya Sajnani Philanthropist | Entrepreneur | Public Speaker

Dr. Jaya Sajnani is a dynamic entrepreneur, philanthropist, and public speaker based in London, UK. As the founder and CEO of YG Travel Ltd, Xplore London, Global Talent Solution Hub, and Helping Hand Foundation Ltd, she has successfully established a portfolio of organizations focused on education, empowerment, and community impact.

With a vision to bridge global educational opportunities, Dr. Sajnani created the Global Talent Solution Hub, a platform that connects students and institutions from the East and West—particularly India, the USA, and the UK—to facilitate international learning experiences. Her companies also specialize in transport services and educational tours, innovatively combining logistics with learning.

Dr. Sajnani is a passionate advocate for women's empowerment. Through her NGO and social enterprise initiatives, she actively mentors and supports women entrepreneurs, helping them launch and grow their businesses. She leads a dedicated charity program designed to uplift and connect women through mutual support and collaboration.

Her trailblazing efforts have earned her numerous accolades, including the International Women Recognition Award (2019), Wonder Woman Award at the UK House of Parliament, and Woman of the Year (2021) at the Amazon Everywoman in Transport & Logistics Awards. She was also honored with the Great British Businesswoman Award (2022) and the Community Leader Award (2023) by the South Asian Heritage Association.

A member of the judging panel for the Everywoman UK Transport & Logistics Awards, Dr. Sajnani is also a co-author of four inspirational books and serves on the boards of LOANI Global and one hundred Successful Women in Business (USA).

Originally from a conservative Indian background, Dr. Sajnani's journey reflects resilience, courage, and a deep commitment to social change. She continues to inspire others by showing how determination and purpose can create a global impact.

Dr. Jaya Sajnani

CEO & Founder

Global Talent Solution Hub

https://globaltalentsolutionhub.com/

WhatsApp +4478085 22157

Email: jsajnani@globaltalentsolutionhub.com.

@globaltalentsolutionhub

# Breaking the Silence: The Why Behind M.A.L.H.Y.

*By Amb Dr. Jessica CH Smith President of MALHY,*
*Written by Charla A Keenan*

It didn't start with headlines. It didn't start with a rally, or a mission statement typed in bold font on a brochure. Before it was an organization, before the banners and the booths, before the school assemblies and the candlelight vigils, M.A.L.H.Y. was a cry in the dark. It started with a mother's gut feeling. She was scrolling late one night through a family member's social media—casual browsing at first, until something didn't sit right. A child—only 10 years old—was chatting with someone far too familiar for comfort. The tone, the timing, the secrecy; something was wrong, and Jessica knew it. Every instinct in her body screamed that this wasn't just a conversation. This was a premeditated lure. That was the night, everything changed. Jessica found online messages, where her family member met someone online who was trying to lure her out -it was a human trafficking trap. Right in our backyard. Not in some faraway city, but here—in our community, among the grocery stores and church parking lots. In that moment of reality, something inside her sparked; something deeper than rage or fear: resolve. If it could happen to her family member, it could happen to anyone. That's when Jessica decided she wouldn't let silence win. What followed was a determined pursuit of truth. A flurry of phone calls, digging, questions, and tears. And then, the hardest truth of all: this wasn't just an isolated scare. It was a crack in a much larger system. A break in the line of defense that was supposed to protect our children. As she dug deeper, she saw the pattern—a series of vulnerabilities that wrapped around so many of our youth like a vice: untreated trauma, undiagnosed depression, hidden addiction, predatory exploitation through apps and games. Kids were slipping through cracks that should never have been there. That moment—that terrifying, gut-wrenching realization—is what gave birth to her mission, and she gave it a name: M.A.L.H.Y. — Mental Health, Addiction, Love, Human Trafficking & Youth financial literacy. M.A.L.H.Y. became more than Jessica's spark—it ignited a community movement that defined M.A.L.H.Y.'s "Why." M.A.L.H.Y. isn't just a logo or a fundraising gala (although every dollar raised fuels this mission). It's about being where the kids are—before the predators, before the pills, before the pain becomes a secret. It's about bringing hope to those in need, providing clothing, food, and temporary shelter for children ages 10-25. " M.A.L.H.Y. 's WHY is to raise awareness and advocate for the safety of our youth, "it is our mission to spread knowledge!" It's about looking a child in the eyes and saying, "You are not invisible." Our outreach equips children by sharing real-life training on how to spot trafficking tactics masked as friendship, addiction disguised as coping, and depression hiding behind straight-A's. Our school workshops bring awareness to counselors and staff members, raising the bar so they listen to youth voices, offering real-world support, and bridging gaps between them and their parents who are often unequipped to handle alone. Our goal is to build solid foundations—between the parent too scared to ask, the teacher too tired to notice, the kid too broken to speak, and a system so fractured that our kids are being lost. M.A.L.H.Y. is about showing up. Over and over again. Until awareness becomes action. M.A.L.H.Y. is a community movement. It's the place you call when you don't know who else to call. It's the reason middle schoolers know how to spot the signs of grooming. It's the reason families in crisis have access to counseling, emergency aid such as food and shelter, and it is a network of people who won't let them feel alone. It's the late-night phone calls from frightened moms, the after-school workshops, the local community event support, the youth ambassadors sharing their truths at rallies, the teacher who finally had the training to save a student's life! It is people like you, reading this story, realizing that silence does not provide safety. Still fighting, still saving, M.A.L.H.Y.'s "Why" isn't just one child or one issue. It's a promise—to defend our kids from danger, to bridge isolation with connection, to bring hope after loss; because our kids are worth fighting for and the predators aren't waiting. Healing takes a community and saving only one child is never enough. No one should have to walk the path of recovery, survival, or fear alone—and thanks to M.A.L.H.Y., they don't. At M.A.L.H.Y., we believe that if you have kids, this isn't just our story — it's yours too. This is M.A.L.H.Y.'s "Why." The truth is chilling—we want to believe our children are safe, but they aren't. Human trafficking is no longer some faraway problem. It's here. Lurking behind screens, in parking lots, on apps disguised as games. Children are being manipulated, extorted, sextorted and groomed—and no one is talking about it loudly enough. Suicide is a secret killer, stealing our children from us—often before they realized they could ask for help. Addiction is the silent threat, hiding in plain sight within our homes, schools, and communities; it quietly takes hold before anyone realizes it is there. M.A.L.H.Y. is here to shatter that silence. M.A.L.H.Y. stands for Mental Health, Addiction, Love, Human Trafficking Awareness, and Youth Financial Literacy. But those aren't just words. They're battles. They're wounds we see every day on the faces of children who feel invisible. They're calls for help hidden behind the smiles of students who show up to class but carry the weight of trauma no one else sees. Their future is why M.A.L.H.Y. was born—and why we continue to fight every single day for love, for healing, for our youth, for all of us. Their safety is our responsibility. Their silence is our call to action! When people ask what M.A.L.H.Y. does, the answer is simple: we show up. Hope wears sneakers and a backpack, which is the M.A.L.H.Y. way. We are in classrooms to teach life-saving digital literacy. We teach students how to spot manipulation, how to recognize danger disguised as friendship, and how to protect themselves online. We hold workshops on mental health, addiction awareness, and coping strategies because vaping, fentanyl, and depression are showing up younger and stronger every year. M.A.L.H.Y. is a voice for the voiceless. Every time we speak to a classroom or walk into a school office, we carry with us the stories of the kids we've met. The teenage girl who didn't want to go home because the only adults she could trust were the ones wearing M.A.L.H.Y. badges. The 11-year-old boy who asked, "How do I make the scary messages stop?" The high school senior who cried during our fentanyl awareness talk and later shared that her brother had overdosed just weeks before. It is for every parent who still thinks "it won't happen to my kid," there's a predator counting on that silence. These are the moments that fuel us. These are the reasons we won't stop talking—won't stop raising awareness. M.A.L.H.Y. is not just a nonprofit—it's a movement. A rally cry for every mother, father, teacher, counselor, and friend who has ever felt helpless watching a young person struggle. Why does M.A.L.H.Y. continue this fight? Because a child was almost taken—and we were lucky enough to get them back. Because too many families aren't so lucky. Because even one child lost to trafficking, addiction, or suicide is one too many. Because this work is not optional—it's essential. Why is M.A.L.H.Y. in this? Because we have no other choice. Looking away is no longer acceptable because awareness saves lives and brings healing! What gives us motivation? It's every hug from every child saved. Every text that says, "You helped me see I'm not alone." Every parent who tells us they learned how to talk to their child. Our mission is to Empower. Educate. Protect. At the core of it all—beneath the banners, behind the workshops, and woven into every act of service—is love. M.A.L.H.Y. exists because of love – a fierce, unwavering, courageous love for our children. Love that dares to say, "Not our kids." Love that confronts evil with education. Love that builds bridges instead of walls. Love that shows up, listens, and never gives up—no matter how hard the journey. What ignites our souls isn't a sense of duty. It's love. It's anger. It's knowing that for every child we reach, there's one less slipping through the cracks. The kids are M.A.L.H.Y.'s "WHY" And we will not be silent! If you or someone you know needs help, please contact M.A.L.H.Y. at 951-704-0025 or visit malhy.org.

## Dr. Jessica Celina Hernandez-Smith

### MALHY Community Outreach Protective Services Inc.

### President

Meet Jessica, a beacon of inspiration and leadership as MALHY President of her organization. With a heart dedicated to serving others, she motivates those around her to become better individuals through active involvement in community service.

Born in El Paso, Texas, Jessica's roots trace back to an immigrant background, which has shaped her journey and experiences. For over two decades, she has been a vibrant member of the Temecula/Murrieta Valley community, dedicating her time to various non-profit organizations. GSFE has supported MALHY in a yearly toy drive to raise over one thousand toys for youth in our local community.

Her impressive resume includes roles as Past-Chair of the Salvation Army Rehabilitation Center, Past-Make-A-Wish March Madness Committee Member, and Past-Chair of the Riverside Community Health Foundation, among many others.

Jessica's volunteer work is extensive and impactful. She has served as the VP of the Community Reinvestment Act in San Diego and Inland Empire, Membership Coordinator for BNI, and has been involved in children's ministry, local food pantries, and as a Girl Scout Leader. Currently, she is a proud member Vice President of the Southern California Inland Empire Black Chamber of Commerce.

With over 20 years of banking experience, Jessica has also been pivotal in managing youth financial literacy programs. As a mother to two remarkable teenage girls, JoyCelina and Daysha, she founded MALHY Community Outreach Protective Services Inc. to support youth aged 10-25 in navigating social media, social anxiety, and peer pressure.

Jessica is not just about work; she finds joy in reading, cooking, and traveling. Adding to her credentials, she is a Process Server, holds a Certificate in Mediation, and is pursuing an etiquette certification to enrich the services offered by MALHY. Educated, well-rounded, and passionate about serving, Jessica is a testament to overcoming challenges and celebrating triumphs, all while staying true to her faith and roots, with Spanish as her first language. As she often reflects, "There's no limit to what God will do in your life." (Philippians 2:13)

## Reach out to Dr. Jessica Smith:

Phone: 951-704-0025

Website url: malhy.org

Email address: malhy.communityoutreach@gmail.com

Social Media Links:

Facebook

https://www.facebook.com/MALHYcommunityoutreach/

Instagram

https://www.instagram.com/Malhy_22/#

TikTok

https://www.tiktok.com/@malhy_22

X

https://x.com/i/flow/login?redirect_after_login=%2Fmalhy_22

# WHY???

*By Dr. (h.c.) Kaye Sheffield, MS, CCC-SLP*

WHY? Why not? Why Mom? Why God? Why her? Why him?

Why is one of the most interesting three letter words in our English vocabulary! It has so many manifestations: questioning, authoritarian, positive, negative, inquisitive, learning, demanding an explanation, and many more uses. It is a word that intrigues me. Where did it come from, but even a bigger question, how did we start using it in our lives?

Being a Mother of three wonderful children and a Speech Language Pathologist, who worked with children much of my adult life, I learned that this 3-letter word was the most frequently used word in a 2- to 3-year-olds vocabulary. I have heard that is used as much as 70 to 80% of the time in a young person's verbal communication...if not more, at times. "Why" is used by the inquisitive child who is growing and learning about the world and where he or she fits in. It actually starts in their brain when a young child begins to use the left side of their brain at about 2 years of age. It is the speech and language side, the questioning and curious side of the brain, the beginnings of socialization and desiring of adult engagement. The word "why" is easily articulated and therefore easily understood by others. These youngsters may also be using or starting to use other "wh" words such as "what, where, who, when," which are also easily articulated and understood by others.

When my children began using the word "why," I was delighted, at least initially, as I knew their curiosity was increasing, new vocabulary was being learned, and they were interacting with adults in a more mature manner than they had been when they were younger. They were expanding their use of language to 2- and 3-word phrases and sentences.

Besides a child's expanding language, curiosity, and exploration development, a child's use of 'why' is used as a way of learning about cause and effect and new vocabulary. It is really a positive and natural stage of development when the child is asking 'why.' Many autistic children don't ask 'why' or use the word or engage in adult conversation. An adult can encourage a young child to use the word 'why,' by saying something similar to: "I wonder why it is raining. Where does the rain come from?" Or "Why do you think that lizard is sitting in the sun?"

The other way a child may use 'why' is demanding, or questioning authority. This questioning authority can drive adults a little crazy!! The child may say 'Why?' when you have asked them to do something. As adults we may say, or want to say, "Because I said so." But another way is to ask a question back to the child. "Why do you think you should stop on the curb and look both directions when you want to cross the street?" It gives the child a chance to think through the reasons for the adult request and gives them a chance to think of cause and effect. Sometimes they gain a sense of pride so that they can figure out the answer to their own question. And we adults can praise them for figuring it out.

'Why' is a very positive learned word for a young child of 2 to 3 years, or up to age 4 or 5. The later young children from 3 to 5 years of age are learning more about cause and effect of their environment. They are inquisitive, curious, and want to learn more. It is a very positive word for students and people to use all through school, and even through life. "I wonder why… is happening." And "I wonder why they made that!" The more curious we are throughout our lives, the younger we are in heart, mind, and spirit.

For young children, 'why' is a maturing word that helps them in learning vocabulary and developing language. It is the social, interactive part of asking 'why' that is good for the child, however sometimes as an adult, we just want to say to the child, "I don't know the answer to that question. I guess you had better just ask Google or Alexa." Another place parents and adults can go to learn more about the use of 'why' in a child's language is to go to: American Speech and Hearing Association, www.asha.org.

How is 'why' learned as a child? It seems to be learned in context, and it may be used in reverse, such as, when an adult asks a child, "Why do you need that jacket? Are you cold?"

As we get older, we learn to regulate the use of 'why' and to use it more wisely. Sometimes we use it powerfully as in, "Why are you letting me go?," or "Why did you do that?" We use it for requesting an explanation and for clarity, "I don't understand why you are asking me to do that."

"Why" has so many uses, besides those mentioned, for safety, for love, for anger, for questioning, for learning, and one of the biggest uses is for communication. When we show up at a meeting or social event, 'why' is a common word in our communication with others. We ask, "Why did you come to this meeting?" or "Why did you move here?" The word 'why' is so common and useful in our communication and learning about others.

When I ask myself the question, 'what is my why?' I am led in several directions. When I started my studies at the university, my 'why' was to obtain that degree. When I started back to the university 15 years later, I had the same 'why', a goal to obtain that master's degree, credential, and Certificate of Clinical Competence (a national certificate for speech pathologists). When I had young children and was suddenly a single parent with a 6-month-old baby, I knew my 'why' was to take care of my three children and keep going. Their physical safety, nutrition, growth, and learning were of utmost importance in my 'why.'

There were times that I reached out to God and cried out "Why Lord?," "Why now?" "Why me?" Each cry out to Him was for help that I could not do by myself. I knew that He was always with me and would not leave me. He promises. I would never have made it through those tough times without Him. I think about some of the tough times and remember, He was there and only He could have helped me through.

I think about getting that degree from the university with exams AND a thesis to write and while getting married and moving... but God was there.

I remember trying to take home my newborn baby, and the doctors said he may have something really seriously wrong with him and may have to stay in the hospital...but God was there and said all would be all right.

I remember 3 years of going to court and three trials to finish a divorce. I remember a serious cancer diagnosis, a melanoma, and surgery. And there was a plane crash in Southern Africa that I, and my family were in. Then another cancer diagnosis came two years after the first diagnosis with a recommendation for chemotherapy. But God! He was there, as He promised He would be. I called out to Him and asked "Why." I found God was there for each one. But God had a different outcome planned than the one I feared would happen.

Do we ever lose our 'why'? I hope not! 'Why' is in our lifelong vocabulary. When we stop asking 'why,' we give up on living.

We always want to stay curious, socializing and having conversations with others to know their 'why.' We need to be wise in our use of 'why' in challenging thoughts, beliefs, and actions that we don't agree with. WHY is a powerful and universal word! In using 'why,' it is wise to keep in mind that we should be "...quick to listen, slow to speak, and slow to become angry." (James 1:19) We should be encouraged to use thoughtful and positive communication and at times be wise in restraining our use of 'why.'

That's My Why! What's yours?

## Dr. Kaye Sheffield, h.c., M.S., CCC-SLP

Kaye is blessed to be the mother of three wonderful, successful children and a grandmother of six great kids. She is a Speech and Language Pathologist who has worked in schools, hospitals, convalescent homes, done private practice, supervised students at California Baptist University and is currently supervising SLP Assistants. She has obtained an Honorary Doctorate Degree in Humanitarian Service. Kaye became a Dr., a Sears, Certified Health Coach and enjoys helping people become as healthy as they can be. She is also an author and has written for the compilation of five books that are national and international Best Sellers. Kaye is currently working on her own book of stories from her life. She loves to dance, both ballroom and square dance, make card crafts, do Bible study with her group of ladies, work in her garden and grow her own produce on the Tower Garden. She enjoys speaking and sharing with others especially on how to put as much fruit and vegetables in your body as possible and grow in all areas of health and wellness.

Dr. Kaye Sheffield, h.c., M.S., CCC-SLP

kaye_slp@msn.com  (there is an underscore after kaye_)

(909) 556-8221

ksheffield.juiceplus.com;  towergarden.com/#kayesheffield

# Rising From the Ashes Like a Phoenix

*By H.C. Dr. Doula Lakeysha Mattis*

There is a power that cannot be shaken. I've known it, clung to it, cried through it, and risen with it—and that power is found in God. My story is not simply one of endurance but divine preservation and intervention. I am not here because I was strong but because God is stronger. Time and time again, my faith carried me when nothing else could. And, even today, God's grace remains sufficient for me to gracefully move through even the most difficult struggles of life wiser, braver, and stronger.

I come from humble beginnings, and those beginnings were filled with love and connection. I was born into a family with a grandmother like no other, who helped me learn how to dream and acted as my weight-bearing walls when the storms of life came through with fiery intent to knock me down for the count. However, my grandmother's tenacity, positivity, and continuing affirmation of her belief in me fueled me to keep the fire going to rise up victoriously out of the ashes of despair, each time resiliently. I know my grandmother's secret; it was prayer. I learned that my grandmother was a warrior wrapped in dignity and reserved strength. I thank God for her soft whispers of prayers; they were declarations and prophetic utterances that shaped my reality.

Through my grandmother, I learned how to be unapologetically me and that I could do anything that I set my mind to. Early in life, I also learned that faith isn't a fair-weather friend—it's a lifeline. I depended on that lifeline many times, and even today, I don't know what I would do without it.

Somewhere down the line, I sought to be excellent in all that I set my hands to do. I raised the standard for myself to earn degrees, lead classrooms and auditoriums of students, train educators, and uplift and serve women and men of purpose. I have walked into numerous rooms where I was the only one who looked like me, and I held my head high, knowing who I was as I heard the soft and gentle whisper of my grandmother within my spirit, telling me that I belonged, and I had what it took to make a difference in someone's life.

Like many, I have had plenty of battles, and at times, those battles have not only left deep silent wounds in my soul but also my resolve to go on. For example, when I was around 8 years old, I remember sitting in a courtroom on the witness stand; the lawyer turned to me and said," Sweetheart, point out the person in this courtroom who did these things to you?" My heart dropped in my stomach, and it felt like time had frozen. I was asked to do one of my life's scariest and most difficult things. That was to point out and testify against the family friend who violated me. There were times when I didn't want to try anymore, and I wanted to stay down and not get back up because life had given me hard blows that I wasn't sure I could come back from. For example, when my husband came home, he told me he was moving out! It was a hard blow, and I didn't want him to leave me or the kids, but he had already decided. I tried to reason with him and pledged to do whatever it took to make things right. But the words I spoke to him seemed to go into one ear and out of the other. I was left alone to raise and fend for my kids. You see, the choice had already been made for me, so I had to deal with the aftermath of all that was to come. For many years, behind my smiles were silent battles, and the glimpse of hope that I once carried within my spirit and soul felt as if it had been extinguished. I took grief, burnout, and unspoken disappointment every which way I turned, and I was tired! I was tired of lifting so much weight and always being strong, so my soul grew weary. And though I kept moving forward, something inside me slowly burned out, and I felt so broken and numb. I soon went into survival mode.

The storms of life got even fiercer, and I felt like the jaws of life were swallowing me up and shredding me to pieces. Like when I had to stand over the hospital bed, looking at my 23-year-old baby girl in a coma, hooked up to all types of machines that were keeping her alive as she fought for her life! She was diagnosed with a rare autoimmune disease, and we could never have imagined that something like this could have happened to her, but it did. Being in the ring of life is no easy feat, and I soon learned that no one is exempt from life's storms.

Life can bring some tough knocks! A few months before this happened to my daughter, my sister found herself battling breast cancer, and unfortunately, she lost the battle. Rewind two years before that, I lost my best friend out of the blue; she didn't feel well, went to the emergency room, and never made it back home. Rewind again a couple of years before my best friend passed; my grandmother fell ill and passed. Fast forward to today, and as I am writing this chapter, two weeks from today, I experienced a bittersweet miracle of my dad slipping away to glory, and he went peacefully with God. I know because I was there with him. And that was one of the hardest hits I have taken in my life. I learned that you never know how strong you are until you're faced with the heaviest battles of life.

Through all of these hard knocks, I prayed and wailed, and as the tears rolled down my face, I sometimes even wanted to turn my back on God. But I pushed through and worshipped through song when I had no words. I read and recited promises from the bible and found God's promises speaking directly to my tired and broken heart, saying: "I will never leave you nor forsake you." And many times, I had no energy to believe. And I realized that He never did leave or forsake me. He was always there through life's good and bad times. Sometimes, He was so quiet, and when things didn't go as I had prayed, I thought I had done something terribly wrong to make God turn his back on me.

But I soon realized that God was using these trials and hardships as an opportunity to develop my faith. Yes, even those ugly moments that I felt would scar me for the rest of my life. But even in that chaos, my faith in the sovereignty of God held me up. I remember falling to my knees more than I can count, not in defeat but surrender. Oh yes, things began to fall into place when I learned to stop trying to force things and do what I thought needed to be done instead of asking God to order my steps and direct my path.

As the storms of life continued to beat across my path and I walked through my wilderness of life, I knew that God would never leave or forsake me. And it was there—in the barren, broken places—that God began to breathe new life into me. What the enemy meant to destroy me, God used to birth a purpose within me that now allows me to function as the Rebound and Reset Doula. I am dedicated to guiding individuals—especially women—through the transformative journey from hardship to healing, from despair to purpose.

Out of all the pain I have experienced in my life came clarity. I began to see myself not through the lens of failure and exhaustion but through the eyes of God—a woman Queen in reign called to serve, to speak life, to build others up from the ashes of their own adversity to rise to greater heights in their lives despite all odds. And that is how the Rebound and Reset Doula was born.

From a conversation with my former business coach, Apostle Alicia George, while in a meeting, she asked me what I felt I should be called based on my purpose in life. I thought about it momentarily, and what bubbled up in my spirit was "doula." And she confirmed it was the same name that she was thinking of. The term doula was not birthed from ambition but from purpose and assignment. I didn't stumble into this work - The Rebound and Reset Doula; instead, I was called to it.

Everything I offer—the Awaken to More courses, the Rebound and Reset framework, the Book Club, the Podcast, and the Reignite Her Season Cohort—was built on the foundation of God's faithfulness in my life. He turned my mourning into purpose. He transformed my private pain into a public rebounding, resetting, and healing platform. My Rebound and Reset framework is more than a book of strategy—it's a spiritual pathway. It moves women through acknowledgment, stillness, vision, identity, boundaries, healing, purpose, action, and sisterhood—not just as steps but as sacred stops on a journey of restoration, rejuvenation, and renewal. These steps are grounded in the belief that God wants us whole, not just functioning or surviving, but thriving!

I remember a specific day, broken and melancholy, sitting in my car, overwhelmed by grief and stress. I cried, "God, I don't know how to keep going." And in that silence, I heard Him: "You don't have to go alone." That moment changed everything. It wasn't about being strong but learning to surrender and remembering if God was for me, who could be against me. Yes, like in the old negro spiritual song, I know that "I have come this far by faith leaning on the Lord, trusting in His holy word, He's never failed me yet, oh oh oh, can't turn around, I've come this far by faith." Don't get me wrong; I am not religious by any means, but I am a spiritual person who believes in the power and authority of God. It is my foundation and power source, and when I surrender and tap into His power source, I can weather any storm that life brings as I put my faith and trust in God to see me through. It is not an easy task to undertake, and at times, I have found myself snatching back the driver's wheel and steering it the way I thought it should go, only to take me on a longer route than necessary, which caused me unnecessary stress and worry.

But, when I decided to hold to his hand, God's unchanging hand, faith taught me that I didn't need all the answers. I just needed to trust the One who did have the answers. Many say that trust is earned and not simply given, and I agree. And, from where I'm standing, when I look back over my life, God has given me ample reason to trust Him and take Him at his word. That trust has carried me through transitions, loss, caregiving, starting over, and every "how will I make it?" moment. And now, I walk in the truth that God never wastes our pain. He repurposes it if we allow Him to do so. What pain have you been holding onto that needs to be repurposed? You can take your lemons and make lemonade if you choose. Yes, it's easier said than done. Yes, it's going to be a challenging feat to accomplish. But all the same, so is holding on to the agony, hurt, pain, misery, regret, and unforgiveness. What do you have to lose?

To the woman reading this who feels like she's at the end of her rope—I want you to know this: you are not forgotten. You are not alone. God sees you. He hasn't abandoned you. Your tears have been counted, and your cries have been heard. You're not too far gone. You're not too broken. You are simply in the process of being developed for a higher purpose. Now, you must have the power to choose to awaken to more. To acknowledge what has occurred in your life, assess it for what it is, and decide to make something beautiful out of it. It's time to move forward and grow into the beautiful, capable, anointed, talented, and unstoppable woman you were created to become! This is not your ending—it's your awakening.

I've walked through fire, but it did not consume me. The same God who sustained me will sustain you. And if you let Him, He will breathe new life into the dry places in your life. He will give you beauty for ashes, strength for fear, gladness for mourning, and peace for despair. That's not just Scripture—that's my story, and if you are ready to rise to greater heights, your story will be even more awesome! You know that the number one challenge facing people today is rebounding faster from a setback. How can anyone rebound and reset their life after they've been taken by surprise and hit hard by life? Let's be honest. Setbacks will happen multiple times in our lives... no one is exempt... and no one knows when. But we all know that setbacks will happen numerous times, so how can anyone rebound faster to get their lives back on track to rise to purpose?

The real caveat is that when life knocks you down, how fast can you rebound from the punches? Some of you have experienced or are currently experiencing multiple rounds of punches in a short amount of time, which can leave you down for the count! Time stops for no one; life keeps on moving, so during the most difficult times, how can you bounce back and not stay stuck in the adversity you are facing? I am on a mission to help people ready to rebound get back on track—to reclaim their lives and rediscover their purpose for life because life can be beautiful, and it's worth fighting for to live a life of purpose.

Sometimes, we only get one shot in life, so go ahead and take your best shot in life. You were created with purpose. You were chosen for more. And no matter what you've lost, you still have something worth living for. You still have a reason to rise all the way to the top! It's time to tap back into life and bet on you. You were built for this; you were made for more. It's time to awaken to more blessings, opportunities, fulfillment, joy, peace, happiness, purpose, hope, faith, and love. This chapter is my peace offering. It's my "won't God do it" personal testimony. And it's my invitation to you to trust God in your storms of life and know that even when you're walking through the valley of the shadow of death, and the ashes remain, He can give you beauty for your ashes. Let Him rewrite your story. Because if He did it for me, He will do it for you.

He's never failed me yet—and if you take Him at His word, you won't forget. Are you ready to hold to His hand, God's unchanging hand, surrender, and let God have His way in whatever battle you find yourself in today?

## H.C. Dr. Doula Lakeysha Mattis

H.C. Dr. Doula Lakeysha Mattis is a purpose-driven Rebound & Reset Doula and Facilitator, Author, Speaker, and founder of LaKeysha Mattis Enterprises LLC and Oasis of Hope International. She empowers women navigating life's hardest transitions to reclaim their identity, reignite their passion, and rise to greater heights with clarity and confidence. With a heart for transformation and a gift for nurturing resilience, H.C. Dr. Doula Lakeysha Mattis designs sacred spaces—both virtual and in-person—for women to heal, rebuild, and walk boldly into the life they were created to thrive in. Through her signature framework and spiritual-centered programs, she helps her clients not just survive but thrive with purpose and power to reign.

**Connect with me:**

WhatsApp: wa.me/15599991163

FB: @lakeyshamattisenterprises

IG: @lakeyshamattisenterprises

# What is my WHY?

*By Dr. Latrice Jones (h.c.)*

To live a life well lived is my greatest desire. It is my ultimate "WHY". But what is a life well lived? It's not just the mere accumulation of material things. For me, a life well lived is about living in the blessings that God, the creator has bestowed upon you. That is my WHY!

I am Called and Chosen to empower God's people. To serve as a catalyst for change and evolution. As a believer, I am committed to live in purpose and walk boldly in my faith. My WHY begins with a pursuit of excellence, excellence in myself, in my relationships, in my doings, my actions, and in my thoughts. I'm not talking about perfection, for there is no perfect human on this Earth. But I have a commitment to doing my best, to giving of my best and of being of service.

It is not always easy to know your WHY. But the more we get to know ourselves and the plans that God, the Creator, has for us, the more we get to know and understand our WHY. In essence, the deeper we dig, the more buried treasures we will find.

## Finding Your WHY

We all have gifts, talents, and callings. I believe they are all the tenants that help us to identify our WHY. As we go through life, we find what we are drawn to & what is drawn to us. We discover what gives peace to our soul, warms our heart, and makes us smile. These experiences will influence and shape us into the person we shall become. Every day that we draw nearer to our purpose and our calling, we get closer to our WHY.

Discovering my WHY takes me back to the days of my childhood. I have always had an inkling for leadership and service. As early as elementary school, I participated in student council, served in classroom leadership roles, and used my voice and talents to make change in my environment.

Planning, mobilizing, executing was a spirit that would follow me throughout my life, as stated beginning in my early years, carrying over into my adolescence, deepening in my teenage years, flourishing in my young adult phases & continuing to guide me well into and throughout my adulthood. In every phase of my life, I can recall a time that I took on a role that would put me in position to not only affect change, but that would also give voice to others, inspire excellence, and seek community.

My WHY, the desire to live a life well lived, could be witnessed during my collegiate years. My extracurricular activities, my college major of administration, my profession, and my community service spoke to my love of making this world a better place, giving of myself, and uplifting others.

This passion carried on to my professional career. It began with my years working with youth and seeing young people striving to make their dreams come true, believing in the power of education, looking for opportunity, seeking breakthrough and opening the door to success, wealth, and careers. Uplifting others included the young pregnant moms that I worked with when I graduated college, as well as the young adults I would encounter in church and the community. Those young people, faced with the demands of the big world, pressured to make positive decisions and live up to expectations. Young people who would doubt themselves, becoming disillusioned, and question their abilities because things didn't quite work out. It was my walking in purpose to inspire and motivate others that fostered my desire to help them during such a vital point in their lives. To be an advisor, a friend and a mentor, someone who would come along beside them and provide guidance, support, and encouragement. My WHY, to help others find their light and keep shining.

## Deepening the Relationship: My Path to Discovering my WHY

As I deepened my relationship with God, the Creator, I discovered I not only had a gift of administration and a love for education, but I also had a gift of leadership and a natural gift to inspire and empower others. This is where I found my footing in life. As I leaned into my gifts, my gifts leaned into me. I encourage you to LEAN IN! The more I operated in my gifts and calling the more God opened doors and provided breakthrough and greater clarity.

My WHY expanded and became better defined. Not only was it my desire to create community, be of service and make the world a better place. But I would do that and accomplish my mission by pouring my life work, my heart and soul into WOMEN, the bearers of life. I had an epiphany and realized if I could empower a woman, then I would also empower her children. If I could show love to a fellow woman, then she could then also show love to those within her sphere of influence. By restoring a woman's hope, meant she would better prepare to live her dreams.

And I knew from my own experience, that a woman who would seek purpose, walk in faith, and live out her dreams, would ultimately create a world that was a better place. It all began to make sense. It all began to come full circle. I had spent years serving my peers in elementary, middle school, high school, and college. I spent years in my adulthood, giving back to the community, teaching young people how to go to college, ensuring young adults had success in their careers, and now I was drawn to the center of it all, women, my sisters.

My WHY had led me to a spiritual place where I now understood that the love God had shown me, could be shown to someone else through me. God was using me to uplift others. God, the Creator had called upon me to MOVE, to ACT, to do MORE and out of obedience and delight, my business. LJ speaks was born! LJSpeaks is a platform where women would find inspiration, motivation, faith, and encouragement, but more importantly would be celebrated and empowered. A space where they too would understand the importance of living a life, well lived.

To encourage women to live their best life, to heal from within, to seek purpose, follow their dreams, and to walk in faith became my mission. It was about teaching a woman to never give up on themselves, to never lose hope. To live an inspired life!

## The Dreamer Within

I've always been a dreamer. I dreamed of my life, my future, and my destiny. I didn't know it as a child, but those dreams were connected to my calling and to my purpose. But they were, and so are yours. Our dreams teach us about ourselves. Following our dreams is about exploring the possibilities and considering the impossible. It's in these moments that we are birthing life into our WHY! I tell you, the more that you take those quiet moments to learn more about yourself, the more the dreams begin to live out loud! I began to live a life that was well lived, a life that was exceedingly abundant. I began to see "it", I begin to realize "it" and was empowered to walk in "it."

It happened for me! I knew "it" was my purpose. My life began to feel aligned!! I was LIVING!!

## Setbacks in Knowing & Living out my WHY?

I'm living a life well lived. I'm aligned with my WHY! Life is GOOD, maybe even GREAT!

And then, just like everyone else, life hit me, there were trials, tribulations, death loss, divorce, disappointment, frustrations, I experienced it all, and I, just like anyone else, found myself off kilter, questioning who I was. "WHY is this happening to me?" I asked. "How did I get here?" I asked. "What happened to all of my dreams, my hopes and the plans that I had for my life?" I asked.

You see, one day we as women, wake up and we are in full adulthood, we may be married, we may have children. We may find ourselves divorced or widowed, or we may find ourselves still seeking that perfect soulmate. It's at this stage of our lives that we begin to question our decisions, we start reflecting on our lives, asking if we've done things, right? As women, we may have set aside some of our dreams as we took on the role of being Mother, wife, partner, caregiver, and not that we regret it: but we just come to the realization that we've lost ourselves. And it's right at that moment, when we're feeling lost, when we're confused and when things are looking dark, that we need to go back to our WHY. It's our core. It's our anchor. It's the heart of who we are! You ground yourself; you remember everything that you have learned about yourself. Ask yourself what made your soul happy? What gave you a smile? What encouraged you? And then you remind yourself how great you are.... GO BACK TO YOUR WHY!

## Seeking Purpose, again... What is my WHY?

Yes, we sometimes find ourselves seeking purpose again, re-evaluating ourselves. We start trying to measure ourselves against other women. We compare ourselves to what society said our life should have been based on our age, we're thirty, we're forty, we're fifty, we're sixty, we're seventy, we're eighty. There are all these rules of which we should have lived life by. I'm here to say, my WHY today, is to tell each one of you, that you are "wonderfully and fearfully made," that you are unique and there is no one way to live your life other than to live well. As I said earlier, we have a purpose here on earth and we don't need to second-guess it, instead, EMBRACE it! Enjoy the journey on your path to Greatness. Enjoy the present and look forward to the future. Every day that we have breath means we have another opportunity to live life to its fullest, an opportunity to seek our purpose and discover our WHY!

It's time to step out of those spaces that we no longer belong to, step out of those shoes that no longer fit us, release what no longer serves us and begin to create new relationships, establish new goals, and dream new dreams. It's never too late. Go find your WHY!

## Life is for the Living: The WHY!

I believe "Life is for the Living." To live exceedingly and abundantly and to live in expectation of what the Creator has for me, that is my WHY! It all points to living a life well lived.

We create our own legacy. We determine what our life will look like. We have that POWER! BE EMPOWERED! So, I ask you, "What is your WHY?" Write the book. Sing the song. Start the new career. Find a new hobby. Cook the fancy meal. Drink the

champagne. And please book the DREAM vacation trip!

Mark Twain said, "Twenty years from now you will be more disappointed by the things that you didn't do than by the ones you did do. So, throw off the bowlines. Sail away from the safe harbor. Catch the trade winds in your sails. Explore. Dream. Discover."

That is my WHY! A life well lived full of exploration, dreams, and discovery.

*My WHY demonstrated...*

- Living in purpose is my WHY.
- Walking in faith is my WHY.
- Building Gods Kingdom is my WHY.
- Starting over is my WHY.
- Following my dreams is my WHY.
- Seeking better for myself is my WHY.
- Wanting more for my children is my WHY.
- Living life boldly is my WHY.
- Living life to the fullest Is my WHY.
- Seeking more of God in my life is my WHY.
- Enjoying life is my WHY.
- Traveling the world is my WHY.
- Being comfortable in my own skin is my WHY.
- Embracing my past is my WHY.
- Embracing my mistakes is my WHY.
- Accepting my setbacks is my WHY.

- Living in the present is my WHY.
- Having no regrets is my WHY.
- Feeling good about myself is my WHY.
- Pouring into the lives of others is my WHY.
- Encouraging another is my WHY.
- Uplifting the community is my WHY.
- Inspiring youth is my WHY.
- Making this world a better place is my WHY.
- Motivating another woman to seek her dreams is my WHY.
- Giving comfort is my WHY.
- Providing solace is my WHY.
- Paying tribute to my grandparents and keeping my mother's memory alive is my WHY.
- Honoring my parents who are still living is my WHY.

But most importantly, being a living testimony of God's greatness here on earth, is my WHY.

GO LIVE YOUR "WHY"!

## Dr. (h.c.) Latrice Jones

Latrice Jones, hailing from Southern California, is a dynamic servant leader, mentor, strategist, and motivational speaker renowned for her commitment to empowerment and community upliftment. As a first-generation college graduate, Latrice earned her BA in Administrative Studies from UC Riverside, a Master's Degree in Public Administration from CSU Long Beach, and a Master's Degree in Leadership from Grand Canyon University.

In recognition of her outstanding contributions to humanitarian efforts, Latrice was bestowed with an Honorary Doctorate in Humanitarianism, further solidifying her dedication to serving others.

Latrice has served in various administrative and management capacities, including City government, the non-profit sector, and currently serves in the Chief Executive Office for the County of Los Angeles. Balancing her roles as a public servant, an Entrepreneur, and as a devoted mother to Lauryn, a Labor & Delivery RN, and Jared, a Boy Scout, community leader and scholar athlete, Latrice continues to exemplify excellence in all her endeavors. She is the visionary Founder of LJ Speaks, a platform dedicated to advocating, mentoring, empowering and inspiring women to pursue their purpose, follow their dreams and live their best life.

Beyond her professional achievements, Latrice is an accomplished author, co-authoring a journal and books on empowerment, healing, spiritual growth, and personal development. She remains deeply engaged in community service, serving as a Children's Church and Sunday school teacher, an Advisory Board Member for the University of California Riverside School of Education, a Member of the Los Angeles County African American Employees Association, and a City of Pomona Civilian Oversight Committee Member. Inspired by her passion of travel and creating memories, she is also a travel advisor, where she takes pleasure in planning travel experiences for all.

With over 25 years of experience in leadership and personal development, Latrice is renowned for her ability to inspire, motivate and empower others through workshops, conferences, one-on-one mentoring, group coaching, and public speaking engagements. She prides herself for being a catalyst of support and growth.

Guided by her unwavering belief in the transformative power of purpose, change and empowerment, Dr. Latrice Jones continues to encourage others to embrace their potential and make strides towards positive outcomes. When asked why she does it all, she replies "It is my mission to be the change in the world that I want to see. I believe in the empowerment of others. Greatness is our Journey, if only we believe in the power of living in Purpose. I encourage all to walk in FAITH and prepare themselves to make BOLD MOVES!

Email: Lj.ljspeaks@gmail.com

Follow her on Facebook: LatriceMarie or LJSPEAKS and on IG: @latricemarie8311 or ljspeaks_empowerment

# Love, Just Love

*By Laura Dunn*

*The mediocre teacher tells.*
*The good teacher explains.*
*The superior teacher demonstrates.*
*The great teacher inspires.*
*William Arthur Ward*

Why do I do the things I do? As an educator of 25 years, I realized early on that many of my students spent more time with me than with their own parents and so the saying is true, "It takes a village to raise a child."

I have been blessed by the presence of several good people in my life, but there was this one unique teacher. She had the "IT" factor. We all felt it. Mrs. Shirley Sutherland in Room 22 was everyone's favorite teacher. Mentor, teacher, friend, and cheerleader to so many, Mrs. Sutherland stole the hearts of students and families in the communities of Stanton and Garden Grove in Southern California. She taught for over 35 years and taught more than 1,000 students.

She's still a woman who resonates classic feminine grace, kindness, and total dedication to the art of teaching. Even at the age of ninety, she still carries herself with that same spirit. She has been married to her husband Cecil for over 65 years, and they still live in the same house that they purchased shortly after getting married and having two children of their own.

This past year, the community honored Shirley on her 90th birthday in which she jokingly convinced us that it was only her 65th birthday. This moment in time was like a dream come true for all of us. There was this distinct presence of light and love on that day. All you could feel was peace. Everything seemed perfect. There were men and women who showed up to honor her as a person who inspired them to be great. We all felt like little kids again. I had the privilege of calling her my second-grade teacher in 1984, and she is also my lifelong mentor.

When we talk about our "why," mine has everything to do with the fact that someone alongside the wisdom and guidance of my own mother took the time to encourage and inspire me. Shirley taught me and all of us students to dream BIG and shoot for the stars because in reality, "The bottom is far too crowded!" Getting to be in her class was like winning the lottery! Imagine having that much power in the hearts of children. No matter where we came from, she had a way of making us feel like we were special and that we mattered, despite our circumstances.

Growing up, I wanted to be just like her. My story is special because even as I moved on throughout my education, my second-grade teacher and I stayed in touch. We would write letters back and forth and she always would end each letter with a reminder that if I ever wanted to go to college, she would help me. So, when I reached my Senior year of High School and I needed a place to stay, both her and her husband let me move in so that I could attend Cal State Fullerton. That was a special time in my life.

After finishing college, my first official offer was to teach second grade just like her. I later went on to complete a Master's and a Dance Credential and even taught out of my own room 22, which made me laugh, but beyond all my accomplishments, the belief that I have in myself because of her, is the "why" in life. Despite what others may think, I know who Laura is and I know what I am capable of because of the love and compassion that Mrs. Sutherland has poured into me. I am more than what my titles or credentials say. I am a human being and woman with a big heart, I am a lover of the arts, athletics, and music. I have also gone on to become a mother of two young men, one who is an elite athlete and the other who is as smart as Bill Gates. I am dedicated to everything I set out to do and I care deeply about other people. Despite my flaws, I am generous, and I love to encourage others because someone special took the time to inspire and encourage me.

Some people do not believe in miracles, but Mrs. Sutherland's love of teaching led to countless touching success stories. At her celebration, and many years later, person after person shared testimonies of how she made them feel and how she made a difference in their life. Some had driven miles to attend and give honor to her. She truly planted seeds into the lives of children who needed something more than just an education. She instilled hope and a sense of excitement in a regular school day. She did things that set her apart from others. Her heart was just bigger! As little kids, we moved to "Mousercise" each morning, we made fancy art projects, we sang songs and performed the play of Peter Rabbit. She hosted swimming parties, took us to the Crocodile farm, and fearlessly drove her car into our neighborhood and would wave and smile when she saw us. We set goals to do well in the areas of math and reading and were always challenged to aim higher. There was always some sort of prize to work towards and sometimes she would pile us into a couple of cars to take us to get a burger, fries, and frosty dessert. When it was time to sit in a circle at reading time, we all wanted to sit next to her. When birthdays, First Communions and Quinceanera's took place, guess who would actually show up? Yes, Shirley showed up year after year, always with a warm smile, a gift in hand and her camera. She created a scrap book for almost every class she ever had.

Many of Shirley's students became amazing contributors to our society: doctors, teachers, police officers, engineers, and business owners (to say a few) and she inspired people like me to have a vision for my life. My why in life comes from a place of gratitude, it comes from knowing that if just one person is really for you, then who could be against you? Most people don't understand that everyday miracles happen through the intentions and actions of ordinary people. They are like hidden gems that show up at the right place and time in our lives. They show up like peaceful soft whispers. These moments enable us to look past the doom and gloom of what the world also brings us.

In my present career as an educator, I've learned that teaching must go beyond content. The great ones teach to inspire. Great teachers instill hope, character, and confidence in students and so now I know it is my turn. Each morning, I set my intentions as I drive to work. On my toughest days I say to myself, "What would Shirley do?" I have been teaching for 25 years, and she still inspires me.

Michelle Obama once said, "Service is a better goal than happiness." She is correct, because through service, one will find their purpose. From there, comes continued happiness which equates to joy that can last you a lifetime. Who has been your greatest mentor of all time? Who has been your biggest cheerleader, friend, or investor of sorts? In a world that focuses more on the "me," instead of the "we," I wish there were a way to show the world how powerful we could be if we would just aim to pay it forward. If that was the case, then we would raise the vibration of our next generation for sure! I pray this book will light a fire in you today to go out and be somebody's miracle. Think of how one little thing a day adds up to hundreds of good deeds over a lifetime. When all is said and done, my prayer is that God will look down on us and say, "Well done, my good and faithful servant."

My why is simple. It comes from the love that Shirley showed me first. This story has not ended. As a community, there's still more work to do, but for now we can exclaim, "We love you, we respect you and we honor you Mrs. Sutherland. Thank you for teaching us the way!"

## Laura Dunn

Laura Dunn resides in Sunny Southern California and has served as an educator in the Val Verde Unified School District for over 25 years. Laura's life mission includes working with students and families in the areas of Elementary Education, fitness, and the performing arts. She is also a certified Aqua Fitness Instructor and proud mother of two teenage sons who have helped her extend the vision of what it means to be a lifelong learner and committed volunteer. She has served as a motivational speaker through organizations such as Friday Night Live and the American Heart Association. She continues to serve as an ambassador of children's health & wellness and aspires to own and operate a family-owned aquatic center after retiring from teaching. Her favorite motto is "If you want something done, give it to a busy person."

# When Life Rewrites Your Why

*By Lauren Raguzin*

*This story is dedicated to my husband,*
*John who I love more than anything in the world!*

Five years ago, if you'd asked me my "why," I would have said: helping others—any way I can.

I've always been the person—the one who feels deeply, listens intently, checks in, and shows up. I believed empathy was innate. But life has a way of deepening our capacity for it through experience.

Still, empathy requires balance. You can't let others' pain consume you to the point where you neglect your own well-being. I've done that—but now I know how to keep it in check, using it to help others feel seen and heard.

Interestingly, I'm an ENTJ—often called "The Commander" in the Myers-Briggs world. Strategic, decisive, goal driven. Yet, my leadership style is grounded in empathy. I mentor, empower, and draw out potential in others—a quality I credit to my first boss, Joe, one of the best mentors I have ever had!!

In business, empathy is often mistaken for weakness. I see it as MY superpower. It fosters trust and collaboration. But without boundaries, it can lead to burnout. It's about showing up for others while honoring yourself.

For most of my life, helping others wasn't just my why. It was my identity. But life has a way of testing and reshaping that purpose.

## April 17, 2023—the day my life forever changed...

It was a Sunday. My husband, John and I were at church, and I was preparing to travel back to my hometown for a special moment, my second book signing with my childhood best friend, Nicole.

I'd recently been published in a collaborative book (my first as a published author) and had also been invited to join the board of NAMI (National Alliance on Mental Illness.)

I was on Cloud 9; this trip was going to be a celebration.

Then everything changed.

As soon as we got into the car, John turned to me and said, "I didn't want to worry you, but I have no feeling on the right side of my body. It started a few days ago."

I knew instantly. He'd had—or was having—a stroke.

We rushed to the ER. The stroke was confirmed. But three days later came a second, devastating blow:

Cancer—Again.

It was his third.

Years earlier, he'd survived thyroid cancer. This time, it was lung cancer that had already spread to his brain—a rare mutation caused by thyroid cells. No symptoms. No warning.

They found 25 to 30 brain metastases and a 2 cm lung tumor. Radiation wasn't an option—20 years prior, he had non-Hodgkin's lymphoma. You can't be radiated in the same area twice.

The hardest part was that they told him before I could get there. I walked into his hospital room and found him slumped over, crying—alone.

That moment is forever etched in my memory.

I had to call my boss before I could even process what this meant for our lives. I'd just started a project with a brand-new client. Everything had been fresh and full of promise. Now, I had no idea when—or if—I'd return.

And the truth? I couldn't.

My husband needed me—completely.

His care became my full-time job.

## Caregiving: A New Role

I've always seen myself as kind and caring. But in the following months, I uncovered a hard truth: I wasn't naturally a caregiver. My mother had been. Why wasn't I?

I'd never been in that role before. I hadn't cared for an aging parent. I'd never navigated serious illness up close. And suddenly, I was thrust into being my husband's full-time caregiver, ready or not.

And it was hard. In ways no one prepares you for.

The hardest part?

Patience, let's say... I wasn't exactly first in line when they handed that out. In fact, I'm a very impatient person, something I work on every day!

I wanted to do everything right. Make sure he ate well. Took his medication. Drank water. Rested. Stayed hopeful. Fought hard.

I was trying to control the situation. But I didn't realize—John was the one going through it, not ME!

No number of schedules or reminders could take away the weight of what he was feeling—physically, emotionally, spiritually.

I was doing the best I could. But I had to let go. I had to relax. I had to learn a new way to love—one rooted in presence, not performance.

I'm still working on that.

Caregiving isn't just about managing someone's needs. It's about surrendering yourself.

Showing up—even when you're exhausted, scared, and stretched too thin and wonder where you will get the strength to face another day of heartache.

I've inherited many positive traits from my mother, but this was one trait— caregiver—I wish I had learned better from my mother how to master it; I felt like I was failing miserably!

I had never been in that role. I didn't grow up caring for a parent or navigating serious illness, you see my Mom did, she took such great care of my Dad until he passed suddenly of a heart attack when I was nineteen.

## My New Why Emerged

Caregiving is hard. It's physically, emotionally, and mentally draining. You lose sleep, time, and parts of yourself.

And yet... through all that, something began to shift inside me. My new why started to evolve.

Not from helping people—but toward understanding them more deeply. Toward compassion without control. Toward showing up even when I had nothing left to give.

I didn't know how to handle it at first. But now, I know this truth:

Sometimes, your why finds you in the quietest, most challenging moments. And when it does, it doesn't just reshape your purpose, it reshapes you. It teaches you. It changes your life.

My career has always defined me. I poured myself into my

work—often at the expense of my own well-being.

But when your partner is your best friend—when you love someone more than anything—there's nothing you won't do to bring them back.

Or at least go back to a place of healing, where life feels livable again.

So, I made a difficult decision: I took a six-month professional sabbatical and supported us financially—Yikes!!

Yes, I was approached—again and again—with consulting projects, part-time work, short-term gigs.

But I couldn't do it.

I couldn't focus.

I couldn't give my all—because I didn't have my all to give.

Not yet.

Because for me, work has always been about showing up fully. And the only place I could do that was right by John's side.

Something unexpected happened—my empathy for others, especially strangers, deepened in ways I never saw coming.

Empathy isn't always something we choose to grow. Sometimes, life cracks us open, and it floods in. I thought I was already deeply empathetic. But walking through pain—illness, loss, caregiving—shifted everything.

You begin to see the quiet ache in others. You stop needing to fix or explain. You just sit with them. You stay.

For me, empathy became less about understanding and more about *feeling*—raw, real, and unfiltered.

Because now I *know* what it's like to be exhausted, to carry what no one else sees.

So, when someone is hurting, I don't ask why—I just know.

Hard experiences carve space in our hearts. And in that space, empathy takes root. It grows wild and strong—not because we want it to, but because now, we *can't* live without it.

## Faith and Gratitude

Life continued. It was hard—there were days I didn't recognize myself. Days I felt more like a shadow than a person, wishing I could sleep and wake to find the nightmare over. But that didn't happen.

I'd spend hours wrapped in a blanket, cuddling my dogs, sobbing—ugly, aching sobs. Thank God for my precious fur babies—they never left my side.

Watching someone you love suffer is its own kind of torture. You feel powerless. Invisible. Defeated. And yet, somehow, you get up and do it all again.

Not because you're strong—because love doesn't give you a choice. It pulls you forward when everything else wants to stop.

Caregiving carries a quiet grief—for what was, what may never be, and the life you thought you'd have. But in that darkness, I found something else:

A new kind of strength.

Not the kind that leads meetings or gives speeches, but the kind that says,

*"I'm here. I'm not going anywhere."*

And during that time, a new part of "my why" emerged.

I couldn't return to full-time work yet—but I could still give.

So I showed up online—writing, reflecting, engaging on LinkedIn and Facebook. Not to share my new normal—I wasn't ready—but to lift others up, even in my sadness.

I wrote about what I could control: gratitude, kindness, perspective.

I also dove into learning about cancer—stories, research, podcasts—anything to help me understand how others survived caregiving and illness.

Because the more I learned, the less alone I felt.

Still, I kept asking myself:

How can I practice gratitude when my life is falling apart?

For me, the answer was simple:

## My Faith

In my first book, I shared how being laid off triggered a year-long depression. That experience prepared me for this one. Back then, I felt lost. But I learned I wasn't alone—and I wasn't now either.

My faith in Jesus and God carried me.

Everyone's on their own path, but I'll be honest—I don't know how I would've made it without my faith. Because my real why now—the one that grounds me—is this:

There is nothing I can't get through without God's help.

That belief helped me lift others up, especially in my own sadness.

Practicing gratitude became my anchor. I focused on what I had, not what I feared I was losing. Every day, I found something to be grateful for—no matter how small. And I wrote it down. I started a gratitude jar.

Here's the amazing thing: we always have at least one thing every day to be thankful for. You just have to look deep inside.

My favorite part—at the end of the year, I read them and discovered:

Wow. Not only did you get through it, but you were also truly blessed!

And then gratitude showed up in a powerful way.

By December 2023, I'd been out of work for eight months. I couldn't apply for unemployment—I hadn't been job searching yet. I was living off savings.

And then, a gift:

My husband's parents' house sold, they went to be with God, first his Mom in 2021, then his Dad in 2022.

We received a lump sum—just when we needed it most.

That money sustained us. It gave us time. I hadn't touched it until my savings were gone. That wasn't a coincidence.

That was God.

Because of that gift, I didn't rush back into job searching. I had space. I had clarity. I could take my time and still focus on John!

Eventually, I started applying. It was tough. Declines. Ghosting. But this time—no panic. No depression. I knew something would come.

Then, one day, I saw a role on LinkedIn—1,900+ applicants by Day Two—and over 3,000 by Day 4. I applied anyway.

That same day, the recruiter called me. I was one of the few selected. Three interviews. The offer was extended in three weeks.

That was not luck. That was faith. That was gratitude. That was God taking care of me!

**So where am I now?**

I'm working remotely with a supportive boss and doing work I enjoy—writing daily!

I talk to five new people a week (usually strangers), helping however I can—because I know what it feels like to need support.

Most importantly, I'm still caring for my husband. His cancer is stable. We take life one day at a time.

This has been the most brutal period of my life.

I've lost my dad. I've lost two best friends, one to cancer, one to suicide. I've watched loved ones suffer in ways that break you.

But through it all, I've learned this:

Yes, life is what happens to us.


**But more than that—life is how we respond.**

And when you respond with faith, grace, and gratitude, even in the darkest times—you can get through it. (My dear friend Cristy told me that, and she is right.)

Not perfectly. Not painlessly.

But through it.

Gratitude doesn't ignore the pain; it honors it and still finds something beautiful to hold onto.

My faith has been my shield.

Gratitude is my lifeline.

Caregiving is my greatest challenge—and my greatest teacher.


**NAMI: Another New Why Emerged**

And yet, through everything I've been through, a new purpose emerged—one deeply rooted in all I've lived, lost, and learned.

When my husband was first diagnosed, I had just returned from my first book signing. I donated every dollar from that event to a cause close to my heart: NAMI—the National Alliance on Mental Illness.

With chapters in every state, NAMI provides free education, support, and advocacy to individuals and families affected by mental illness. I gave to our local chapter, NAMI Johnston County.

Shortly after, their team reached out and asked if I'd consider joining the board. I was honored and moved—but with my husband's health declining, I couldn't commit. I had to put that dream on hold.

Until recently, in October 2024, I officially joined the NAMI board—and we just held a major fundraiser this May. I shared my story. I'm proud to serve as Director of Marketing and Communications.

It's one of the most meaningful decisions I've ever made.

Now, I'm exploring certification so I can teach NAMI's free classes. That's right—every NAMI program is free. And I want to help deliver that kind of life-changing support.

I want to teach. I want to help. I want to walk alongside those who are struggling—especially those who've considered self-harm or lost someone to suicide.

This is my new why.

It's my passion. It's my purpose.

Why? Because I've been there.

I've battled depression after losing a job. I've watched my husband fight for his life. I've lost one of my closest friends to

suicide—someone I spoke to the very day she died.

I know what pain looks like. I know what silence feels like.

And I know how isolating mental illness can be.

That's why I'm here now.

To serve.

To give.

To help others hold on just a little longer. Because I don't live to please people anymore. I live to please God.

And if I can use the pain, rebirth, and renewed perspective to lift someone else up—then that is the most authentic version of "my why" I've ever known.

## Lauren Raguzin

Lauren Raguzin has been passionate about writing since she was 10 years old. She began her career as a secretary at a large advertising agency and has spent the past 20 years building a career in communications. While she has an entrepreneurial spirit, much of her professional journey has been within corporate organizations. A writer at heart, Lauren, always dreamed of becoming a published author—this marks her second book publication.

Lauren's love for teaching and mentoring has led her to spend the last 15 years as an undergraduate and graduate instructor, where she finds her greatest joy in helping others discover their passion, especially in the field of communications.

She lives in Clayton, North Carolina, with her loving husband, John—her soulmate and best friend—and their two beloved Cavalier King Charles Spaniels, Cinnamon, and Skippy. In her free time, Lauren enjoys cooking and sharing healthy recipes through her healthy cooking Facebook page.

https://www.facebook.com/healthylauren?

A lifelong learner and fearless risk-taker, Lauren embraces change and credits every achievement to God's grace. Her faith and spiritual journey are the most cherished parts of her life.

To connect with Lauren, email her at lraguzan123@gmail.com. She also loves connecting on LinkedIn—where she's the only Lauren Raguzin on the social media platform.

# What Is My Why?

*By Lady Ambassador Dr. Lenora Peterson-Maclin, Ph.D., H.E.*

## Why do I do what I do?

Because I believe no act of service should go unseen.

Because I believe those who give their hearts to heal the world deserve to be honored while they are still here to receive it.

Because I know firsthand how transformative recognition can be—not just for the honored, but for entire communities.

My journey began over 35 years ago, rooted in a vision to create bridges of love, dignity, and acknowledgment. I saw too many unsung heroes—selfless individuals who uplift their neighborhoods, volunteer without applause, and mentor youth without asking for anything in return. These were people making the world better, yet no spotlight ever found them.

## That had to change.

In 2016, I founded the Global International Alliance (GIA) and GIA Advocate University, a private nonprofit initiative rooted in humanitarianism, community service, and the power of honor. GIA was never about creating titles—it was about creating moments of recognition that validate the soul's labor. Over the years, we've honored more than 5,000 people around the world—from Atlanta to London, Paris to California, New York to Maryland, Texas, and beyond. And we're not done.

My "why" is the feeling I see in someone's eyes when they're told their life mattered—that their years of compassion, sacrifice, and service were seen, valued, and uplifted. It is the moment when a quiet grandmother who ran a soup kitchen for decades stands on a stage and hears a room full of applause. It is when a youth leader who never thought they were "good enough" receives a certificate, a sash, and an award that tells them otherwise. It is when a teacher, a veteran, a nurse, a pastor, a foster parent, a dreamer—finally feels seen.

**That is my why.**

Through GIA Advocate University, we offer honorary certifications in Humanitarianism, community leadership, and peacebuilding. These are not merely accolades; they are tributes to heart-driven living. Each event we host—be it in Atlanta or overseas—is orchestrated with excellence and love. From the Trailblazer Women of Excellence Awards to our global People's Choice ceremonies, we celebrate those who uplift humanity.

People often ask me how I have the energy to keep going. The truth? I draw strength from the very people we serve. Their stories of courage and community feed my soul. They are reminders that there is so much good in this world—and my mission is to make sure it's celebrated.

**Humanitarianism is my language. Honor is my ministry. Unity is my goal.**

I have been blessed to receive international recognition, but none of it compares to watching someone cry tears of joy when they realize their life of service was not in vain. I serve alongside global peace organizations such as National United for Peace, United Nations Women USA, and the Commonwealth Entrepreneurs Club, because unity demands action and partnership.

I was deeply humbled to receive the 2023 Top Global Ambassador and Humanitarian Award from the International Association of Top Professionals (IAOTP), and now, to be named the 2025 IOATP President's Award Honoree is a surreal reminder that the work is far from over.

From receiving the Nelson Mandela Award to the Princess of Peace honor and a Congressional Certificate from the late Congressman John Lewis, every milestone has reminded me that we're making a difference—but the true reward has always been in the lives changed.

At our core, GIA isn't just an organization—it's a movement.

## We educate, uplift, and most importantly, honor.

We are approved by the Licensing Boards Division of the Secretary of State of Georgia, endorsed by United Nations Women USA and the National Council of Negro Women, and accredited through LPM Consulting Services – Higher Learning Program LLC. Our training programs follow the standards set by U.S. regional accreditation bodies and the Association of Christian Schools International (ACSI).

Our programs are open to all—regardless of race, age, nationality, or socioeconomic status. That's because service has no borders, and love knows no limits.

One of the highlights of my year is organizing our All-White Dinner Gala, where we honor Trailblazing Women of Excellence and global changemakers. These are not just events—they are sacred moments, lighting up lives and inspiring others to serve.

I hold a Ph.D. in Theology and have studied Humanitarian Response to War and Disaster through HarvardX. I'm certified in business and human rights consulting from the United States Institute of Diplomacy and Human Rights. But again, titles mean little if they're not used in service of others. Every degree, every skill, every resource I've acquired—I've channeled it back into the mission: to give voice, light, and legacy to the unheard heroes of our world.

My nonprofit, Vision in You Outreach Foundation, continues to advocate for youth, seniors, and underserved communities. I want every person to see the vision in themselves—and more importantly, believe it.

My "why" is deeply personal. It's about legacy. It's about love. It's about ensuring that no good deed goes unnoticed, and no servant-hearted soul leaves this world feeling invisible.

As long as I breathe, I will keep building stages, printing certificates, sending emails, making calls, and lifting up the people who carry our communities on their backs.

My prayer is that everyone who crosses my path knows: You matter. You are seen. Your kindness has power.

Because when we honor others, we heal the world—one soul at a time.

## Lady Ambassador Dr. Lenora Peterson-Maclin, Ph.D., H.E.

Lady Ambassador Dr. Lenora Peterson-Maclin, Ph.D., H.E., is a globally recognized humanitarian, peacebuilder, and visionary leader who has devoted over 35 years to honoring those who serve from the heart. As the founder of Global International Alliance (GIA) and The People's Choice Awards, she has created international platforms to recognize and uplift over 5,000 individuals for their service, compassion, and commitment to community.

Through her organization GIA Advocate University, Dr. Peterson-Maclin offers honorary certifications and global awards programs in humanitarianism, peace, and leadership. Her efforts span across major U.S. cities and international locations including London and Paris. As a passionate advocate for unity and recognition, she believes that everyone—regardless of age, ethnicity, or background—deserves to be seen for their contributions to humanity.

Dr. Peterson-Maclin is also a Certified Global Goodwill Ambassador with United Nations Women USA and the CEO of The People's Choice Awards nonprofit. She holds a Ph.D. in Theology and has completed humanitarian response coursework through HarvardX, as well as consulting certifications through USIDHR. Her extensive accolades include the Nelson Mandela Award, Princess of Peace Award, and a Congressional Certificate from the late Congressman John Lewis, she is also a United Nations Diplomat.

She continues to serve with organizations such as National United for Peace and the Commonwealth Entrepreneurs Club, and she is the founder of Vision in You Outreach Foundation, a nonprofit committed to community advocacy.

Dr. Peterson-Maclin's legacy is one of love, honor, and empowering everyday heroes to realize their global worth.

Reach out to Dr. Peterson-Macklin via Email: giaprocessing@gmail.com .

# Why I Empower Midlife Women to Defy Age and Design Their Destiny

*By Dr. (h.c.) Lynnette LaRoche*

There came a moment—silent but profound—when I stood at the threshold of my own life and realized I've been living someone else's story. I know now, I was not alone.

This is also the story of many midlife women who in a moment, came to the realization that she did not recognize her own life.

Maybe it was the strip of her identity that came at the finality of a divorce decree, the eerie quiet that replaced the laughter that once filled the house since the children left home, or the sudden feeling of emptiness after losing that long-held career or is it watching the passage of time creep across her reflection in a mirror to the point that no longer reflects who she truly is.

Maybe it was living the life of safety - safe career (for women); safe mate who didn't challenge you; safe suburban environment; safe hobbies and interests; safe friends that didn't have risky dreams.

Maybe it was simply the multiple decades lived under the weight of expectations—being the dutiful daughter, the perfect wife or partner, the tireless employee, the selfless mother—until she no longer recognized the woman staring back at her.

And maybe it was fear - fear of living her truth because she feared rejection, not being accepted, being talked about, not fitting in, being judged.

**I work with that woman.**

I am a life architect. My mission (and I chose to accept)—my why—is to empower midlife women to break free from the old scripts and design a life they love. A life where age is not a limitation, but a trophy of the wisdom gained through life's lessons. A life where past pain and difficult life transitions become the blueprint for building a vibrant and fulfilling future they get to design. A life where they are no longer invisible, unheard, or unloved—but radiant, empowered, and unshakably confident.

This is not just a calling. It's personal. Because I was her. I was at this threshold of multiple major life transitions.

And as a life architect, I use the metaphorical bulldozer, sledgehammers and pick axes to bring down the walls of the self that is not true, not living to passions, values, and purpose.

I give midlife women the tools to demolish what does not work for them anymore and together we draft the blueprint of the life they have always wanted.

## The Invisible Years

There was a time it seemed like I had it all. And before I could see it coming, the time came when I believed my life had run its course, that there was nothing more for me. Alone. Fearful for my future. Like many women, I had played my roles as if in a theatrical play to much resounding applause—raising children, beating corporate milestones, supporting others, holding everything together while silently falling apart inside.

Then life began to unravel. Transition after transition—some expected, many not—came crashing into my world. Divorce. Career loss. Weight gain. Weight loss. The empty nest. Multiple relocations. The dissolution of the friendships/networks that were only there if you could help them or could prove by results that you are at the top of your game. Loss after loss after loss. Then the emotional exhaustion. All the labels – all the masks – I wore began to peel away, and what remained was a woman I barely recognized. I felt lost. Stuck. Shrunken. Broken. Forgotten by the world. Forgotten by myself. Ashamed of who I had become.

**I was lost, but not beyond redemption.**

Midlife is not a crisis. It is a call to rise. It's a catalyst for transformation. It's a stage of life that demands first agitation and then reinvention, not resignation.

The world doesn't talk about women like me. Like us.

Instead, it glorifies youth, idolizes perfection, and whispers cruel reminders that time was no longer on our side. Commercials show wrinkle creams, surgical procedures, exercise adverts for our sagging body, and diet pills, as if aging was a disease that we have that needs to be cured. Media paints aging women as myself as undesirable, over the hill, irrelevant, EXPIRED. We are no longer seen as beautiful, alluring, sensual, ambitious, charismatic, or powerful. We were simply... fading.

But deep within me was a flicker. A spark. A fire began raging. A whisper that said, "It's not over. It's not the end. This is a beginning."

That whisper is now a shout-out to the world: look at me. Look at us! Really see us! As we are a force to be reckoned with. According to the National Institute of Health, in 2017, women over fifty comprised over 17.2 percent of the total population. That's almost 1.4 billion women! We can't be hidden. We won't be ignored. We will DEFY the stereotypes on aging.

## Midlife Is Not a Crisis. Midlife is the Time to Be an Agitator.

Midlife is not a crisis. It is a call to rise. It's a time to agitate the status quo that has now become your life. It's the moment when a woman realizes she has spent half her life living someone else's dream, living by the expectations or opinions of others or society and she's ready to take back control and write her own story with all the pitstops that will make her fulfilled and bring her joy.

It is not about what's ending—but what's finally beginning. A beautiful unfolding.

This is where I come in.

The women I work with come to me hollowed by sadness, loss, and fear, paralyzed by change. Some are empty nesters who no longer know who they are outside of motherhood. Some are at the precipice of loss of a career that defined them. Others are divorced, unsure if they'll ever love—or be loved—again. Many have sacrificed dreams on the altar of obligation. They're exhausted by expectations that were not their own. Frozen by the fear of becoming invisible, of becoming "expired." They feel like their best years are behind them. That they are too old to start anew; to finally chase the dreams and desires they have buried deep in their heart.

But I tell them this: "There is no expiration date on your brilliance, your beauty, or your purpose."

You are not too old. It is not too late. As George Eliot said, "It's never too late to be who you might have been." And the life you dream of, the person you desire to be, is still waiting for you—if you're brave enough to build it, to become HER.

## Becoming a Life Architect

I don't call myself a life coach. I'm a life architect.

I was lost, but not beyond revivification. That is why I do this work—because I know the way back to the true self.

Midlife is not a crisis. It is a call to rise into the greatest version of you. It's a catalyst for a metamorphosis. It's a stage of life that demands moving through discomfort and letting go, not acquiescence.

I facilitate the rebuilding of midlife women lives—one pillar at a time. We strip it all back: the limiting beliefs, the roles, the regrets, the self-condemnation. We expose the bare foundation, taking away everything that was not truly theirs. Then, with intention, love, gratitude, and clarity, we craft a blueprint for a new life.

The architecture of reinvention rests on four pillars—emotional, mental, behavioral, and spiritual. These are what I call the anterooms of transformation.

In the emotional room, we explore the suppressed pain, the grief, the shame. We give voice to the stories they've been too afraid to speak. We release the weight of "shoulds" and guilt that have anchored them for too long.

In the mental room, we rewire old narratives. "I'm too old." "It's too late." "No one will love me." We dismantle these lies and replace them with truths that ignite possibility.

In the behavioral room, we examine the patterns that have kept them stuck—people-pleasing, perfectionism, procrastination. We implement new habits that align with their desires and goals.

In the spiritual room, we reconnect them to their deeper self— their intuition, their inner wisdom, their soul's yearning. This is where they rediscover what truly matters.

We then begin designing their future. How do they want the rooms of their life to look? How do they want the rooms of their life to feel? What do they want to furnish them with—joy, freedom, passion, love, purpose? Who do they want to invite in—relationships, careers, opportunities, communities that reflect their truth?

And we don't just talk about it. We script it.

## Scripting the Soul's Blueprint

One of the most powerful tools I use is scripting. It's more than journaling—it's visualization on paper. It's writing out the life you desire as if it has already happened. It's infusing words with feeling, with detail, with unwavering belief. Beyond belief, actually. It is infusing the words with KNOWING. Knowing that the life you desire to create is yours.

Scripting activates the mind and spirit to believe. And when a woman believes in her power, the world shifts.

## The World Needs Midlife Women to Rise

Why do I do this work?

Because the world needs women in their 40s, 50s, 60s, and beyond to stop shrinking and start shining. To stop apologizing and start living boldly. To stop making excuses to be less than and start living fully.

We are the untapped power source of the world—overflowing with wisdom, inspiration, creativity, empathy, and strength. We have raised generations. Built businesses. Survived heartbreak. Endured loss. Loved deeply. Fought fiercely. And still—we rise.

Envision a world where midlife women weren't made to feel invisible but were celebrated as visionaries.

See a world where your wrinkles and sagging skin were not flaws, but cherished memories and proof of a life fully lived.

See yourself stepping into a world where we stopped apologizing for taking up space and instead claimed our place as alchemists, leaders, lovers, creators, and catalysts.

That is the world I'm building—one woman at a time. This is my WHY.

## My Why

My why is not a slogan. It is not a plea for pity or sympathy. I take full accountability. It is my story. It's the story of so many midlife women that has been held in secret.

I do this work because I was the woman curled up in fear, shame, abandonment, wondering if life had anything left to offer me.

I do this work because there was no one to speak life into me. No one to say to me, "You're not done yet. You're just getting started. There's still work for you to do, impact to make."

I do this work because I know that when a midlife woman rises, she becomes a lighthouse over the ocean of other women seeking to raise the sails of their ships, showing them that they can do the same.

Every time I witness a woman step into her power, take control of her life, reclaim her voice, rewrite her story—I know I'm exactly where I'm meant to be.

That is my why.

This is my mission.

This is my joy.

**My Why? To Facilitate Rewriting of Your Story**

To the woman reading this who feels unseen, unheard, uncertain, broken, empty—this is your sign.

You are not alone.

You are not too old.

You are not too late.

You are not worthless.

You are not ugly.

You are not used up.

You are a phoenix that has just begun to erupt in flames.

It's time to let the old story burn and rise into the woman you were always meant to be.

Grab the pen and hold against your heart and ask: What do I really want (for me)?

Now start writing.

You are the architect.

You are the masterpiece.

YOU ARE THE WHY.


## Lessons in Reinvention

What I've learned—and what I teach—is this:

1. You are not broken (and useless). You are being called to evolve, to agitate the status quo.
2. Regret or disappointment in your life is not your story's

ending. It is a signpost pointing toward what you truly desire if you are willing to run toward it.

3. There is no shame in starting over. There is only power and so much to gain in choosing to do so.

4. You are not meant to be everything to everyone. You are meant to be everything to yourself. To want yourself more than anyone else can want you. To do more for yourself than you have ever one for anyone else.

5. Beauty is not in youth—it is in aliveness. A woman lit up from within is powerful, magnetic, sensual, and unstoppable.

## Dr. (h.c.) Lynnette LaRoche

Lynnette LaRoche is a life architect who empowers women with the belief that they are their lifelong passion project! She is committed to facilitating the transformation of women who have faced life-altering transitions to rediscover themselves and rise, reinvent and curate the blueprint of a life lived boldly with purpose and passion.

Lynnette is committed 💙 to guiding midlife women who have experienced major life transitions through transformative changes. With her proven 4-part formula - R.I.S.E - she empowers midlife women to **REMEMBER** their voice and vision as they **ILLUMINATE** their purpose and passion whilst they **SURRENDER/STRENGTHEN** body, mind and spirt and **EMBODY** their bold, new chapter full of impact 👣 and free from old expectations to create a future they love!

Lynnette is a drug development powerhouse with two drug approvals during the height of the pandemic and a legacy of building and leading high performing teams. She is also a 4-time best-selling author and recipient of an honorary doctorate degree.

CONTACT: info@risewithlynnette.com

# The Values and Beliefs That Guide My Choices
*By Ambassador Dr. (h.c.) Marcy Decato*

I come from a loving family in a small city called Manizales. We are in the coffee region of Colombia, my dad, Carlos, my mom Norma, my only brother Andres and I. Both my parents worked at the main telecommunications company of Colombia back then, Telecom. We had a very simple life, but with a great deal of love, they gave my brother and I an example of compassion for others and generosity, many people came to live with us if they were going through hard times, so there was always someone at home besides the four of us, and I learned from each one of them.

I can say that my values started at home with mom and dad: love for others, compassion, integrity, responsibility, charisma, generosity, and resilience.

My beliefs have been formed throughout my life influenced a great deal by my spirituality, I don't consider myself a very religious person, but I live my life with one main philosophy "to love my neighbor" with that in mind, everything else follows, respect, compassion, understanding and tolerance.

## What Is My Why?

For a long time, I thought my "why" would come from having the kind of life I imagined growing up—marriage, children, a family of my own to grow old with. But life unfolded differently. I've been divorced twice. I never had children. And there are moments when the fear of growing old without a traditional family structure creeps in and lingers.

But what I've learned is that your "why" doesn't always come from what you have—sometimes it comes from what you give. Mine is rooted in love, connection, and resilience. It's grown from the spaces between loss and healing. And it continues to reveal itself through the people I choose and the values I live by.

## Love for Others & Compassion: My Anchor

Even without children or a romantic partner by my side, I have been deeply blessed by the friendships I've cultivated. These friendships aren't just companionship—they are family. They remind me that love shows up in many forms, and that chosen family can be just as meaningful as the one we're born into.

I show up for people, and they show up for me. That reciprocity—grounded in compassion—keeps me going. I don't take it for granted. In a world that often rushes past pain, I try to slow down, to notice others, to be present. That's part of my why.

## Integrity & Responsibility: How I Move Through the World

Integrity, for me, means owning my story—even the chapters I never expected to write. It means telling the truth, showing up with consistency, and doing what I say I'll do. I take responsibility not only for my actions, but for how I care for the people in my life.

That includes my parents, who live 3,000 miles away. I speak with them daily. I visit them twice a year. I do everything I can to make sure they feel supported and loved—because even from afar, family matters deeply to me.

## Carisma & Generosity: Giving Light

Despite everything, I carry light in me—and I try to share it. Whether it's through a warm presence, a word of encouragement, or simply making someone laugh on a hard day, I want to be a person who leaves others better than I found them.

My charisma isn't loud, but it's authentic. And my generosity isn't about grand gestures—it's about giving of myself in small, intentional ways, every single day.

## Resilience: The Quiet Strength Behind It All

It's easy to celebrate life when everything goes according to plan. But true resilience shows up when life doesn't. I've had to let go of some dreams. I've faced the ache of loneliness. I've wrestled with fear about the future. And still—I rise. I keep building, I keep loving, I keep choosing joy.

That, more than anything, is my why: to keep showing up with love and integrity, even when the picture doesn't look the way I once hoped it would.

## In the End

My life is far from perfect, but it's full of meaning. My "why" is to create connection, offer compassion, and live with deep presence and honesty. I may not have the traditional family structure I once dreamed of—but I have people who love me, values that guide me, and a life that, in its own way, is full.

And I've learned that sometimes, the most beautiful lives are the ones that were reimagined along the way.

# Marcy Decato

Born and raised in Colombia. Marcy Decato has a bachelor's degree in advertising, and three associate degrees, Marketing, Business Administration, and Computer Graphics. Marcy combines creativity and credentials to develop powerful and effective marketing campaigns. Marcy is an exceptional designer and branding specialist. 14 years in the Direct Mail industry and 40 years in the Marketing and Advertising industry make her an expert in these fields.

Marcy Decato co-owns with Gigi Mindreau-Banks a very successful business, Creative Solutions Marketing & Printing, Inc., offering promotional items, branded apparel, graphic design, web design, and commercial printing.

Marcy has received several recognitions and awards for her leadership roles in the community of Corona, California. She has collaborated in several books, and she enjoys public speaking.

Contact:

Marcy Decato

marcy@creativesolutionsmktg.com

FB: facebook.com/marcy.decato

951.707.6338

www.creativesolutionsmktg.com

# What's Your Why?

*By Dr. Marietta Aguido Reformado (h.c.)*

## Introduction

### What's your Why?

Your Why isn't just a statement — it's the heartbeat of your mission. It shapes not only how you move through the world, but why you move at all.

For me, discovering my Why shifted my life from being success-driven to purpose-led. I moved from simply achieving to intentionally serving. My Why is rooted in love for humanity, a passion for justice, and a lifelong commitment to building bridges where others see walls. It's about uniting people, amplifying silenced voices, and leaving a legacy that transcends generations.

Every step I take in leadership, philanthropy, and entrepreneurship is anchored in one unwavering belief: Humanity.

In this reflection, I share not just what I've done—but who I am. This is not simply a story of a businesswoman. It's the story of a humanitarian, a unifier, a woman who dreams of a world healed by compassion and connection.

## The Journey to Discovering My Why

My journey toward discovering my Why wasn't immediate or easy. Like many, I began with ambition and drive, fueled by a desire to succeed, support my family, and earn respect. But over time, those goals—though meaningful—were no longer enough. I began to ask deeper questions:

What impact am I truly making?

Who am I serving beyond myself?

What legacy will I leave behind?

Growing up in a multicultural society offered me both opportunity and adversity. I witnessed the struggles of marginalized communities and the disparities in education, opportunity, and access. These early experiences shaped my understanding of leadership—not as power, but as service.

As I stepped into the business world, I discovered a passion for helping others succeed. I began consulting and advising businesses, and the more I helped others rise, the more I felt called to something greater. I realized I wasn't just building businesses—I was building lives, supporting communities, and reshaping futures.

The defining moment came when I was asked to consult on a project supporting displaced women and children. Listening to their stories broke something open in me. These individuals, often overlooked, displayed a resilience that deeply moved me. That moment cemented my Why: to be a voice for the voiceless, a bridge for the marginalized, and a force for unity.

Since then, every personal and professional decision has been aligned with this purpose. I took on leadership roles not for recognition, but for impact. I joined humanitarian organizations, broadened my global partnerships, and used my platform to uplift others.

Discovering my Why turned my work into a mission—and my life into a message.

## Living the Why Through Action

Knowing your Why is only the beginning—living it out is where transformation happens. Purpose without action is a whisper; purpose with action becomes a movement.

In my role as a strategist and consultant, I integrate purpose into every project. I seek out clients and partners who believe in inclusive growth, ethical leadership, and social responsibility. From mentoring women entrepreneurs to guiding multinationals in cultural integration, I lead with a service-first mindset.

One of the most profound expressions of my Why has been through humanitarian and peace-building work. As Head Representative of the United Nations World Peace Association (UNWPA) in Malaysia, I've led initiatives that protect, empower, and uplift vulnerable communities. During the COVID-19 pandemic, we facilitated donations of essential supplies to hospitals—not just as aid, but as acts of solidarity.

My work with the United Refugees Green Council, where I serve as a spokesperson on human trafficking, has been especially transformative. These efforts exposed me to the hidden pain many endure—and the extraordinary strength they possess. I've come to understand that true empowerment is not just about providing resources but restoring dignity and enabling autonomy.

Business has also remained a key channel for living my Why. As President of M Worldwide Holdings and Vice President of Beisage Global USA, I promote values-based innovation, environmental sustainability, and inclusive growth. Through partnerships with organizations like the International Peace Corps and the Worldwide Wellness Club, I help facilitate wellness initiatives and intercultural collaborations grounded in humanity.

Whether mentoring young leaders, supporting small businesses, or advising global institutions, my goal is always the same: to create meaningful impact. Purpose is not reserved for public speeches or titles—it shows up in how we lead, how we serve, and how we treat one another.

For me, every action stems from this foundational belief: All Means All. Every person matters. Every voice deserves to be heard. Every life holds value.

## The Power of Unity

Meaningful change—in business, education, human rights, or health—begins with connection. At the core of everything I do lies a deep commitment to unity. My mission has never been about personal gain, but collective elevation. I believe in the power of we over me.

Unity isn't passive agreement—it's courageous understanding. It means choosing collaboration over competition, even in the face of difference. In my role as Vice President of the International Peace Corps and in diplomatic circles, I've witnessed how diverse minds united by a common purpose can drive real, lasting change.

This commitment extends beyond formal institutions. I actively support underprivileged schools, women's shelters, and refugee communities. Whether through literacy programs, safe spaces for survivors, or youth mentorship, I aim to restore hope and reignite potential.

These efforts are not about charity—they're about justice. I've seen girls transform into leaders because someone believed in them. I've seen survivors become advocates because they were given a platform. That is the multiplying power of unity.

Even in global forums, I advocate for collaboration that is cross-sectoral and cross-cultural. In a country as diverse as Malaysia, cultural fluency isn't optional—it's essential. True connection begins when we honor each other's stories and extend empathy beyond borders.

And yes, this unity includes partnering with global figures and influential leaders who use their platforms for advocacy. Together, we amplify the truth that love-driven leadership can reshape the world.

So, when people ask what fuels my mission, I respond:

Unity is my compass.

Collaboration is my strategy.

Humanity is my heart.

## Inspiring the Next Generation

Each generation has the power to change the world. But turning potential into purpose requires opportunity, mentorship, and representation. That's why empowering the next generation—especially young women—is one of my greatest passions.

Today's youth aren't just future leaders; they are leaders now. Unfortunately, their voices are often dismissed or overlooked. I believe in changing that reality by opening doors, offering guidance, and equipping young people with the tools they need to lead with integrity, clarity, and compassion.

Through forums, mentorship programs, and humanitarian outreach, I've supported youth from all walks of life in discovering their own Why. Under the banner of United Hands of Hope, we've provided food, clean water, school supplies, sanitary pads, and emotional support to communities in need.

For many girls, something as small as access to hygiene products determines whether they stay in school. That's why our initiatives focus not just on aid, but on dignity. These are not handouts—they're declarations of worth.

Whether through sponsorships, scholarships, or leadership training, my goal is to light the path forward for those coming after us. The most meaningful legacy is not what we leave behind—it's who we lift up.

The next generation is watching—not just for inspiration, but for direction.

Let's lead with purpose.

Let's lead together.

## Conclusion

In a world hungry for healing, clarity, and courage, discovering your Why is not a luxury—it's a necessity.

My Why is rooted in unity, service, and transformation. It lives through every person I serve, every story I elevate, and every act of intentional leadership.

Wherever I go—boardrooms, classrooms, rural villages, or refugee camps—I carry this truth.

Every human deserves dignity, opportunity, and belonging.

This journey is far from over. I remain committed to rising, serving, and leading with purpose—so others can do the same.

So now, I ask you:

What's your Why?

Because when you find it, everything changes.

And so do you.

# Dr. Marietta Aguido Reformado

## Global Entrepreneur | Humanitarian Leader | Peace Advocate

Dr. Marietta Aguido Reformado is a globally respected entrepreneur, peace ambassador, and humanitarian visionary whose work spans continents, industries, and cultures. She is a catalyst for change, known for her unwavering commitment to purpose-driven leadership, sustainable development, and global unity.

A dynamic force in both the corporate and humanitarian arenas, Dr. Reformado currently serves as the President of Beisage Global LLC, Vice President of Global Risk International, and Professional Partner at GBP International, where she drives East-West trade and fosters cross-cultural business alliances. Her unique expertise in implementation, facilitation, and strategic consulting has empowered businesses around the world to achieve sustainable success while embracing social responsibility.

Dr. Reformado's leadership has also been instrumental in bridging global markets through Malaysia's multiracial landscape, positioning her as a trusted voice in navigating diverse economies and building inclusive partnerships.

In recognition of her impact, she has been appointed Loani Globalwill Ambassador and Kenya Chairperson and proudly joins the International Board of Directors at Leaders of All Nations International (LOANI)—an honor that reflects her profound influence on global leadership and advocacy.

Beyond business, Dr. Reformado is a tireless advocate for human rights, equity, and compassion. Her humanitarian work spans Africa, Southeast Asia, and the Middle East, where she has championed initiatives addressing period poverty, human trafficking, and the plight of refugees.

Her ongoing contributions include:

- Consultant & Spokesperson, United Refugees Green Council
- Founder of period poverty initiatives in Kenya and the Republic of Guinea
- Patron of PwD Smart FarmAbility, promoting disability inclusion in agriculture
- Organizer of LOANI's upcoming Kenya charity mission, focused on underserved communities
- Crisis relief leader during COVID-19, facilitating vital medical supply donations

She also serves as Mama Dorcas, a patron for vulnerable children and orphans, offering love, support, and tangible hope to the next generation.

Leadership Rooted in Purpose

Dr. Reformado holds numerous influential positions, including:

- Vice President, International Peace Corps (Diplomatic Relations)
- Governance Council Member, United Nations Association Malaysia (UNAM)
- Advisor to international organizations including Malaysia Corruption Watch, Worldwide Wellness Club, and others
- President, World Jomasar Martial Arts (Asia), reflecting her dedication to empowerment through discipline and resilience

Her work is grounded in a single belief: compassion and collaboration can move nations. She leads with humility, driven not by recognition, but by the lives she transforms.

Dr. Reformado's exceptional service has earned her numerous accolades, including the Global Leadership Award and honorary title Dr. Hc Dato' in honor of her contributions to cultural diplomacy and humanitarian impact.

A powerful mentor and role model, she inspires a generation of women, youth, and social innovators to lead with heart, vision, and courage. Her legacy is not in titles—but in lives uplifted, communities restored, and futures reimagined.

**Contact :**

Email: mariettareformado@gmail.com

Website: https://www.globalrisk.international.com

Phone : +254113546196

# A Shared Vision of Wellness and Beauty

*By Melissa Khan*

My name is Melissa Khan, and my journey is deeply rooted in a powerful "why." As a wife to Nadeem Khan, a dedicated doctor, and a mother to two beautiful daughters, Italee and Irelynd, I have dedicated my life to empowering women and girls to embrace their unique beauty and cultivate confidence. This mission is not just a career path; it is a calling driven by my own experiences and the belief that every individual deserves to feel beautiful and strong in their own skin.

Growing up, I faced significant health challenges that often left me feeling vulnerable and out of place. The hospital was a frequent backdrop in my life, and during those formative years, I discovered that caring for my skin and experimenting with makeup provided a sense of control and normalcy, not to mention a look and feel of a healthy happy young girl, instead of a pale sick weak person I had previously seen staring back at me in the mirror.

Each time I looked in the mirror, I saw not just a girl grappling with health issues but a resilient individual who was fighting to reclaim her identity. The act of applying makeup became a ritual that empowered me, allowing me to project strength and confidence, it made me feel healthy and as if I was well and back to normal, even when I didn't feel it inside, it gave me strength and will power to get to a healthier state. This experience taught me a crucial lesson: our image and appearance can profoundly influence how we perceive ourselves and how we navigate the world.

The struggles I faced in my youth ignited a passion within me to help others, particularly women and girls, find their own confidence and beauty. My "why" is rooted in the desire to teach them that they are incredible just as they are, and to provide them with the tools and knowledge to look and feel their best, no matter what their situation is.

I understand the pressures that society places on women regarding beauty and appearance. My mission is to create a supportive environment where women and girls can explore their beauty without fear of judgment. I want them to know that confidence comes from within and that every individual possesses unique qualities that make them special.

Throughout my journey, I have been fortunate to connect with a diverse community of women who inspire and uplift one another. Together, we have created a network of empowerment, fostering confidence and sharing knowledge about self-care and health, through my platform, and my beauty brand Radiant Rhythm.

I believe that knowledge is power, and I am committed to educating women about their bodies, self-love, and the importance of healthy product consumption. By sharing my insights and experiences, I aim to equip others with the tools they need to make informed choices about their beauty routines, product consumption and overall well-being.

My family has been a cornerstone of my journey. My husband, Nadeem, has been my unwavering support, inspiring me with his dedication to health and well-being. His knowledge and support in formulating beauty products has been the foundation to my beauty line. He not only helps me to understand every aspect about health and wellness and how to properly care for my skin and body, but he constantly educates and teaches my daughters everything he can about living a healthy life and embracing their own beauty through self-care and proper wellness.

As a mother, I am passionate about instilling in Italee and Irelynd the understanding that beauty is multifaceted, and that self-worth is not dictated by societal standards. I encourage them to embrace their individuality and to express themselves freely, whether through skincare, makeup, or any other creative outlet. I want them to feel empowered to define their beauty on their own terms.

My "why" is not just about my journey; it's about creating a legacy for future generations. I envision a world where every woman and girl recognizes her inherent beauty and feels confident in her own skin. I am committed to fostering an environment where self-care and self-love are celebrated, and where women support one another in their journeys.

I aim to spread the message that confidence and beauty are accessible to everyone. I want to inspire women to embrace their unique qualities and to find strength in their individuality.

My journey as Melissa Khan is a testament to the power of resilience, empowerment, and the unwavering belief in the beauty of every woman and girl. My "why" drives me to inspire others to embrace their true selves, cultivate confidence, and prioritize self-care. Which is why I created a beauty brand which is safe and effective for all skin types and all ages of skin. A beauty brand where mothers and daughters, grandmothers and granddaughters or any group of women or girls can learn and do skin care together and learn makeup tricks together with healthy safe products. Products that aren't loaded with chemicals. Radiant Rhythm is just one more part of my contribution to women and girls to understand how to embrace and preserve their beauty.

Together, we can create a movement that celebrates the strength and power of women—one that encourages every individual to recognize their inherent beauty and to feel confident in their own skin. To create a world where individuality is so special that no woman or girl strives to be like one another to fit in but strives to be her own self! As we move forward, I remain committed to my mission: to empower women and girls to embrace their beauty and to live boldly and authentically. Follow me on my social media (Instagram) @mrsmelissakhan and Facebook Melissa Murphy Khan, or my business page on Instagram, @radiantrhythmstore, to follow my journey or empowering women and girls to love themselves and their own unique individuality. Let's create a beautiful confident world together.

## Melissa Khan

Melissa Khan is a dedicated mother and entrepreneur, known affectionately as the "mother of Italee and Irelynd Miller." She is married to Dr. Nadeem Khan, and together they manage their thriving medical offices and Medspa business. As a passionate aesthetician, Melissa combines her expertise in beauty and wellness to enhance the lives of her clients.

In addition to her professional pursuits, Melissa is an active "dance mom," "cheer mom," and "gymnastics mom," supporting her children's extracurricular activities with enthusiasm. Her love for animals shines through in her affection for her pet French Bulldogs, who are cherished members of the family.

Recently, Melissa launched a new venture, a beauty product line called Radiant Rhythm, which focuses on clean beauty and effective serums suitable for all ages. Through her innovative approach to beauty and wellness, Melissa Khan continues to inspire those around her while balancing the joys of motherhood and entrepreneurship.

Instagram: @mrsmelissakhan & @radiantrhythmstore

Facebook: Melissa Murphy Khan

Websites: www.radglam.com & glam.science

# What's Your Why: Coaching Beyond the Field

*By Dr. (h.c.) Coach Mikki St. Germain*

I didn't start coaching football just to win games. Sure, winning is exhilarating. The roar of the crowd after a touchdown, the scoreboard ticking in our favor, the celebration with the players after a victory, those moments matter. But they are not the why. The trophies gather dust. The headlines fade. What lingers is who those young men and women become long after the last whistle blows. That's why I coach.

My journey into coaching began out of love for the game. It started late compared to most. I was forty-five when I first stepped onto the football field as a coach. Some said I was too old, too inexperienced, or simply out of place, especially as a female in a male-dominated arena. But I didn't step onto that field to prove something to the doubters. I stepped onto a field to stand beside kids who needed guidance, leadership, and belief, sometimes more than they needed a playbook.

Football is more than X's and O's. It's a metaphor for life. Every snap represents a choice. Every play is a reflection of preparation. Every win or loss teaches accountability. I saw early on that most of my players weren't struggling with football; they were struggling with life. Broken homes, low self-esteem, peer pressure, anger, fear of failure. These challenges walked onto the field with them every day. So, my why became clear: *I coach football to coach life.*

I teach my players that discipline is freedom. When they learn to show up on time, pay attention, push through the drills, and respect the game, they're not just becoming better athletes.

They're developing habits that will serve them in college, in careers, and in the pursuit of their biggest dreams. Every rep matters because it trains more than muscles. It trains the mindset.

I've watched kids transform right before my eyes. One quiet and withdrawn player barely spoke during his first year with us. Football became his outlet. He started coming early and stayed late, eventually becoming the team captain. He found his voice, not just as a leader on the field but as a young man who learned he could take ownership of his life.

Another player battled anger issues. His first instinct was always aggression, not strategy. I taught him how to channel that fire, how to turn anger into focus, and how to play with control and poise. Years later, he shared how learning to manage himself helped him face life's bigger challenges.

Football teaches how to lose, too. Life won't hand you a win every day. Sometimes you do everything right and still fall short. I want my players to know how to handle setbacks with grace. I tell them, "You're either winning or learning. There's no losing here." Resilience is one of the greatest gifts I can give them. When they graduate and face real-life fourth downs, layoffs, heartbreaks, and failures, they'll remember they've been here before and know how to push forward.

Goal setting is at the core of what I instill in them. Every season begins with setting clear, measurable goals, not just for the team, but for each player individually. Whether it's improving speed, mastering a play, or earning more playing time, I encourage them to write their goals down and revisit them often. Success doesn't happen by accident. It happens when preparation meets purpose. Setting goals teaches them to work with intention, track their progress, and hold themselves accountable.

Self-reliance is another cornerstone. On the field, I push them to solve problems. If something breaks down mid-play, they need to think fast and adjust. I don't hand them solutions; I guide them to find their own. I encourage them to take ownership of their actions and decisions off the field. Learning to rely on themselves, while also understanding the power of teamwork, creates a balance that serves them in every area of life.

What makes me proudest is not how many touchdowns they score, but the calls and messages I get years later. The young man who became a business owner and applies our "team first" mentality to his company. The athlete who overcame a troubled past and now coaches' others, passing on the torch.

They are my why.

Football gives me a platform to reach them. The game builds camaraderie, teaches accountability, demands perseverance, and sharpens goal setting and self-reliance. But at its core, football is the vehicle, not the destination. My mission is to prepare them for when the pads come off and life gets real. I want them to know how to show up, communicate, lead, and face adversity with their heads held high.

I tell every player who wears our jersey: *You may not play football forever, but you will always play the game of life. Learn it here. Master it here. Take it with you.*

Coaching is not easy. It requires sacrifice and late nights. Emotional investment. Sometimes, heartbreak. I've lost games, lost sleep, and even lost players to life's harshest battles. But I've also gained a family that spans far beyond the sidelines. My players know I'm in their corner, long after they hang up their helmets. And that trust, that lifelong bond, is priceless.

So why do I coach?

Every practice, every game, and every life lesson disguised as a drill is a chance to impact the next generation.

Because I believe that building better athletes is good, but building better people is everything.

Coach Mikki St. Germain – www.4thand1mindset.com

## About Dr. (h.c.) Coach Mikki St. Germain

Coach Mikki is a trailblazing football coach, international speaker, and author devoted to helping people win both on the field and in life. With 17 years of coaching experience, she transforms the lessons of the gridiron into powerful tools for personal growth. Through her signature *4th and 1 Mindset*, bestselling book, and inspiring talks, she teaches athletes, business leaders, and everyday champions how to push past fear, set bold goals, and persevere through adversity. Her mission is rooted in building self-belief, staying disciplined when no one is watching, and helping others create a legacy driven by courage, heart, and purpose. Whether from the sidelines or the stage, Coach Mikki is passionate about guiding others to rise, lead with confidence, and become champions of their own story.

www.4thand1Mindset.com

# What's My Why?

*By Minh Dannerstedt, Ph.D.*

This fundamental question—"What's my Why?"—may seem simple at first glance, yet it is one of the most profound inquiries we can make about our lives. We all, at some point, reflect on the real meaning of life and the motivations behind our daily actions. When we face difficulties or navigate uncertainty, our deep real purpose, the very reason we get up in the morning—becomes a guiding light. It defines the clarity of mind of our decisions, fuels our resilience, and shapes the direction of our journey.

In the fast pace of daily life, it's easy to get swept up in routines— working, caring, learning, planning, duties, responsibilities, reacting—without pausing to ask what truly matters to us. Yet that pause is vital. To live meaningfully, we must regularly step back and assess: Are my actions aligned with my deep purpose? Do I live consciously, or am I simply reacting to demands and distractions?

The modern world is filled with noise. Social obligations, responsibilities, digital stimulation, and constant demands on our attention can blur our inner compass. Amid this, it's easy to forget what we once set out to achieve and fulfill—or why we chose the path we're on in the first place. But when we quiet the noise, a deeper voice emerges—the voice of purpose. The "Why" beneath the surface.

## The Journey Inward

Clarity comes from within. I've come to understand that our

mindset—how we interpret, react, and choose—emerges from the beliefs and values rooted in our habits and patterns we have received. As I look back on the phases of my life, I can see how each stage has invited reflection, growth, and a deeper understanding of my Why.

Growing up in a country torn by war deeply affected my worldview. The images of suffering, loss, and uncertainty I saw on television weren't just distant events—they shaped my thinking and reflections. They awakened in me a yearning for peace and harmony, not only as abstract ideals but as living principles I wanted to cultivate within myself and share with others.

This yearning quietly steered my actions and thoughts. I understood I was guided by a great light from within. As a young girl observing the adults around me, I began forming my deep understanding of the big picture and the impact of kindness, the importance of balance, and the value of living with purpose and intention, our big Why.

## Building My Life Around Purpose

As I grew older and entered different life roles—daughter, sister, wife, mother, grandmother, and friend—my Why evolved, guiding me to continue to pursue. It expands and deepens. I realized that every action, no matter how small, has an impact. My choices shaped not only my own life, but the lives of those around me.

Motherhood was a defining chapter in my life with positive experiences in understanding children and adults. Raising four children was both a responsibility and an enriching one. I witnessed their growth from infancy to adulthood, and in nurturing them, I too had learnt to be creative for the harmony of the family, being organized with some planning when it's necessary, for certain predictability and for the family dynamics.

My Why during those years centered on being present, with family principles and instilling values that would help my children grow into thoughtful, responsible, and compassionate adults.

While taking care of my children, I was evolving as an individual at the same time. I was always interested in Nature, the Universe and the Great Energy governing the whole Universe. I had an opportunity to learn and develop our Human Spiritual potential and how to self-heal with Universal Energy. I was fascinated by the connection between the seen and the unseen—the visible behaviors we display and the invisible forces, beliefs and energies that shape them to expressions and actions in the material world.

I learned about the human energy field, about spiritual intelligence, and how we carry the potential to self-heal and heal others. This led me to pursue advanced studies in spiritual energy healing, culminating in a Doctor of Philosophy in Spiritual Energy Healing by the Open International University for Complementary Medicines, in 1998. My purpose expanded: I was not only raising a family, but I was also helping others discover their inner healing power and spiritual potential.

## Serving Others Through Healing and Connection

While taking care of my children, I felt a great joy when sharing what I had learned. I began mentoring, teaching, and traveling internationally. These experiences offered a broader lens through which I could view and learn more about the unique role of humanity through their learning experiences and evolution on planet Earth. I met people from different cultures and walks of life, each with their own stories, challenges and hopes, with great spiritual lessons for me to discover and expand my knowledge and experiences.

Through it all, one truth remained clear about people and their values on how they approach others, in different situations: people long to be seen, understood, and heard. No matter our background, we share a desire to live meaningfully and in harmony with others. But too often, we misunderstand each other, as we lack the tools to know how to truly connect and communicate, especially in moments of tension or when there is a difference in the perception of values that defines a difference in approach and communication.

This realization brought a new layer to my Why.

Five years ago, I discovered a transformational approach to human connection—one that complemented and expanded my life's work. I became certified as a Coach and Trainer in Communication and Relationship Dynamics, focusing on understanding people's personality code values.

This science of personality codes offers insight into how people make decisions, communicate, and under which lens they see the world. It allows us to understand one another at a deeper level—how we can learn to speak each other's "code value language," reducing misunderstanding and misinterpretation, and increasing empathy and connectivity.

This contributed to the evolution of my Why: to bridge gaps between people, foster connective communication, once we recognize and understand our own personality code values and allows us to develop a skill to speak the code value of others, for a connective communication.

## Living in Alignment

My Why has now crystallized and I now can pursue my life mission: to empower people to live consciously, self-heal and heal others, as well as teach a system of skill set for people to find out what is their values code, understand others' values code, speak their code for more comprehension and predictable approach, and how we can communicate with empathy, heal relationships—both for ourselves and for others.

We are mind, body, and soul. We are light beings with an unlimited capacity for growth, connection, and contribution. When we align our thoughts, emotions, and actions with our deepest values, we step into a higher state of being. We become creators of peace, inspiring people around us. This doesn't mean life becomes free of challenges. But it does mean that we meet those challenges with a clear heart and an open mind to adapt and create. Whether we are leading a family, guiding a team, supporting a community, or navigating personal change, our Why becomes the anchor that steadies us and the compass that shows us the direction.

## The Bigger Picture

In today's world, where stress, disconnection, and division often dominate, the tools of spiritual healing, emotional intelligence, and value-based communication are not luxuries—they are fundamentals and necessities for human's foundation. These tools allow us to tap into the spiritual potential of the human consciousness.

Imagine a world where each person knows in clarity their Why—where individuals live with purpose, families thrive in harmony, and communities rise through mutual communication and understanding. That's the vision that fuels me. That is my Why.

So, I ask again—not just of myself, but of you:

What's your Why? What fuels your heart, shapes your decisions, and moves you forward? What would change if you brought more of your heart and soul into communication, your relationships, your work, your thoughts?

Why are we here? What is our spiritual potential? Why do people make decisions the way they do? What triggers them? How can we speak their personality code language? How can we speak the same personality code language wherever we go? How can we learn the personality code system? How can we build connections and how to approach people based on personality code values?

Let's be creative. Let's be conscious. Let's create from the heart and soul. Let's tap into our emotional and spiritual intelligence.

Let us live—intentionally, purposefully, and in harmony—with our deepest Why.

Minh Dannerstedt, Ph.D. Certified Coach & Trainer in Communication & Relationship minhdann@gmail.com https://codebreakerglobal.com/crackyourcode/communicating

### Dr. Minh Dannerstedt, Ph.D.

Dr. Minh H. Dannerstedt started with Spiritual Energy Self-healing workshops in Europe and was invited to teach in several countries on different continents.

She received a Certification Doctor of Philosophy from The Open International University for Complementary Medicines in 1998.

She is also a Certified Hado Instructor trained by Dr. Masaru

Emoto.

Dr. Minh H. Dannerstedt is a Certified Coach & Trainer in Communication & Relationships for Business & Personal life.

https://codebreakerglobal.com/crackyourcode/communicating

minhdann@gmail.com

#oneworldonelanguage #makepeoplematter #makekidsmatter

# Why is My Why

*By Pastor Dr. Monica Gomez*

*AKA: Monica Go*

When my dear friend and leader, Robbie Motter, asked me, "what was my why?" I paused—not because I don't know, but because words often feel too small for the calling I carry. I am a humanitarian. I am a pastor. I am a public figure. I am a wife. I am a mother. But more than all this, I am a servant. That is my why. That is the drumbeat that echoes through every chapter of my life. Why is my why. And my why is always about others— about lifting, healing, equipping, and loving in the name of Jesus far greater than myself.

## The Seeds of Purpose

I wasn't born into a platform. I was born into purpose.

Growing up, I watched my world shift around me like sand in a storm—cultures, countries, communities. I lived between borders, carrying the weight of multiple identities while trying to discover my own. And yet, even as a young girl, I knew I wasn't called to simply exist. I was called to impact. Even in moments of silence, I could hear the whisper: "You were made for more." My daughter.

Service began at home. As the oldest daughter, I learned quickly how to care for others, how to listen when my siblings needed encouragement, and how to be the glue when things felt broken. My heart was tender, but my spirit was resilient. God was already forming my character—not through glamorous moments, but through hidden ones. Through wiping tears, through choosing compassion, through taking responsibility when it would've been easier to walk away.

That was my first understanding of ministry: not a pulpit, but a posture.

## Called to Heal, Not Just to Preach

My journey into ministry was not a career path. It was a surrender. I didn't wake up one day and decide to become a pastor. God awakened the calling in me through people. I was the one they called when marriages were crumbling, when children were sick, when dreams were dying. I was the shoulder, the prayer warrior, the one who refused to let others give up.

People think pastors are preachers. But real ministry is messy. It's walking into someone's lowest valley and sitting with them until hope rises again. It's crying until the heavens break open. It's laying down your own pain to carry someone else's. I've done all of that. I still do. Because my why is service, and service looks like love on its knees.

Ministry for me has never been about building crowds—it's about building people. Sometimes that happens in front of thousands. Sometimes it happens in the dark, with no applause, no cameras. Just two souls and the Spirit of God between them. That's enough. That's everything.

## The Humanitarian Heart

Being a humanitarian is not a title I wear—it's a conviction I carry. I don't believe you can claim to love God and ignore the pain of His people. That's why I've given years of my life to serving the underserved—orphans, widows, war-torn communities, women who've been silenced by trauma.

I remember visiting a rural village where children were drinking from the same water source as livestock. My heart shattered. But I didn't just cry—I acted. That's what love does. It moves.

We've built wells, brought medical care, offered education, and established leadership programs in nations that are often overlooked. But more than anything, we bring dignity. Because every person deserves to know they matter.

And I don't do it alone. I've been blessed with a team, a family in faith, a tribe of warriors who believe in justice, mercy, and transformation. Together, we're not just doing outreach—we're rewriting legacies.

People ask me, "How do you have the strength to keep going?" The answer is simple. I don't rely on my strength. I rely on His. My hands are just the instruments; He is the composer. And He writes beautiful stories through willing hearts.

## A Voice in the Public Square

As a public figure, I've learned that visibility is not about popularity—it's about responsibility. God has entrusted me with a platform, not so I can be seen, but so others can see Him.

The world is loud. And in the noise, truth often gets buried. That's why I speak—not to be heard, but to awaken hearts. Whether it's through social media, television, podcasts, or live events, I speak from a place of conviction. I speak life, purpose, healing, and challenge. I speak not to entertain, but to empower.

Being in the public eye comes with scrutiny. But I've made peace with the fact that not everyone will understand me. I'm not here for approval—I'm here for assignment. And if my words can rescue one soul from despair, if my life can model integrity and boldness, then every criticism, every sacrifice, is worth it.

## A Wife with a Mission

Marriage is not the finish line—it's the foundation of legacy. I am honored to walk life with a man who doesn't just share my dreams but prays them into reality. Together, we serve not as two separate entities but as one united force.

Our home is our first ministry. It is where vision is born and where character is tested. Being a wife has taught me that love is not a feeling—it's a choice, a covenant, a commitment to becoming better together.

We laugh. We cry. We disagree. But we never quit. Because our why is bigger than our wants. Our why is God. Our why is kingdom. Our why is generations we may never meet but will still impact through our obedience.

## A Mother with a Mantle

Motherhood changed me forever. There is no ministry more sacred than raising children. It is leadership in its purest form. It is the unseen labor of shaping souls.

My sons have seen me at my highest and lowest. They've seen me preach and weep. They've seen me fight for others and come home to fight nighttime battles. And through it all, I pray they've seen love. Not perfection, but presence.

I don't just want to keep teaching my adult sons about the greatest lesson of all, God. I want them to experience Him through me. I want them to know that purpose is not a destination—it's a daily surrender. I want them to understand that greatness is not fame—it's faithfulness.

So, I pray with and for them. I speak over them. I build them up with truth and tenderness. And I remind myself, even on hard days, that my greatest legacy may not be what I do on stages—but what I deposit in their hearts.

## Faith as My Foundation

None of this would be possible without my faith. It is not just a part of my life—it is my life. Every decision, every risk, every act of service flows from an unshakeable belief in a good, faithful, and purposeful God.

I believe in miracles. I believe in the power of prayer. I believe in redemption stories and second chances. I believe that every person is created on purpose, for a purpose. And I believe that the deepest fulfillment comes not from achieving, but from aligning—with His will, His timing, His love.

There have been seasons of wilderness. Times when I questioned if I was enough. Times when doors closed, people betrayed, strength failed. But in every valley, I found Him. And that's where I learned that your why can't come from applause—it has to come from a place so rooted in God that even storms can't shake it.

## Why is My Why

My why is not a brand. It's not a slogan. It's not a strategy. It's a revelation.

I serve because I was rescued.

I give because I was given grace.

I lead because I was led through fire.

I love because I was loved back to life.

Every time I look into the eyes of someone who thinks they're forgotten, I see myself. And I remind them of the truth that healed me: You are seen. You are chosen. You are not your past. You are not your pain. You are God's masterpiece, and there is still so much more ahead.

That's why I do what I do. That's why I keep going even when it's hard. That's why I speak when it would be easier to stay silent. That's why I believe when the world says it's hopeless. Because my why is Him. My why is you. My why is every soul still waiting for someone to show up and say, "You matter."

## The Legacy of Why

When my life is over, I don't want to be remembered for how many followers I had or how many events I hosted. I want to be remembered as someone who made others believe again—in themselves, in love, in God.

I want my children to say, "She taught us to serve."

I want the poor to say, "She treated us like royalty."

I want the broken to say, "She saw beauty in our ashes."

I want heaven to say, "She finished her race."

Why is my why. Because life without purpose is just existence. And I refuse to merely exist.

So, I live with urgency. I lead with compassion. I love with abandon. I speak with truth. I serve with joy. And I walk boldly in the calling over my life.

This is not just my story—it's my offering. A life laid down. A heart set apart. A soul on mission.

And in all of it, my deepest prayer is this:

That those who cross my path will not just remember my name, but they will remember the God I pointed to.

Because in the end, that is the only why that matters.

I just give it a GO every day of my life.

### Pastor Dr. Monica Gomez
### AKA: Monica Go

Pastor Dr. Monica Gomez is better known as Monica Go. She is the LOANI Global Chair, Women Spiritual Mentor, and International Speaker. Reach out to Dr. Monica Gomez at, 1-407-684-4111 or scan the link below.

# Lady Amb. Nanette Meneses' Why:
# A Journey of Miracles, Resilience and Empowerment
*By Lady Amb. Nanette Meneses*

From a young age, I've been driven by a deep belief that healing and hope extend far beyond traditional medicine. I've dedicated my life to empowering others to discover their own paths to wellness—because no matter what the challenge, there is always a way. Let me share the incredible miracles in my life, for I believe they may empower you as well.

## Humble Beginnings and a Heart for Service

I come from humble beginnings, the daughter of Cuban immigrants who rebuilt their lives from scratch after arriving in the United States. My parents left behind everything they knew, stepping into a foreign land with nothing but their dreams and an unbreakable spirit. They faced language barriers, financial hardship, and the daunting task of starting anew. And yet, despite their struggles, they never hesitated to lend a helping hand to others and to foster children.

I remember vividly how my mother would cook extra meals and quietly deliver them to neighbors and the needy. My father, even after a long day of grueling work, would teach English at a local college and help others find jobs. That spirit of service and compassion was deeply instilled in me from a young age. It was never about what we had; it was always about what we could give.

## The Birth of a Passion for Helping Others

At just seven years old, I remember standing on the playground, watching children in wheelchairs sit on the sidelines, unable to join in the fun of running, playing, and laughing. I felt an ache in my chest, an awareness that some children didn't have the same freedoms I took for granted.

Inspired by Jerry Lewis and his unwavering dedication to the Muscular Dystrophy Association, I decided to take action. With the boundless enthusiasm only a child can possess, I organized a mini-carnival where kids could play games for just ten cents, raising money to support the cause. The joy I felt in making even a small difference was indescribable. By the time I turned thirteen, I had convinced our local roller rink to host a 24-hour "Roll-a-Thon" for Muscular Dystrophy. The event was a huge success, and I saw firsthand the power of collective action. Even as a child, I understood that together, we could make a difference.

That experience taught me something invaluable: one person's passion can spark a movement. When we open our hearts to the needs of others, we become part of something far greater than ourselves.

## A Personal Journey of Healing

As I grew older, my passion for helping others only deepened. I had always believed in the power of the human spirit, but it wasn't until I faced my own battles that I truly understood the resilience within us all.

My mother was a firm believer in natural remedies. While we respected modern medicine, she also turned to herbal solutions, holistic practices, and traditional healing methods that had been passed down for generations. At the time, I didn't fully appreciate the wisdom she practiced. But life has a way of teaching us lessons when we need them most.

As an active young athlete, I lost my voice during a critical time in my life. Doctors recommended medication but they failed. I had little or no voice. Surgery was recommended to my vocal cords. My father was able to arrange for me to be seen by the best doctor, the doctor that treated Frank Sinatra. He specialized in voice issues, and had a lengthy credential of success, but the recommendation was the same, surgery on my vocal cords. We were warned the surgery in those days would have significant risk of permanent scarring and may not have fully restored my voice. I watched my father take on the challenge of finding a natural, better solution that would have no side effects. Calling forth a miracle, he would discover the power of applying kinesiology, an area of medicine back then that was in its infancy. He was able to learn that my vocal ailment was actually an allergy to a certain food group. Once I stopped eating that food group my vocal cords healed without traditional medical treatment or surgery. At the time everyone agreed it was miraculous. That was the first time I truly experienced the power of natural healing.

Still, it wasn't until I faced one of the greatest challenges of my life that my faith in alternative healing along with modern medicine was too powerful to ignore.

## A Miracle Beyond Medicine

The day I was diagnosed with pre-malignant cervical cancer, I was terrified. As everyone knows, cancer can be a dream killer. Despite my observations as a youth of the power of natural remedies, I chose to undergo surgery for the cancer, but I was left with continuous cramping and pain related to endometriosis. I was a guinea pig for pharmaceuticals' latest and greatest pills for

7 years.

At 27, I was told that clinically I could never have children, and it was strongly recommended that I have a hysterectomy to avoid recurrence of cancer. The weight of that news crushed me. I wanted to be a mother someday. I realized we were not treating the problem, an unhealthy body, we were simply attempting to treat the symptom.

I refused to accept the "impossible." I began to revisit my past successes. I began to consider alternatives to traditional medicine and turned to the holistic practices I had once taken for granted. I decided to stop relying solely on the advice of one area of medicine, or on the belief that there was only one solution to a medical problem, or even the idea that modern medicine was superior to other solutions used throughout the world. This **Mental Shift** became the basis of much of my later life accomplishments.

With the guidance of a medical doctor that also believed in integrative medicine, the importance of healing your body and spirit, the capability of the human body to heal itself, and the recognition that symptoms are simply the manifestation of an illness, not the cause, I embraced change, which included changing my diet, adding herbal and nutritional supplements together with alternative modalities. I really had to believe that my process would heal me. I had to be willing to change my mindset and overcome my doubts and the doubts of others. I had to affirm a deeper **trust in God**. I would pray and ask for strength. With a strong belief the mind can heal. I surrounded myself with positive energy and unwavering faith.

The results were nothing short of a cure. On later scans, ovarian cysts had disappeared, the endometriosis that plagued me since my teens was a thing of the past, cramps, and pain stopped and most importantly, for the first time in my life I was "regular." Although these successes were powerful, another miracle would soon reveal itself.

Against all odds, I became pregnant and became a mother of two beautiful children—both born after the age of forty. The moment I held my children in my arms, I knew that I had been given a gift, not just in motherhood, but in the lesson that had been reinforced: There is always a way!

## Bridging the Gap Between Traditional and Alternative Healing

Millions of people endure unnecessary pain and discomfort every day. We are blessed with extraordinary medical professionals who work tirelessly to heal and save lives, but even they have limitations. They can't know every solution, especially when it comes to the wealth of alternative options available. Regulations restrict what they can offer, leaving many searching for answers beyond the walls of a doctor's office.

Our modern medical system relies on clinical trials, studies, and proof of effectiveness, but consider the reality that many tried and true remedies have had little or no clinical trials. Instead, these remedies have been proven by generations of success in the treatment of ailments, but there is little financial incentive to study these remedies. After all, clinical trials are expensive and to prove a remedy works, most entities need to be able to support the study and effort with a promise of profit beyond the outcome of the study. Modern medicine promises solutions to symptoms at significant cost, not usually because the cost of the product is high, but because the profit of inventing is necessary to reimburse the discovery effort. While this process has produced success, it has banned many natural remedies to obscurity. Only recently has attention to this troubling dilemma been uncovered. My personal Why led me to revisit natural remedies, and now we need to create a new movement, one that doesn't just allow clinically studied remedies, but studies that advocate natural remedies as well.

My husband, as I write this, was afflicted with aggressive stage 4 cancer. The traditional treatment was a temporary solution, postponing the inevitable. But is it? If we challenge the traditional, open to the availability of other remedies, and address the underlying problem causing the progression of his cancer, then we will have achieved more than was promised at his diagnosis. Our journey through his treatment choices has introduced us to countless individuals who are becoming increasingly aware that doctors alone do not always hold the answers. He is in remission with a blend of medical and integrative treatment, and so are the many people that we have encountered along the way. While alternative medicine can have a stigma of Voo Doo, we need to shed that idea and replace it with a positive attitude or investigation and searching for effective options.

My Why includes the vision that there is a community of those seeking answers, that the community shares experiences and knowledge, and discovers natural remedies to stand next to medical knowledge. Not a library written and approved only by a portion of the medical community devoted to clinical trials, but also those in the integrative field, and those that are also experiencing the symptoms and relief. Imagine if you had access to a huge world-wide database of medical and natural remedies, their rated effectiveness, and the identification of those that could provide those remedies?

My Why also had the vision that we are not given limited access to information, either by a governmental entity or the medical profession, in the name of protecting us, but rather let us investigate and apply our judgment to solutions that may not be within the mainstream of modern medical advice.

I have spoken to countless individuals who feel trapped in a cycle of pain or discomfort popping one pill after another. They feel unheard, unseen, and hopeless. But I have also seen the transformation that happens when people take charge of their own wellness, also exploring natural remedies, holistic treatments, and integrative therapies. If there is one message to be heard, it is to be your own Advocate for miracles.

This is **MY WHY.**

I have dedicated my life to empowering others—to helping people find their joy, reclaim their health, and believe in their ability to feel better, mentally, physically, and spiritually. My mission is to inspire individuals to become their own advocates, to embrace alternative paths to wellness, and to never give up. Be your own Hero. This is the reason I created the Happy Hero Foundation. Whether advocating for yourself or supporting someone else, we can rewrite the narrative of pain and suffering.

Being a hero does not mean that you should simply follow the advice of others or try everything offered. The world of charlatans is a large one. However, my Why includes advocating for your active investigation into alternatives by talking to others who are having success, reading, and researching testimonials, comparing your journey to others who have successfully bridged the gap before you, and being inspired that you will find an answer, just keep searching.

To support my point, when my oldest daughter was born, she was born with colic, an insidious problem that medical doctors cannot seem to solve. Time and again I was told that her insistent crying could not be helped and that she would grow out of it at 6 months old. Many of you have experienced the sorrow of colic, and so you know that there is no deeper frustration than that of your baby crying endlessly, all day and sometimes all night. I applied what I have been advocating for this problem, and the results were nothing short of another miracle. I created a safe natural external herbal remedy. When I applied it to her belly, she stopped crying, instantly. Our pediatrician used it on his own grandchild and convinced me that the world needed this remedy. Happi Tummi was born 21 years ago and is a manifestation of my Why. It was not invented by me because I am special. It was invented by me because I became an advocate for my newly born daughter. There must be a way, and we will find it. Happi Tummi is a prime example of determination, collaboration, and the application of my why to a real-life challenge.

## Creating a Ripple Effect of Empowerment - Thus A Happy H.E.R.O.

Healing is not just about curing ailments. It is about restoring Hope. It is about Empowering yourself and others. It is about being Resilient. And it is about Outreach to others to find a solution or to share your successes and create a community where everyone inspires each other. I envision a world where more people feel empowered to seek out solutions that truly work for them. Where mothers can soothe their colicky babies without relying on harsh medications. Where people suffering from chronic pain find relief through methods they never knew existed. Where individuals facing dire diagnoses discover that they are not powerless—that they have options, hope, and community.

I want to create a ripple effect of empowerment. I want to inspire people who will inspire others, who in turn will inspire even more. Together, we can build a community of hope, healing, and infinite possibilities.

You don't have to suffer. There's joy and hope to be found in the process of transformation. Keep going, keep believing, and let's make this life's journey one of purpose, connection, and impact while having FUN!

## Let's Keep on Keeping On—Together

Life is full of challenges, but it is also full of opportunities to grow, laugh, heal, and uplift one another. My journey has taught me that even in our darkest moments, there is always a light waiting to be found. Sometimes, that light comes in the form of a simple remedy. Sometimes, it comes from the kindness of a stranger. And sometimes, it comes from within ourselves.

So, to everyone reading this—no matter where you are on your journey— Truly embrace it, Have Fun, Inspire others, know there are Infinite possibilities! And there is always a way!

## Lady Amb. Nanette Meneses

Lady Nanette Meneses: A Visionary's Journey from Humble Beginnings to Global Impact

In the world of business and philanthropy, few stories resonate with you and I as deeply as that of Nanette Meneses. With her roots firmly planted in the rich soil of resilience—born to Cuban exiles who arrived in Miami, Florida, with little more than hope and determination—Nanette embraced the rights and benefits of America, and has crafted a legacy defined by compassion, innovation, and leadership.

Nanette's professional journey is marked by significant achievements, not the least of which is the invention of Happi Tummi, an award-winning product that has brought relief and happiness to more than 1.5 Million babies and parents worldwide. Her creation has garnered attention on national platforms such as the Today Show and has been celebrated as the best product in its category for many years.

Her prowess in marketing and strategic vision was evident early in her career. By the age of twenty-seven, Nanette had already ascended to the position of VP of Marketing for a Fortune 500 company, playing a pivotal role in its evolution into the largest company of its kind in the world. Her innovative marketing and customer acquisition strategies found partners in prestigious sports entities like the Los Angeles Rams, San Diego Chargers, and the LA Lakers.

Beyond her corporate success, Nanette has dedicated three decades to coaching CEOs and entrepreneurs, sharing her insights on overcoming adversity with curiosity and perseverance,

Her commitment to the support of others is evident in her leadership and entrepreneurial spirit for philanthropy. She founded a non-profit, A Happy Hero Foundation, dedicated to helping others find unconventional solutions to difficult medical, and life challenging circumstances. The foundation will research and discover answers to perplexing medical issues, which receive little or no financial attention, natural solutions that are often overlooked for more harmful medications. Her success with Happi Tummi is a founding example, creating an all-natural solution to colic in babies and pain and discomfort in teens and adults. Nanette was knighted by the Knights of Malta in 2002, and most recently knighted by the Royal Order of Constantine the Great and Saint Helen for her continued humanitarian service. Nanette has been active in many non-profits, and leveraged her talents to support various charitable causes, notably presenting a $100,000 check to Jerry Lewis on national television for the Muscular Dystrophy Association.

Her mission, deeply personal and universally impactful, focuses on alleviating the suffering of the most vulnerable—babies to the elderly. Nanette envisions a world where every person facing a difficult malady or challenge has a companion when finding effective solutions. This vision is a testament to her belief in the power of innovative solutions to everyday problems, a principle she applies not only to product development but to life itself.

Nanette Meneses embodies the spirit of resourcefulness, teaching others to live a balanced life that draws on individual strengths to face fears and adversities. Her life's work encourages us all to manifest our dreams into reality, proving that with determination, compassion, and a bit of ingenuity, we can make a significant impact on the world. Her motto "Happy is good" is a message needed in the world today.

In sharing her story, Nanette does not seek accolades but rather aims to inspire others to join her in a collective effort to bring comfort, kindness, joy, and relief to those in need. Her journey from the daughter of exiles to a leader and philanthropist serves as a partner of hope, inviting us all to contribute to a world where suffering is diminished, and dreams can flourish.

Nanette is a mother of four wonderful children and married to the man of her dreams.

Lady Amb. Nanette Meneses  866-744-2774
or info@happitummi.com, https://www.linkedin.com/in/nanette-meneses-77bb0a9/, IG:@happitummi
IG: @Ladynanettem, FB:@NanetteMeneses,
Website: www.happitummi.com

# Fuel by Passion: The Drive Behind Our Purpose

*By Ambassadors and Drs. Randi D. Ward and*
*Chaudhry Masood Mahmood Bhalli*

My new husband Masood and I are extremely passionate people about performing our work and fulfilling our dreams. One of things that first attracted us to each other was that we share the same strong moral values; we also share the same "WHY" we do the things we do. Together our relationship both personally and professionally has been successful so far because of these reasons. Our unique qualities also enhance our partnership and make us the humanitarian people we truly are. Here are some of our individual WHY's.

I am a lady who dreams bigger than many people. I love stepping out of my comfort zone and taking risks (not dangerous ones but risks many people might think are a little crazy or difficult to achieve). I always believe almost everything is possible if I work hard enough and never give up. Reinventing myself to achieve all my dreams is a challenge I happily pursue.

So WHY do I do the things I do to fulfill my huge dreams? I believe all of us have talents and skills that we are not utilizing. I am constantly on a life journey to discover my "hidden" God-given gifts and then find ways to use them to create a better world. As a true humanitarian and a lifetime educator, I love helping people with these skills I have developed.

As a child, I dreamed of being an entertainer---an actress, singer, and dancer---but God had other plans for me. I was destined to be an educator. Coming from a family of educators, this was not a surprising choice for me. At the age of 22 years, I began my 37-year American, English, Language Arts, and Gifted Education teacher career in West Virginia and concluded it in Georgia. I loved watching young people grow intellectually and mature into successful adults. As well as teaching them subject content, I did my best to encourage them to believe in themselves and dream bigger. As I follow many of them today on social media, I am so proud of who they have become.

When I retired in May 2008, I was naturally excited. Even though I still loved teaching on my very last day in the classroom, I would now have more time to spend with my now late husband Bill, to be able to travel whenever I desired, and not have to wake up at 5:30 a.m. (A horrible time even for a morning lady like me.) However, after a few months, I became so bored. I no longer felt I had a purpose.

In 2010, I joined Facebook and started connecting with people around the world. As an extrovert, this was a wonderful way to fill my free time. What I now consider to be one of my "mini miracles" occurred. I received an invitation to teach at an English adult school in Cairo, Egypt, in 2011 from a Facebook friend who had opened a center. The idea of teaching in a foreign country was intriguing. However, a violent revolution had just recently ended in January with the overthrow of Egypt's 30-year dictator, so my family did not want me to go. After much serious contemplation and numerous dreams during the night I believe were from God, I accepted the three-month teaching position. My husband and son were not happy, but as a risk-taker, I believed I would be safe there.

Against my family wishes, I boarded a plane to Cairo in early November 2011. Little did I know that one week after my arrival the second violent revolution would begin, and I would be living three blocks from Tahrir Square, the main center of the revolution. In my dreams, God had promised to keep me safe, and He did that even though I was surrounded by violence frequently and even listened to twelve protesters die and 160 people get injured by the bullets of the military police one-half block from my apartment.

During the next three months, I taught six classes in four levels of English proficiency and had the greatest teaching experience of my life. I successfully taught my adult students some new English skills, but they also taught me how to become a much-needed Egyptian woman for survival. Teacher Randi became a welcomed Student Randi again. I always love learning new things, so this was a blessing.

When I returned to my home in Georgia, I knew I had to do more. My adventure in Egypt was not done. The night dreams started again. The Voice told me to write my memoir of my life in Egypt. Thus, five months later Because I Believed in Me (My Egyptian Fantasy Came True) was completed and published in November 2012. Shortly after that with three Egyptian friends, my two Egyptian schools were created. Having talked to so many students about the quality of their Egyptian schools, I felt the need to create mine to help. The first one was an adult English and German center called Rise Up which opened in January 2013 followed by 6 October Nursery one year later in which I created nursery rhymes and children's stories. I taught these young children from my home in Georgia via Skype. I was so proud of both schools, but sadly they both were forced to close several years later due to things beyond our control. I do not consider them failures though. I learned a lot about being a new entrepreneur and will always treasure the memories made working with these students. I am still connected to many of my former Egyptian students via Facebook and have had the pleasure to see them become more fluent in English and grow into successful adults.

My actual classroom days have ended but not my teaching. I just use different platforms. I now write in all genres, except a screenplay, but I hope to do that one day. It is definitely on my bucket list. I am a novelist with two published novels Random Wanderings and the sequel Wandering No More, a poet, a blogger, a magazine writer/editor, a short story writer, an essayist, etc. I also have become an international speaker and have spoken on over seventy-five platforms in seventeen countries either in person or virtually. From 2015 until 2019, I also did volunteer private online English tutoring with students in Egypt, Morocco, Algeria, and Tunisia that needed my assistance. Often the poor internet in their countries interfered with the success of those sessions, but I feel they did benefit from our interaction. My lessons, writing, and speeches are always designed to inspire and entertain as well as to educate. Many of them teach life skills necessary to live happy, successful lives. I will always be an eternal teacher.

Two current passion magazines are so important to me. With a young Moroccan friend named Ayoub Kadi who is also like a son to me, we created an online magazine called Morocco Pens. It provides non-native English people the opportunity to write articles in English and become published authors for free. I am the Editor as well as a Contributing Writer. I am so proud of this magazine and the work we do. My second magazine is Inspirations for Better Living with publisher and dear friend Johnny Tan (From My Mama's Kitchen). Once again, I am the Editor of this incredible magazine but also write a monthly article. Our goal, our WHY, is to help Millennial Mothers create better lives for their families via motivational and educational articles from renowned authors and successful people.

In 2020, I became certified in four coaching categories, including NLP. Another "WHY" was added to my life plan. I decided to become a Book Writing Coach. As an English teacher, this was another easy career transition. I strongly believe everyone has an inspiring or interesting story to tell, but many do not know how to tell it. I love helping those people write their stories to share to the world and then edit their work to enhance the beauty of their words. It brings me great joy when I see the pride these people have in their finished written products---books, articles, etc.

My wife Randi has shared her Why's. Now I will happily share mine. I am Ambassador Dr. Chaudhry Masood Mahmood Bhalli from Pakistan but also live in the USA with Randi. My friends and family call me Masood. As an international Humanitarian, I have humbly received several prestigious awards and honors. I received a 2023 GIA University Honorary Doctorate (USA) for Humanitarianism and a 2024 Global Iconic Changemaker Entrepreneur of the Year plus Recognition in United Nations Platforms. I am the Global Male Ambassadors for GSFE (Global Society for Female Entrepreneurs), USA and LOANI (Leaders of All Nations International), UK, the LOANI Pakistani Global Ambassador, and an Ambassador of Happiness awardee by Queen Eden of Birland. I was awarded Worldwide Superhero from LOANI and Institute of Global Professionals. I have Co-Authored the most Worldwide Famous Best-Seller Expert World Leaders Book featuring Successful International Leaders published by LOANI, Best-Seller Voices of Peace—A Global Perspective, #1 Best-Selling Book Leading with Your Heart and Soul---a book with twenty-seven other international humanitarian leaders, and Iconic Global Changemakers, Vol. 2. I am honored to be in Lady Amb. Dr. Robbie Motter's Legacy book A Leader with a Heart of Gold. I am an even character in

Randi's new novel Wandering No More which will be launched in Kenya in July 2025.

Because of my incredible, loving parents, especially my mother, and the highly professional and excellent teachers I was provided due to my mother's desire for me to have the best education possible, I am a highly educated and intelligent man. My parents raised me in the most respectable ways. I was taught to respect and help others as well as myself. Family and genuine friends are a huge part of my life. I try my best to help them when possible. My parents encouraged me always to do my best and use my God-given talents and gifts to my fullest potential to help create a good future for humanity as well as myself. I have done that and will continue to do that. The teachings of my Islamic faith have also instilled in me the highest of moral standards and values. God always directs my daily life.

Because of these blessings, I am a loving, caring, patient man who has huge dreams and passions and enjoys helping others achieve their dreams. People from all over the world often come to me for personal and professional advice. During my life, I have helped many people and students in South Korea, Spain, my native country of Pakistan, etc. and with the use of social media, people in other international countries. I have gladly shared my acquired wisdom and the skills I have learned with them. I love to see hard-working people overcome personal issues and succeed in their lives.

I have spent much of my professional career in the area of Hospitality and other related services. Originally, my college/university courses were for pre-engineering and involved time-consuming and difficult courses such as physics, chemistry, and higher-level mathematics. Being able to excel in these courses was not a problem, but I wanted to start a job, so I needed a more practical and less intense course of study. Because I was also raised to appreciate the finest things in life, I developed a passion to live a glamourous life. Thus, I chose to study all areas of the Hospitality Industry. As a forever student who wanted to be completely prepared for this industry, I have completed dozens of courses in my master's program. This professional field would allow me to travel the world and explore new places---meet interesting new people---and dress in high fashion. This dream came true; I experienced this wonderful lifestyle and career in major hotels in Asia with top-paying salaries and much prestige.

When COVID tried its best to destroy our world, the Hospitality Industry was deeply affected as we all know. Using my vast knowledge as an experienced entrepreneur, I needed to recreate myself and find a new career path. Thus, the creation of my new business with Randi. We are so proud of RM Infinite (OneStop Possibilities). As the name implies, this is a multi-service company. Since my WHY continues to be to help others, RM Infinite focuses on the individual needs of our clients. Randi and I are experts in our fields. Since one of our many services is book publishing, Randi serves as our Book Writing Coach, Master Editor in all Editing Areas, Ghost Writer, and Expert Adviser on Book Writing Concerns/Questions from clients. My skills include many diverse services. I manage our team for the actual book publishing process from Book Cover Design, Formatting/ Composition, Printing, and even Marketing if requested by the client---the entire publishing process. I am a very skilled Marketer using unique methods to sell products using the areas of Advertising, Branding, Creative Projects, Event Planning, Graphic Designs, Motion Graphics, Productions (including Documentaries, Infomercials, etc.), 3D Animations, TVC, Public Relations, and even Translations (since I am fluent in many languages).

Part of my training in the Hospitality Industry also made me an expert in other areas of National and International Travel. I am highly adept at organizing and managing Domestic and International Tours. As a world traveler having visited more than half of the world, I understand many cultures and know the best things to do, to see, etc. and how to provide economical packages for clients or luxury packages if desired. I am a skilled Worldwide Immigration and Visa Consultant and can recommend and arrange the perfect travel insurance policies. I have proudly assisted clients in these areas to enable them to fulfill their travel needs and dreams.

My creative talents and love of high fashion mentioned earlier will also be revealed one day with the designs of my future high-quality, elegant, exquisitely handmade ladies' shoes (appropriate for brides and ladies with great taste), handbags, and jewelry made with gold, silver, fine metals, and genuine gemstones). I will also design special "Made to Order" requests. This is my future "dream" project in the USA. With God's blessings, I will make this new business happen.

Masood and I want to share our final WHY which relates directly to this inspiring book. Because of Lady Ambassador Dr. (hc) Robbie Motter, our beloved friend and GSFE sister, we were given an amazing opportunity to share our life WHY'S with the world, so naturally we had to participate as Co-Authors. Thank you, dearest Robbie, for always being our role model and reminding us constantly of the importance of "showing up." We hope our stories will inspire others to "show up," discover their "WHY'S," and follow their dreams. Life is precious, so Masood and I do our best to live it to the fullest.

Blessings and Best Wishes to all you Readers,

Randi and Masood

## Ambassador Dr. (h.c) Randi D. Ward

Ambassador Dr. (hc) Randi D. Ward, 2020 IAOTP Educator of Decade/Top 50 Fearless Leaders; Co-Owner ---RM Infinite; CEO Randi D. Ward, Author and Editor; Visionary Book Coach/14-time Best-Seller Master Editor; 16-time International Best-Seller Author/Speaker; 2 Humanitarian Honorary Doctorate Degrees; an Education Honorary Doctorate; one Humanities Honorary Doctorate; LOANI Visionary Global Goodwill Ambassador; Humanitarian; Multi-Award Recipient; International Student Mentor.

+1 678 634 0069  (WhatsApp)

Email: randiteach@yahoo.com

Facebook: https://www.facebook.com/randi.ward/

Website: https://www.randidward.com

## Ambassador Dr. (h.c) Chaudhry Masood Mahmood Bhalli

Ambassador Dr. (hc) Chaudhry Masood Mahmood Bhalli is an Entrepreneur, CEO and CO-FOUNDER of "RM Infinite" (International Multiple Services), Expert Administrator, Advertiser, Brand Developer, Communicator, Conceiver, Creator, Productions, Designer (Females Specified Handmade Bags, Jewelry, and Shoes) Documenter, Encourager, Establisher, Events Planner, Generator, Hotelier, Immigration and Travel Consultant, Initiator, Introducer, Listener, Marketer, Promoter, Translator, and Continued ...

+1 470 534 0072 (WhatsApp)

Email:  consultneed1@gmail.com

m.me/consultneed (Facebook Messenger)

# What's My Why

*By Rima Aboulhosen*

## The Question That Changes Everything

Have you ever paused long enough to ask yourself, Why am I here? Not in a fleeting, existential way, rather with the weight of knowing that this question holds the power to shape how you live, love, show up, and BE in the world?

I have. And what I've discovered is this: My why isn't a destination—it's a living, breathing force that evolves as I do. It's the compass that guides me, the fuel that keeps me going, and the answer to how I rise after every fall.

## The Road That Led Me Here

I come from a land shaped by both beauty and war. Lebanon— my birthplace—taught me resilience before I even understood the word. The sounds of laughter and gunfire intertwined in my childhood, teaching me early on that joy and pain can coexist. Yet it was in the in-between moments, the quiet ones, where I found something deeper: the unwavering desire to create light in the midst of darkness.

Life uprooted me and placed me in a new land, a new culture, a new way of BEing. The United States became my second home, offering opportunities and also demanding reinvention. My experiences—war, caregiving for loved ones, witnessing loss, and navigating my own struggles—shaped my heart and provided me an unshakable knowing: I am here to connect, to uplift, and to remind people that we are one human family.

## When Life Breaks You Open

There are moments in life that fracture everything you thought you knew. Moments that shake you awake, forcing you to see the world—and yourself—differently. For me, one of those moments wasn't only a moment. It was a childhood shaped by war, by division, by a world where love and hate existed side by side, separated only by a thin, fragile line.

Lebanon, a country of breathtaking beauty—a land where the sea kisses the mountains, where laughter and music fill the air, where families gather around tables overflowing with food and stories.

Lebanon was also a country at war; and war has a way of turning even the most familiar places into something unrecognizable.

## When Neighbors Became Enemies

One of the hardest things to comprehend as a child was how people who once shared meals, laughter, and life could suddenly see each other as enemies. I remember watching people from a nearby neighborhood—once like extended family—as war slowly poisoned their hearts. Fear turned into suspicion. Suspicion into anger. And anger into something even darker—hate.

People who once greeted each other with warmth now crossed the street to avoid one another. Doors that had always been open, filled with the smell of home-cooked meals, were now shut tight—barricaded against the unknown. Invisible walls rose between us, turning neighbors into strangers, and strangers into threats.

I didn't understand why. How could someone's heart change so drastically over labels, politics, or religion? How could someone who once smiled at me now carry a weapon in his hands?

It would have been easy—so easy—to let anger settle inside me, to let fear turn into bitterness, to see the world through the same lens of division that was being handed down from generation to generation. Even then, something inside me knew that wasn't the way.

I remember one night—the sound of bombs rumbling in the distance, shaking our home just enough to remind us that nothing was truly safe. I was working on a school assignment, exploring the questions of hatred and revenge. It became a doorway to something deeper, inviting me to search for wisdom within. That moment stayed with me. I had seen what hate could do, and even then, I knew: I didn't care to live that way.

So, I made a choice.

A choice that would shape the rest of my life.

I would never let the world dictate the size of my heart!

Instead of letting war harden me, I let it soften me. Instead of carrying bitterness, I carried compassion. Instead of seeing enemies, I chose to see the wounded hearts behind the anger, the fear behind the aggression.

I chose love. I chose kindness. I chose understanding.

## War Taught Me the Power of Connection

War could have taught me that division was inevitable. That people would always find reasons to turn against each other. That hate was easier than love.

It didn't. It taught me the exact opposite.

It taught me that beneath the noise of politics and religion, beyond the walls we build between ourselves, we are all the same. We care to be safe. We care to be seen. We care to be loved.

I began to notice small moments where humanity still shined through, even in the darkest times.

A woman offering her last loaf of bread to a neighbor—despite being on "opposite" sides.

A soldier pausing before pulling the trigger, remembering that the person before him was someone's child, someone's parent.

A child, no older than I was, reaching out for another's hand—not as an enemy, but as a friend.

*These moments were proof to me that love was always stronger. It just needed to be chosen.*

## How This Shaped My Why

Looking back, I realize that my why—the core reason I do what I do—was born in those early years. I saw firsthand what happens when fear overrides love. When people let division define them. When kindness is forgotten, I knew I cared to spend my life doing the opposite.

That's why I speak about unity. That's why I created Planet of One—because I know we are one. That's why I remind people that love is the answer—because I've lived in a world where people forgot that, and I've seen the destruction it causes.

I don't just believe in kindness. I have witnessed its power.

Every time I meet someone new, I don't see their religion, their nationality, or their political beliefs first. I see them. The human being in front of me. Their heart, their story, their struggles. And that has made all the difference.

## Loss, Love, and Strength

The war wasn't the only thing that shaped me. The loss of my sister and my father taught me even more about love, resilience, and what truly matters. It all forced me to confront the impermanence of life. Within that, I found something sacred: the essence of being mindfully present.

Watching my sister battle cancer, she was a warrior in the truest sense of the word—she fought cancer with grace, strength, and an unbreakable spirit. She taught me that love isn't about the time we have but about how deeply we connect. She showed me that even in suffering, there is beauty. That even in loss, there is love.

And my father? Standing by my father as dementia unraveled his mind and feeling the ache of goodbye—He was a man who lived with laughter in his heart, even when the world gave him reasons not to. He taught me how to find joy in the simplest of moments, how to laugh even when life was heavy. When I lost him, I realized something powerful: Detaching from suffering doesn't mean detaching from love. It means allowing love to exist beyond pain.

Grief has a way of refining you. It strips away the unnecessary, leaving only what truly matters. And what mattered to me was this: Love, Presence, and Connection.

These experiences didn't break me; they broke me open. They deepened my why, sharpening my focus on what I am here to do. So, I carry them with me, not in grief, but rather in love. They are woven into my why, into every conversation I have, every person I reach, and every heart I touch.

*I don't know where life will take me next. I don't know how many more moments will shape me, break me open, and teach me. Yet I do know this:*

No matter what, I will choose love.

No matter what, I will choose kindness.

No matter what, I will see people as they truly are—not enemies, not labels, not strangers, simply human beings.

And maybe, just maybe, if enough of us make that choice, the world will finally remember that we are not meant to be divided. We are meant to be one.

## A life driven by why isn't always easy.

I've learned that why isn't about grand gestures—it's about the small, consistent choices you make daily. It's in how you treat the person next to you, how you show up in difficult conversations, and how you choose love over fear.

Your why is reflected in:

- The energy you bring into a room.
- The way you listen—not just to respond, to truly understand.
- The impact you leave long after you're gone.

## The Connection Between You and Me

I believe in the unbreakable thread that binds us. We are not separate; we are deeply interconnected. And when you step into your why, you give others permission to do the same.

I see this truth in every conversation I have, every podcast I host, every soul I encounter. The moment we recognize our shared humanity; we break down the illusions that divide us.

Your why isn't just about you—it's about the imprint you leave on the world. It's about the way your presence changes someone's day, the ripple effect of your kindness, and the way your courage inspires another to rise.

## The Lightness of Letting Go

One of the hardest lessons I've learned is that attachment can cloud your why. We cling to identities, relationships, and expectations, believing they define us. And yet, true freedom comes when we release what isn't ours to hold.

Letting go doesn't mean you don't care. It means you trust. You trust that life will unfold as it's meant to, that people will walk in and out of your life as they need to, and that your why will remain—unshaken, unwavering.

My father taught me this in his own way. Even as his memory faded, his essence remained. His laughter, his warmth, his presence—it was all still there, beyond the physical. He showed me that love isn't about holding on; it's about BEing.

## Owning Your Why

Living your why means owning it fully, **with no need for permission or validation.** It isn't about having all the answers or checking boxes. It's about being present in your own journey— knowing that the small steps matter just as much as the big leaps.

There's no single formula for finding your why. It's a process, a practice of BEing, a lifetime of exploration. Your why will fill you up, guide you forward, and remind you every single day that you are here for something beautiful and meaningful. Will you listen to it? Because your why isn't waiting at the finish line. It's speaking to you now.

## Rima Aboulhosen

Rima Aboulhosen, the visionary CEO behind Planet of One, is a heart-centered empowerment creator, podcaster, educator, and dynamic speaker.

Born amidst the turmoil of Lebanon, Rima's journey led her to embrace a new chapter in the United States, where she and her family redefined their lives. This transformation became the foundation of her unique philosophy: "Life, Liberty, and the pursuit of Mindfulness."

With a deep appreciation for the preciousness of each moment, Rima founded Planet of One—a beacon of inspiration designed to help individuals step into their true potential and live with authenticity, ultimately elevating our shared world.

A passionate advocate for kindness, respect, understanding, love, and gratitude, Rima lives by her mantra: "Let's be what matters, a loving human family." Her unwavering dedication to fostering positive change makes her a shining example of how one person can transform the world through compassion and purpose.

Join Rima in awakening the best within us all. Together, let's be the force that shapes a world woven with love, kindness, and unity.

Rima Aboulhosen

Founder & CEO: Planet Of One

Host: Attitude Of Altitude Podcast

Email: Rimaa45@gmail.com

https://linktr.ee/planetofone

# Finding My Why: A Journey of Transformation
*by Lady Amb Dr. Robbie Motter (h.c.)*

In a world filled with challenges and disturbances, the quest for self-love and personal growth can often feel like an uphill battle. However, within each struggle lies the seed of potential, waiting for the right conditions to flourish. My journey toward discovering my 'why' has been a winding path filled with experiences that have shaped me into the person I am today. It's a journey of resilience, transformation, and a deep commitment to helping others uncover their unique gifts. This is my story— how I learned to love myself, elevate my talents, and inspire others by encouraging them to step out and step up.

## A Journey Begins in Paradise

I was born and raised in Hawaii, a breathtakingly beautiful place characterized by its stunning landscapes, rich culture, and vibrant communities. Yet, beneath the surface of paradise, my childhood life was tumultuous—a grand mosaic made up of moments of joy shadowed by pain and uncertainty. Growing up in foster homes from a young age, I learned early on about the fragility of life and the importance of resilience. Each home presented its own set of challenges, but amidst the chaos, I found solace in the lush green mountains and the sound of the waves crashing along the shore in Hawaii and the beauty in other states that I lived in foster homes.

By the time I was fourteen, life had become overwhelming. The instability of my upbringing and the burden of moving from home to home had stripped me of any sense of permanence. I found myself thrust into the world far earlier than most teens, forced to navigate life on my own. It was then that I decided I would not let my circumstances define me. My why began to take shape: to cultivate a deep-seated love for myself and to discover the talents I possessed—talents that would allow me to rise above my struggles.

## The Awakening in San Francisco

At fourteen, I looked older and back in those days they did not ask your age, so left the foster care system in CA and I landed my first job in San Francisco, a bustling city pulsing with life and opportunities. I remember standing on the corner of Market Street, wide-eyed and filled with both excitement and anxiety. For the first time in my life, I felt a shred of independence. My job taught me more than just customer service; it instilled in me a sense of responsibility and discipline. It set me on a course of exploration—of self-discovery.

Living in San Francisco in a boarding home on California street, opened my eyes to countless possibilities. I began to meet individuals from a melting pot of cultures—people with stories as diverse as my own. Their experiences ignited a flame of inspiration within me, encouraging me to embrace my journey. Amidst navigating my own challenges, I took time to support the women around me; at that time, many women were not supporting one another.

This sense of camaraderie became another of my whys. As I worked in various top jobs across the country, I made it a priority to champion women in their pursuits as during that time women where not helping each other. While I was a mother—raising three children through the trials of divorce—I understood the dual role of being a caretaker and a force of empowerment.

Embracing Challenges as Opportunities

As the years rolled on, I explored various states—Ca, returned to Hawaii, then to Texas, Virginia, New Jersey, New York, Washington, D.C., and finally Southern California where I live today. Each transition taught me invaluable lessons and broadened my perspective. I embraced every new opportunity, believing that continuous learning was vital in shaping a brighter future for myself and my children.

Throughout my professional journey, I encountered numerous obstacles—moments when doubt crept in, nudging me to question my abilities. Yet, through every challenge, I discovered my unwavering capacity to turn setbacks into steppingstones. I always, even to this day, believe that challenges offer us the opportunity to find another way and the importance of being resilient becomes apparent, especially as a **cancer survivor**. My health struggles reminded me to savor each moment while dedicating my life to being there for others.

It was in the face of adversity that I realized my ultimate why— to guide women toward understanding that they are perfect just the way they are, and that they can achieve their dreams.

## Building the Foundation of My Non-Profit

Years of experience in various industries equipped me with a wealth of knowledge, and I was inspired to channel that into something greater. I founded my nonprofit, Global Society for Female Entrepreneurs (GSFE) a 501 (c)(3) in 2017. It is a community devoted to uplifting women and fostering a sense of collective empowerment. With nearly **four hundred members**, our organization provides support and connections to women, youth, and others from all walks of life, breaking down barriers and building bridges of compassion.

I wanted to create a community that fosters collaboration and growth—where women, youth and individuals can be nurtured yet challenged to step out of their comfort zones. Through workshops and events, I strive to offer opportunities that not only build skills but ignite a sense of self-worth. My aim is for every participant to feel they are in a space of love, warmth, and understanding—a place where they can embrace their uniqueness and celebrate their journeys.

Our motto echoes through all we do: "We are ONE, we are not here to Compete; we are here to Complete each other." This mantra encapsulates our goal to foster a sense of belonging, reminding each member that there is strength in unity.

## The Many Whys of Life

In my journey, I have come to realize that our lives are comprised of many whys. Each time we achieve a goal or fulfill a desire, a new why surfaces—an opportunity beckoning us to explore further. This realization has enriched my life profoundly; it keeps my spirit hungry for growth and learning.

I encourage those who cross my path to identify their whys. What ignites their passion? What causes them to leap out of bed each morning? Each member of our community has untapped potential waiting to be explored. Together, we can create a culture that celebrates growth, resilience, and progress—where every challenge is not perceived with fear, but with excitement for the possibilities that lie ahead.

The journey is both personal and collective, and I believe in the power of sharing our whys with one another. When we come together to support each other in our quests for self-discovery,

we cultivate a compassionate community that thrives on inspiration and kindness.

## Inspiring Stories of Transformation

Within the tapestry of my non-profit, numerous stories of transformation illuminate the impact of empowerment.

During a workshop, I met a young woman who had been battling anxiety and depression for years, feeling trapped in a cycle of self-doubt. Within our program, she discovered her love for writing—a talent she had lost sight of. With encouragement and a nurturing environment, she found the courage to express herself through her words.

Before long, she completed her chapter for the book, unveiling her story to the world and many words in the story that she had never shared with anyone. That day the book was launched I watched her transformation; and since then, she has gone on to write chapters in more books. I again realized my reason for being. It was more than just helping others; it was about witnessing their liberation—the fiery resurgence of self-love and creativity. Each woman who stepped into our space deserved the chance to shine.

These success stories, filled with love and courage, ignite the flame of hope in others. My heart swells with joy when I see our members achieve their dreams, as it fuels my belief that we must first start with loving ourselves.

## Creating a Supportive Community

As the non-profit grew, so did the community surround it. Women began to come together, sharing their stories and supporting one another—building a network that fueled every member's personal journey. We hosted events that allowed individuals to showcase their talents, whether through art, spoken word, entrepreneurship, or other creative expressions.

Our gatherings offered a welcoming atmosphere where vulnerability was celebrated, not shamed. Participants became more than just beneficiaries; they evolved into advocates for one another, amplifying their voices and lifting each other up. It was a testament to the beauty of community—a reflection of the support we all yearn for.

In this supportive environment, I remain committed to the belief that everyone has something valuable to share; there is always room for growth. Witnessing the bonds formed within our community further solidified my purpose—reminding me of why I started this journey in the first place.

## Facing Setbacks with Strength

While the journey may have been rich with growth and joy, it was not devoid of challenges. When covid came I faced moments of overwhelming doubt, times when I questioned whether I could meaningfully impact others. The non-profit world can often feel like an uphill battle, where funding is limited, and resources can dwindle.

During this particularly challenging period, we no longer could meet live and that threatened the continuation of our programs. Just when I felt the weight of despair settle in, I turned inward and reminded myself of my why. I reached out to our members and the community—the very women I sought to uplift—and shared our struggles authentically.

Their response was overwhelming. Women whom we had supported stepped up, volunteering their time, effort, and resources. Together, we learned about Zoom a word and system many of us never heard about, but we found someone to teach us and immediately we started our meetings online and magic happened we became international with a network in Canada and England and women from all over the US joining us. such a powerful reminder of the impact we can make when we rally together.

Through this experience, I learned the true meaning of community and collaboration—the beauty of creating a space where individuals feel empowered to step in to help one another. Each challenge reaffirmed my belief in the importance of continuous learning and sharing insights, both of which fortify our collective resilience.

## Continuing the Journey

As I stand here today, I look back on every experience, challenge, and triumph that has shaped my life's journey. Creating my non-profit is an ongoing adventure—each day bringing new opportunities and lessons to absorb.

I recognize that as I evolve, so do my whys. A few whys I was never able to find the answer to like "Why my mother did not want me and Why I never knew my dad, but I learned your past has nothing to do with your future, so you just move on. Today, my intention is to create a ripple effect whereby the impact of my work magnifies far beyond what I can achieve alone. Every person I help inspires others to step into their power and shine, forming a cycle of empowerment that has the potential to touch lives for generations.

My 'why is not just about me; it is about creating spaces for countless voices to be heard, amplifying the collective spirit of humanity. It is about ensuring every individual knows they possess the ability to transform their narrative—to speak, to write, and to create without limitations. It's about forming meaningful collaborations and continuing to serve others.

## Encouraging Others to Find Their Why

In conclusion, I embrace the concept of many whys throughout my life of 89 years. Growth is a lifelong journey, and the desire to help others discover their paths remains a driving force in my life. As we navigate the complexities of existence, I hope to remind everyone that embracing oneself—learning to love every facet of personal history—opens doors to boundless possibilities.

I encourage anyone reading this to reflect on their own journey. What are your whys? What obstacles have you faced, and how can you transform them into steppingstones? Know that it is never too late to embark on a journey of self-love and empowerment. Every step taken is a testament to your strength.

Together, we can create a legacy where self-love flourishes, talents are nurtured, and no dream is deemed impossible. In this collective quest for growth, let us rise, step out, and step up—celebrating every unique thread woven into our lives.

### Lady Amb. Dr. Robbie Motter (h.c.)

Lady Amb. Dr. Robbie Motter (h.c.) is the Founder/CEO of GSFE, a 501(c)(3) global organization, she is also an award-winning author and coauthor of many books, international certified speaker, coach, and mentor, she has been received numerous awards over the years for her work with women and prior to being an entrepreneur in 1985, she spent over 25 years in corporate America in top positions. She can be reached at rmotter@aol.com, cell 951-255-9200 she is also on WhatsApp and the websites are GSFEUS.COM and robbiemotter.com She can be found on Facebook and LinkedIn as Robbie Motter.

# A Right Now Passionate WHY

*By Sandie Fuenty*

Ask yourself, what is a WHY? Just take a look at a child learning to speak and what is the one word they all know and ask — WHY? And they keep asking WHY till they are satisfied with the answer.

A WHY is a self-chosen passion that drives you forward. A friend of mine called it your "Right Now Passionate Goal." It is what drives you to get out of bed each morning and keeps you going till you place your head on that pillow again. A WHY could be the need for income, recognition, advancement, the desire to leave a legacy, to set an example for others, or just to enjoy life.

WHY's change at different times of our lives. Think of that child as they are growing up and how their WHY will change so many times based upon the differences taking place in their lives. I look at my two granddaughters and how their lives are constantly changing.

Four years ago, my WHY changed drastically. My husband suffered from the aftereffects of Agent Orange from when he served in Vietnam. Agent Orange was a pesticide that was used to defoliate the jungle areas where they were fighting. In 2020 his health changed to the point of his not being able to walk, not being able to care for himself, not being able to drive. He needed care most of the time. As the year progressed and we entered 2021, my WHY became him...to help get him through each day, each doctor's appointment, each medication change, each surgery, each amputation, each episode of a new attack on his body and mind. We were faced with the recurring ER visits and hospital stays of unknown duration. The final one lasted just short of two months. Jim passed peacefully on November 5, 2022.

Luckily, because I was an entrepreneur and had my own business (Director with Mary Kay), I was able to be flexible and remain driven but also calm during most of the time during Jim's illness. The last month my WHY was completely, 24/7, focused on him and nothing else.

After his passing, my WHY was to get through each day, and deal with the arrangements and paperwork that needed to be taken care of. I did not give much thought to the future at that time. Basically, I was numb and in survival mode and on autopilot. About a year after living between homes, I decided to sell the house and move to Orange County to be closer to both of our children and granddaughters. They didn't want me driving back and forth from OC to Lake Elsinore frequently or staying by myself. And I agreed that the drive was getting to me. So, a new WHY appeared. I was busy getting the house ready to sell, fractured my pelvis getting it ready to show and then going through several escrows. Then it was sold, and I had to figure out what to do with myself — my next WHY.

Now that I've moved and become settled in Orange County, I realize that I'm living a life that is good. My WHY is now focused on me. Rediscovering me is what is important now. I've lived my life for my parents, my husband, my children and now it's time to live for me. I've learned I don't want a lot of responsibility; I want to be flexible with my life, and my health is good for my age but not perfect. I love traveling. In our marriage we earned many trips, and he traveled to Brazil with a friend, I traveled to Switzerland, France, Italy, Austria, Budapest, several Caribbean cruises with our office administrator (she loved it). We were even able to take two trips together — one to Fiji and one to Lake Tahoe which was extended due to snow. Jim was reluctant to leave the business running in someone else's hands. Give me an hour and I can have my suitcase packed and be ready to go.

I have learned that every day is a gift from God, and I want to enjoy and make the best of it.

Soon after getting settled in Orange County my WHY became to find a local church because this was so important to my outlook on life, and I missed the fellowship. God was always with me and never left me alone. My daughter was driving down the street last summer, saw something going on outside and it was a summer series of worship services out front of the church. I went back that Sunday to check it out and that has become my home church.

We have two beautiful granddaughters. The oldest, Sophia, is nine. Jim and I were able to spend a day or two each week with her during her infancy, toddler, and preschool years. We lived with her parents while our house was being built from mid-2017 till February of 2018. Once we moved back to Elsinore, we were able to keep her at our house for days and we'd go to the pool and the park. We chose a great community for kids. It was meant to be our forever home, and it was his.

The little one, Penelope was born a month after Jim passed. Jim didn't get to meet her but she has his eyes and her sister talks to her about Papa so she will know him. She also points to the moon and says Papa and somehow equates the heavens to him. I was able to be with her an average of 2 days a week until she started preschool this January. Since I live nearby I am able to go to Sophia's Polynesian Dance, school recitals, sports games and enjoy time with her and her sister.

Once Lindsey (our daughter and my roommate) and I moved

here to Huntington Beach, I realized I was basically living the life I wanted but I did start getting complacent shortly after realizing it.

I was asked to write a chapter in a friend's anthology and that became my next WHY. This is the fifth anthology to which I have contributed. What would my story be about? God kept putting on my mind what we went through leading up to Jim's death and walking through the grief. I wrote about the journey to widowhood and realized it was very cathartic to me and was a very healing project. After doing the chapter, I felt led to commit to writing my own book to help others walking through grief. Stay tuned for my solo book launch later this year.

My WHY when I first met Robbie Motter was to find out what networking was all about, meet others and grow my business. I knew I wanted to get out and expand my business but wasn't sure how to go about it. I found a group on MeetUp and summoned the courage to go. I met Robbie by doing so. Just by showing up in an unknown place, with unknown people and completely out of my comfort zone, I met new friends and a restaurant owner that helped get my business back on a successful track and get me involved in new areas.

I learned to get out and promote myself and my business and its benefits. She introduced me to RJ, the restaurant owner, and told me to "ASK" for what I wanted. I did and he said yes, and we worked together for many years to make Valentine's Day, Mother's Day, and Cancer Awareness Days special; greeting his customers and making them feel welcome and supporting my business and giving me the courage to expand and meet new people. From there I became an author in GSFE's first book, wrote monthly columns entitled Beauty Buzz for a local paper, became a Director of a GSFE chapter, and also promoted myself to Directorship in Mary Kay. I have received many awards from Presidents, Senators, other non-profit organizations, have been a board member of several organizations, and made many life-long friends because of attending that meeting located on MeetUp.

Then Covid hit. A new WHY became necessary for me to embrace. This became a very interesting time in my life, my business, and the world. I am so glad I decided to jump on the bandwagon and learned the new virtual aspect of life. During the Pandemic, I learned Zoom, FB, held virtual GSFE meetings, and virtual MK appointments in my early seventy's. I definitely was not familiar with social media! It was a great and busy time, not without some funny mistakes, like forgetting to sign off a Zoom. I really soared with the newness of everything around me. During Covid I also realized how different life growing up was for me and for my granddaughter and started writing a book to leave as a legacy for her.

My WHY now is to encourage other women to be themselves and to live with grief. I want to be a beacon to remind others that age does not matter and I'm feeling fulfilled and happy to be out in the world again rebuilding me at the age of seventy-five.

What are the benefits of your WHY?

Why do you need a Right Now Passionate WHY? WHY's give you a reason to pursue a passion. They give you a push when you have no desire to do anything. A WHY will give you focus so you can take that next step towards what you want. Otherwise, you will float from one day to another, from one task to another, with no roadmap where you are going.

Your WHY will help you look at options out of the box, set goals and targets to direct you to move forward. A WHY will help you feel good about your accomplishments and your daily wins.

I've learned that material things are not as important as we think, but we hold onto them so tightly because we can see them. We need to learn to hold onto our WHY's just as tightly as we do those material things that will break, disappear, and slip through our fingers. A WHY is usually attached to a goal or something you are trying to achieve.

Go out and try something new. You do not know what is waiting for you and what doors are waiting for you to open them. You cannot make a WHY. It is something inside you that you strive towards, and it sparks your passion.

Remember that little child we talked about at the beginning? Will all their WHY's ever be answered? No, never. But stay tuned because tomorrow or next week there may be a new WHY in place. Just like yours and mine.

### Sandie Fuenty

At the age of seventy-five, and after 32 years with Mary Kay, Sandie has become quite aware of what the "total package" of a woman looks like. She spent many years in male dominated fields of Corporate America and construction and has learned the ins and outs of remaining a professional woman — beauty from the inside out — and able to hold her own.

November of 2022 her husband of 51 years passed. She walked through his deterioration from Agent Orange and Vietnam with him, and she is now in the process of creating a new life for herself while helping to care for her two granddaughters (9 yrs old and 2 years old). She moved back to Orange County to be close to her two children and be able to participate in all lives.

She loves to travel, especially to the Chicago area where she grew up, to spend time with her younger sister. Sandie can have her bags packed and ready to go within an hour!

As an author, columnist, and avid reader, she enjoys time with her dogs and cats, family time, fixing up their new home with her daughter Lindsey, and being active in her local church. She has been featured in five bestselling anthologies and is working on her first solo book which will launch this fall.

Sandie's life is now about encouraging others to pursue life, even during grief.

Reach out to Sandie:

Phone: 714-981-7013

Email: sandiesldy@aol.com

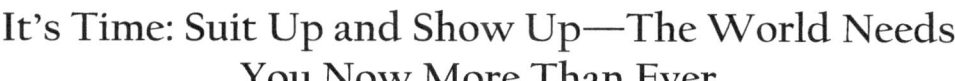
# It's Time: Suit Up and Show Up—The World Needs You Now More Than Ever

*By Shannon Leischner*

"Two roads diverged in a wood, and I—

I took the one less traveled by,

And that has made all the difference."

—Robert Frost

There comes a moment in life when everything changes. A moment that forever draws a line between who you were... and who you are meant to become.

My moment came under a starry sky filled with music, laughter, and thousands of souls dancing freely. It was October 1st, 2017, at the Route 91 Harvest Festival in Las Vegas. But what began as a night of celebration turned into a night of chaos, heartbreak, and unimaginable horror.

In an instant, everything shattered.

Gunfire rained down. People screamed, cried, bled and some never saw morning. Lives were never the same  and some lost forever.

By the second round of shots, my survival instinct shut off and I decided to help as many as I could before I was taken out. Running through the venue, my instincts took over as I pulled strangers to safety, comforted the wounded, and did everything

I could to help others with their injuries.

Then I saw her.

A woman who had been shot in the head. Her breathing was faint, labored. That moment changed me. Her struggle, her fight for every breath, etched itself into my soul. It made me realize just how precious life is. And how quickly it can be taken from us.

As I crouched beside her, whispering prayers into the chaos, I made a vow:

When I make it through this, I promise to live a life of meaning. I will keep going for those who no longer can. I will help others heal, step into their strength, and remember what really matters. I was spared for a reason—and I'll spend the rest of my life living up to that reason.

And I did.

Awakened by the Fire

Before that night, I was living—but not to my fullest potential. I was going through the motions, playing it small, often caught in a victim mindset. I was living but not truly living.

Something changed as I walked through that fire. I was reborn, not with more answers, but with deeper questions.

What am I really here for?
What if every scar is a symbol of purpose?

What if surviving wasn't just for me... but for everyone my message could possibly touch?

Since that night, I've devoted my life to helping others heal. To empower those who feel lost. To guide people back to themselves. And to ignite the flame of purpose inside those who are ready to remember why they're here.

Because let's be honest: you weren't born just to exist. You were born to rise.

## This Isn't Just a Shift—It's a Calling

Over the past few years, the world has gone through a massive awakening. Lockdowns, loss, isolation, and the quiet moments in between forced us all to face ourselves.

It's as if the universe hit "pause" on everything so we could finally ask:

- Am I truly living the life I'm meant to live?
- Am I fulfilled?
- Have I been hiding from my true power?

When the noise stopped, the truth spoke louder than ever.

Many of us had wished for more time, more freedom, a break from the constant grind. Then suddenly, the world gave it to us. Not as punishment, but as a divine invitation.

An invitation to grow.

To evolve.

To wake up.

## What If We're Being Called to More?

I don't believe we create tragedy. But I do believe we create meaning. And in the aftermath of pain, we have a choice.

We can shrink...

Or we can suit up and rise.

The real question isn't, "Why is this happening to me?"

It's, "How can I use what is happening to step into who I am truly meant to be?"

When we shift from victimhood to empowerment, we reclaim our lives. We step into our purpose. And we stop merely existing—we start leading.

Because here's the truth: you are a leader.

Not the kind that needs a title or applause. The kind who carries light into the darkness. Who transforms pain into purpose. Who walks boldly into the unknown with an open heart.

## Suit Up: What It Really Means

To "suit up" means to rise. To remember. To reclaim every part of yourself you've buried under fear, doubt, or trauma.

It means embracing your story—not just the shiny parts, but the messy, raw, and real ones too. Because that's where your power lives.

It means:

- Choosing growth, even when it's uncomfortable.
- Chasing joy, even when the world feels heavy.
- Showing up fully, even when you don't feel ready.

You don't have to have it all figured out. You just have to be willing.

Willing to heal.

Willing to rise.

Willing to lead.

## Stepping Into Your Highest Self

Here's what no one tells you: Becoming your highest self isn't some magical transformation. It's a daily commitment.

It's waking up each morning and choosing to be just a little braver. A little kinder. A little more aligned with your soul.

It's pushing past fear. Speaking your truth. Saying yes to the important things that scare you.

It's understanding that pain doesn't define you - it refines you.

And through every challenge, every moment of doubt, you're being sculpted into someone extraordinary.

The Power of Purpose

We all have gifts.

Some of us heal. Some lead. Some teach, write, build, inspire, create, nurture, or guide. Your gift is sacred. It was given to you for a reason, and the world needs it now more than ever.

If you've been waiting for a sign, this is it!

Your voice matters.

Your story matters.

Your purpose matters.

You are not here by accident. You were chosen for this time in history. You are the answer to someone's prayer.

Seven Ways to Suit Up in Your Own Life

Here's how to begin:

## 1. Honor Your Story

Don't hide from your past. Own it. Share it. Let it fuel your future. Your scars are sacred; they are proof you survived.

## 2. Empower Your Mindset

Shift your thoughts. From fear to empowerment . From "What if I fail?" to "I've Got This!" Speak life into your soul. We came here for a reason to LIVE.

## 3. Pursue Your Joy

What sets your soul on fire? What makes you come alive? What drives you? That's your compass. Follow it.

## 4. Take Daily Aligned Action

You don't need to see the whole path. Just take the next brave step. Momentum builds miracles.

## 5. Surround Yourself with Uplifting Souls

Find your tribe. The ones who see your light and remind you of it when you forget. Community is everything.

## 6. Lead with Love

Whatever you do, do it with love. Let kindness be your currency. Let compassion be your legacy.

## 7. Own your Greatness

You are capable of whatever you set your mind to. Know that your spirit is a powerful being who came here to impact the world. Don't allow anyone to dim your light. You came here to be great. So, own it every day.

You Are the Light the World Has Been Waiting For

This is your moment.

The world doesn't need more perfection—it needs more presence. It needs people who are done playing small. People who are willing to step up and serve. People who are ready to walk the path less traveled.

That's you.

So, take the leap. Trust the call. Honor those who came before you by living fully now. Let your life be the tribute, the testimony, the torch.

You were saved for a reason. You are here for a purpose.

It's time to suit up and show up.

You've got this!

## Shannon Leischner – A Healer Like No Other

For over 20 years, Shannon Leischner has been a guiding light for those seeking profound healing, spiritual clarity, and life transformation. As a world-renowned energy healer, psychic, and medium, Shannon comes from a long lineage of gifted spiritualists, dating back to her great-grandmother. Her innate abilities—combined with decades of experience—allow her to pinpoint the root causes of physical, emotional, and spiritual distress, unlocking pathways to deep and lasting healing.

People seek Shannon when they've tried everything else. From stage four cancer to autoimmune disorders, chronic pain, and mysterious ailments, her clients often come to her as a last resort—only to discover that true healing begins at the soul level. By identifying and clearing spiritual blockages, she has helped countless individuals experience miraculous recoveries, newfound purpose, and an unshakable sense of peace.

Shannon's journey wasn't just one of study—it was one of survival. Having overcome immense personal challenges, she intimately understands the connection between spiritual imbalance and physical health. This deep wisdom fuels her mission: to help others heal from the inside out.

Beyond her private sessions, Shannon is also a respected teacher and mentor, empowering others to harness their own healing abilities. Whether you are looking to heal yourself, develop your intuitive gifts, or reconnect with your higher purpose, she offers the tools and guidance to transform your life.

Shannon has worked with celebrities, CEOs, athletes, and everyday people who are ready to break free from suffering and embrace their highest potential. No matter your background, if you are seeking real, lasting change, Shannon is ready to help you step into the life you were meant to live.

Are you ready to heal on a level you never thought possible?

Connect with Shannon today and begin your transformation.


Shannon Leischner

FB Shannon Leischner

IG Angelicguide

Email shannonleischner@gmail.com

Text (310) 503-9380

# Three Women, One Purpose: Discovering Our Why

*By Dr. Stephanie Ellison-Keys, with Georgia Cannon-Alleyne and Lynnette Steele*

## Introduction

Sometimes, the most profound journeys begin not with a map, but with a question: What is my why?

Not just in a professional sense. Not for the roles we play aka mother, mentor, nurse, friend. But at the soul level. Why am I doing what I do? And does it even matter?

Each of us: Georgia, Lynnette, and I have wrestled with that question in silence. Life pulled us in different directions. One of us was serving people's lives in the hospital. One was rising from brokenness, still caring for her children. Another was navigating grief while coaching others through their transformations. At the time, we didn't know our paths would cross. We didn't know we were all searching for the same thing.

We were each yearning for more fulfillment that lasts and not more stuff, but more meaning overall. More alignment. More peace.

And in finding each other, we found something greater: a shared purpose. A shared why.

## Georgia's Why: Legacy Through Love and Service

When I think of Georgia Cannon-Alleyne, I think of resilience wrapped in compassion. Her story carries the steady heartbeat of a woman who's been in the trenches—who's shown up, day after day, not just in her nursing scrubs, but with a heart wide open.

Georgia shared with me how one morning changed her life. She woke up to her husband Harris in unbearable pain. As a nurse, her instincts kicked in. She rushed him to the hospital where doctors told her he might not make it through surgery due to a dangerous intestinal blockage.

And then they asked her something no one is ever really prepared to answer:

"Do you have your affairs in order?"

She didn't.

But that didn't stop her.

In the middle of that crisis, Georgia became both the caregiver and the crisis manager. She got their will, healthcare directive, and power of attorney prepared within 45 minutes. Right there in the emergency room. And Harris survived.

That experience marked her deeply.

For most of her life, Georgia has cared for others. Long hours. Heavy decisions. She's held hands, calmed fears, and stood in the gap. But she also had to face a hard truth: she had been pouring into others without ever making space to care for herself.

So, she asked herself a question that every caregiver eventually faces: Who takes care of the caregiver?

That question became her turning point.

Georgia began to redefine what legacy really means. It's not just what you leave behind—it's what you build while you're still here. She wanted to build a life of joy, rest, and wholeness. A life that would take care of her, even when she could no longer take care of others.

Now, she supports women, mentors families, and shares her story to help others prepare—not from a place of fear, but from

a place of love. She lives her why with grace and grit. She's no longer operating on depletion. She's giving from her overflow.

Georgia's why is rooted in service—but now, it includes herself too.

That's her why.


## Lynnette's Why: Restoring Voices and Dignity

Lynnette Steele is the kind of woman who carries quiet strength. You'd never guess the depth of her story unless she lets you in. And I'm so grateful she let me in.

After over 25 years in a mentally and emotionally abusive marriage, Lynnette made the incredibly brave decision to leave. She packed up what she could and took her three children with her, not knowing where they'd land.

They moved from hotel to hotel for three months before finally finding an apartment. And in those long nights of uncertainty, she felt it all—fear, loneliness, vulnerability. Especially financially. It was a time when she didn't feel seen or protected.

But Lynnette didn't give up. That hard season gave birth to something powerful inside of her.

Her why became about helping others reclaim their voice—the ones who feel unseen, overlooked, or unheard. She wants to be a light for the single mom fighting to keep her family together. A voice of strength for the elderly facing complicated paperwork. A beacon for the young person trying to step into adulthood alone.

But Lynnette's why is also about rewriting her own story. She's not just surviving anymore—she's healing. She's growing. She's claiming her worth.

She's found community and connection with women like Georgia and me. Together, we've laughed, cried, prayed, and rose. And every time she shares her story, another woman feels less alone.

Lynnette's why is about restoration. It's about courage. It's about dignity.

And it's beautiful.

## Stephanie's Why: Faith, Family, and Freedom

Now for me. I'm Dr. Stephanie Ellison-Keys. I'm a chaplain, transformational coach, author, speaker, humanitarian, and serial entrepreneur. But my greatest titles are still "Mommy" and "Daughter of the King."

My why began the day I held my baby girl Amanda for the last time. She lived just 16 days. And those 16 days changed everything. After her passing, something shifted in me. I wasn't just trying to live life—I was on a mission to live it fully, faithfully, and fruitfully.

I made a promise that day—not just to Amanda, but to God. I would help as many people as possible get to heaven. First, my kids. Then, everyone else He put on my path.

That became my why.

As a single mother of five, I know the weight of needing to provide and the ache of needing to be present. I needed a life that honored my calling and my children. One where I didn't have to choose between showing up for work and showing up for my kids' hearts.

I needed flexibility. I needed alignment. I needed freedom.

Freedom to be at home when one of my children needed to cry.

Freedom to lead a Bible study on a Tuesday morning.

Freedom to support women rebuilding their lives after domestic violence.

Freedom to encourage young people who've never had someone believe in them.

So I built it. Brick by brick. Step by step.

My why is rooted in faith. I believe in God's promises, and I stand on them—especially when life gets shaky.

My why is about family. Not just my biological family, but every person I'm called to serve, love, and cover. I want to build a legacy that lasts—one with joy, meaning, and miracles.

And yes, my why is about freedom. I don't want to live on autopilot. I want to live on assignment.

When I look at Georgia, I see faithfulness in action. When I look at Lynnette, I see strength wrapped in grace. When I look at the three of us together, I see purpose—and I know that none of this was by accident.

This is what happens when women live with intention.

This is what happens when we find our why.

## Conclusion

When our stories came together, it wasn't about promoting a product or a platform. It was about honoring our purpose and anchoring our lives in it.

We're three women from different places, with different paths— but a shared truth: We were made for more. And we want others to know—they are too.

So if you're reading this and wondering if your story matters, let us be the ones to say: It does.

Your voice matters.

Your healing matters.

Your why matters.

When women rise together, communities heal. Families flourish. And legacies are born.

And that... is our why.

## Dr. Stephanie Ellison-Keys, with Georgia Cannon-Alleyne and Lynnette Steele

Georgia Cannon-Alleyne, Lynnette Steele, and Dr. Stephanie Ellison-Keys are passionate advocates dedicated to empowering others through resilience, faith, and legal access. Georgia, a full-time nurse and LegalShield Associate, transformed life's unexpected challenges into a mission to help others since joining LegalShield in 2000. Lynnette, a LegalShield Associate, Certified Jafra Beauty Pro, and co-author of "The Forget Me Not Journal," brings compassion and creativity as an Activities Coordinator and advocate for personal empowerment. Dr. Stephanie Ellison-Keys, a chaplain, author, and international humanitarian, specializes in faith-based transformation and legacy-building, equipping families and women to rise in purpose and influence. Together, they inspire hope, resilience, and empowerment through their work and service.

Reach out to Dr. Stephanie Ellison-Keys via Email: drstephaniekeys@gmail.com

# Legacies on Lakeshore: A journey of Love, Service, and Inspiration

*By Stephanie Lynn Steenstra*

I have such a bright smile as I write these words to you. This is something I have wanted for a very long time, and I am forever thankful to Dr. Robbie Motter and her entire network. Thank you for uniting our voices to answer a call for remembrance, honor our great purpose, and bring forth the beautiful world we were designed for. Thank you, readers, for your time and open hearts. I hope you share this book with someone you love and remind them they are destined for great things.

Years ago, I promised my grandmother I would write a book. She read the entire Bible in a year, never skipped an instruction manual, and always read the fine print. Because she was forever informed, creative, and deeply caring, she guided me to lead with a heart of service and gratitude.

I remember her reaction when she finished reading the journal I kept while studying abroad in Spain. She beamed with pride, and I'm thankful I captured those details as a Rotary Goodwill Ambassadorial Scholar. A big reason I'm writing is to remember what truly matters. I'm always amazed by the crystal-clear memories my grandmother has of her childhood and our adventures. She even remembers more about our European travels than I do. I still laugh when she tells people that I "could fall in manure and come out smelling like a rose."

My mother had me at a very young age, and I was fortunate to meet all four maternal great-grandparents. They were loving and kind. My grandma and I are so impressed with mother's sacrifice and maturity in raising me. We grew up together, and I appreciate her deeply. She recently moved to California with me after my dad died tragically, leaving her a widow at retirement age.

During Easter 2022, 23&Me reunited me with my paternal family. I'm thankful for this brilliant group who encouraged me to write my story. What a gift that both my grandmothers are still alive as I approach my 50th birthday. They are both named Evelyn and live in Illinois. They are fighters with exceptional spirit.

My sacred "Why" weaves together love, remembrance, and gratitude to honor every generation and co-create a better world.

I'm all about building bridges, celebrating those who make a difference, and working together for a deeper purpose. I've always dreamed of a healing center and living library overlooking the lake with an infinity pool. I hope to bring together leaders, creators, artists, and students. I want to honor their stories and achievements with celebrations that feed the soul.

My vision of Legacies on Lakeshore emerged to honor artists, Veterans, and First Responders who shared their talents at Jack's on Lakeshore Drive. They all have stories to tell. Many have created nonprofits and are leading with purpose.

Following in the footsteps of my grandmother and mother, I began my service journey as a junior volunteer at Memorial Hospital. I also taught Vacation Bible School and joined my grandmother on mission trips.

Raised in church, I asked to be baptized on Easter at seven. I loved singing hymns, pretending to read music. My grandmother, a Deacon, worked weekly on dental grants for children and helped ensure they had eyeglasses, bridging doctors and the community to support their success in school.

My grandma's resilience, work ethic, and creativity inspired me and shaped my Why. I always told her she is the wind beneath my wings. She is the matriarch and rock of our family's love.

Her business card read: Evelyn's Busy Hands. I loved helping her wrap hundreds of tiny gifts for children's Advent calendars for Christmas. It was hard to open just one a day. Mine came in a bag because they were too heavy! She always met her goal of making and selling one hundred calendars each year for $5. She made gorgeous quilts, crafts, and gifts, all stitched with care. I'll never forget the hand-sewn tags: "Made with love by Evelyn." She has crocheted hundreds of hats to help patients and students in need. I love that lady with all my heart.

I'm incredibly proud to begin my journey as a Chaplain this year. My mother saw my joy when I was invited, and my grandma was the first person I wanted to tell. She immediately reminded me to stay grounded and not take on too much. She knows I can pour my heart and soul into projects and leave myself depleted.

I envision a world where universities, hospitals, and assistive technology unite to serve humanity. We deserve a society rooted in spiritual care and ethics, guided by compassion and dignity. There are plenty of med school students who can utilize what's available to everyone today to help fix care shortages, re-evaluate "add-on treatments" that worsen side effects, and help create spaces where Veterans, stressed teachers, grieving families, and the brokenhearted can heal.

The idea for this essential collaboration has been ignited by my mother who has been severely affected by these issues. We lost my father in a traumatic way last year and I believe it could have been prevented.

My mother read to me nightly and always had PBS in the background. She nurtured my love for learning and guided me to the dictionary. I loved school but missed much due to allergy-induced asthma. Humidity and seasonal changes affected my breathing. I was hospitalized and placed in an oxygen tent, which scared my family, but I loved my time there.

Thankfully, my school provided an in-home tutor in sixth grade, a pivotal moment in my life. She taught me to study, organize my thoughts, and keep a positive attitude.

Instead of PE in junior high, the library became my haven. I loved it and worked as a librarian through college. Our librarian, "The Pink Lady," always in pink, made every holiday special. Valentine's Day was a highlight as we celebrated our teachers with pink punch, cards & treats. That's where my "Parties with a Purpose" idea was born celebrating with goals and teamwork, not food & drinks. I thrived as a genuine teacher's pet and saw a perspective most students didn't.

Spanish had always been my favorite, thanks to a high school teacher who insisted I take her class over French. I'm glad she did. Her class awakened my dreams. We watched travel videos, made crafts, and cooked together. I believed I could see the world and make it better.

Scholarships didn't cover my entire private college experience. My grandmother sewed hundreds of bunny dresses and turned Renuzit bottles into adorable bunnies holding baskets. She sold them at craft fairs, bringing joy to thousands. A church member and Rotarian told her to make sure that I volunteer. It inspired a lifelong passion for service.

Throughout college, I volunteered, became President of our Kiwanis Circle K chapter, and appreciated representing our club at conventions as a delegate. I loved leadership training and motivational speeches. My capstone project focused on Service Leadership and Community Collaboration.

To teach Spanish, I needed to study abroad. I received a Rotary Ambassadorial Scholarship of $25,000 to study in Spain for a year. Representing Illinois, I gave speeches to Rotary Clubs across Spain. It was life-changing. I traveled to other countries and had the time of my life. I'm thankful to my Educational Psychology professor for her wisdom and Christian lessons like "do not cast pearls before swine."

Returning to the U.S. for student teaching was disappointing. The icy weather and metal detectors were a stark contrast to Europe. The architecture, outdoor cafés, historic universities, and quality of life explain why my daughter, Christiana, now loves living in the Netherlands.

I met her father online in a European chatroom within WBS (World Broadcasting System), later bought by Disney. He is a high-level Dutch car designer with his own company Foresee Car Design (4C): Concept, Car, Computer, Consultancy. The "4Cs" became part of my email and teaching philosophy: Create, Collaborate, Connect, Communities. The C also reminds me of Christiana, our daughter, born in 2001, before the world changed.

We married in Illinois six months after meeting online. I flew to Germany over spring break to meet him. My family was stunned and concerned, but destiny took over. I lived in Germany for a year.

I was offered a job teaching English at the University in Murcia, Spain, but chose marriage instead. I taught English at Berlitz to businesses, and I worked with him at international motor shows. We laughed when I tried VR goggles for the first time at the Amsterdam Motor Show and fell, I was stunned by the realism of concept cars racing on tracks around the world.

He always said I had a natural gift for PR. He introduced me early to design thinking and Photoshop. I'm still in awe of how he pioneered technology to bring his concepts to life. Always a visionary and an optimist, his signature tagline, "Stay Creative," continues to inspire me.

Germany never felt like home the way Spain did. We chose the California dream over Motor City. He later worked for Porsche in Huntington Beach, while I enjoyed a position with AltaVista in Irvine, editing copy for their shopping.com platform.

When Christiana was born, Hyundai offered him a senior design role back in Frankfurt. His work helped transform Hyundai's design reputation.

But my breathing suffered in Germany just like it had in Illinois. Asthma and allergies became overwhelming, and we quickly returned to California, where I could breathe more freely and feel strong again.

We were married for 11 years, I started Stephanie's Photo Magic, capturing events and teaching Photoshop and digital photography at the Community Center. I was so blessed to spend seven years with Christiana and help in her classrooms and YMCA.

One of my photography students, an attorney, hired me as his assistant. I supported him by preparing training materials for Conflict Dynamics. I helped him design trainings for social workers in conflict resolution. It was meaningful work and prepared me well for the next chapter of service.

After the 2008 financial crash, we divorced. Christiana and I moved back to Orange County, where I taught Spanish 1 and 2 online through Connections Academy and later called California Online Public Schools. I served as Adviser for the National Honor Society, mentoring high-achieving students in service leadership. Our goal was one hundred hours of community

service per student, a perfect complement to the online learning model. Helping them connect with the real world was priceless.

One of our standout projects involved working with veterans at VA hospitals. The students created a website that became a central hub for assistive technology resources. It was a powerful example of how young people can make a real and lasting impact.

I also received extensive training in TPRS: Teaching Proficiency through Reading and Storytelling. I believe stories are sacred. They carry power and potential, and they breathe life into the 4C mission: Create, Collaborate, Connect Communities. Earning my Master's degree in Educational Technology gave me the chance to study abroad in Guadalajara, Mexico.

It was alive with color, music, art, history, and architecture. The round pyramids fascinated me, and the healing resorts whispered ancient wisdom. I'll forever be grateful to Cal State Fullerton for their vision in promoting global learning. We experienced true project-based education. We used the internet during exams, and grades were earned through collaboration and creative expression. It was education as it was always meant to be, not memorizing for the test, and forgetting it the next day, rather building something meaningful together.

When 2020 arrived, everything changed. Online education lost its soul. The service-learning projects vanished. Campus tours, field trips, and all the things that made our school so special was stripped away. Students were never meant to be confined to a desk. They were meant to experience life together.

That same year, a longtime employer and honored USMC Gulf War veteran purchased a lakeside BBQ shack in March of 2020. It was a bold move at a difficult time. But with full-hearted commitment, he transformed it into a thriving destination with his son. I joined him in 2021 and got to witness the impact that discipline, routine, and vision can create.

I had the opportunity to lead social media efforts and manage many aspects of administration for the small business. (That needs a lot of reform.) His generosity toward Veterans, First Responders, and Faith Baptist Church, combined with his natural flair for design, helped build something truly legendary.

With live music, excellent food and service, and breathtaking views, the venue became the hot spot. I've had the opportunity to watch his gifted son step into his natural leadership roles. I have had the honor of mentoring him as his learning coach, advisor, and personal paparazzi, I'm excited to see what's next because I know they are destined for greatness.

Together, they created a destination that now overlooks beautiful Lake Elsinore. The city made major investments to clean and revitalize the lake, and the results are stunning. With six firepits and thirty-two picnic tables, the beach has become a place to celebrate life and gather in joy. Watching the community come together fills my heart with gratitude.

I've always dreamed of true freedom. To live and work where I want, with the people I love, doing something that matters. I believe technology holds the key to expanding that freedom, and I want to help build the bridge between where we are and what's possible. Health is a vital piece of that. Without it, there is no freedom & without the remembrance of purpose we can lose our way.

This chapter is lovingly dedicated to my extraordinary family and friends.

To my beloved aunties, thank you for your strength, your commitment to family, and your unconditional love.

To my tough-as-nails, soft-as-a-bunny grandmother: You are the pillar of our legacy. Your devotion to your family, bringing joy, and your example of service and creativity shaped my life's path. I wouldn't have found this circle of kindred souls without you.

To my beautiful mother, the master gardener who can bring flowers and plants back to life: You gave me roots that reach deep into the Earth and a deep appreciation for animals and the environment. I've enjoyed going to estate sales together and having you there to remind me when I forget. Thank you for helping me not cry over spilled milk. I still see your young face reading to me at the edge of my bed, helping me bring stories to life and guiding me to the dictionary to discover more.

To my radiant daughter, Christiana: Watching you thrive in the Netherlands, "living your best life" is my greatest joy. Though I miss you deeply, I know you are exactly where you are meant to be, sharing your art, talents, wisdom, and humor with the world.

To the loyal, strong, and generous men in my life: Thank you for your steadfast love and protection. Your presence has given me courage, and your heart has given me peace.

To my dear co-authors: This journey has been a divine gathering of souls. Your voices are so important, and your courage inspires me. Let's keep designing a better tomorrow together.

May you live a great story.

## Stephanie Lynn Steenstra

Stephanie Lynn Steenstra is an ambassador, educator, designer, and visionary. She aspires to build bridges and inspire lasting legacies through creative collaboration, universal design, and assistive technologies. A proud mother and unwavering optimist, she finds joy in purposeful travel and rejuvenating spa days.

Through community engagement, she seeks to connect leaders across generations, fostering a culture of service, leadership, and mindful living. Stephanie envisions a new era where legacy, healing, harmony, and a higher purpose unite to create a better world.

Social media

www.legaciesonlakeshore.com

www.facebook.com/steph4c

www.instagram.com/joyful4c

https://www.tiktok.com/@joyful4c

www.pinterest.com/steph4c

https://www.linkedin.com/in/steph4c/

https://www.youtube.com/@joyful4c

www.x.com/joyful4c

# What's My Why?

*By Sue Phillips*

Everyone has a "Why." The burning reason that keeps them going, even when the odds feel insurmountable. It's the heartbeat behind the hustle, the fire behind the dream. For some, their Why is hidden deep within, waiting to be discovered. For others, it's always been clear as day.

For me, my Why has always been rooted in **passion, purpose, persistence, perseverance** and perhaps surprisingly—**perfume**.

### The Scent of a Dream

Fragrance is more than a luxury. It's a language. A whisper of who we are, who we've been, and who we want to become. I've always believed that scent carries memory, emotion, and identity—three things I've held onto as I've chased my dreams.

I created my fragrance company not just to make people smell good, but to make them feel something. I wanted to bottle confidence, inspiration, and beauty in a way that touched people's lives. Every drop is a chapter in a story—my story, your story, **our story.**

Perfume is powerful. It lingers. And so do dreams when they're born of passion and persistence.

### From Stage Lights to Scents

Before there were bottles, there were scripts. My love for acting runs just as deep as my love for fragrance. Acting allowed me to step into different lives, to feel the pulse of humanity, and to understand emotion on a profound level. It trained me to listen, to feel, to observe, and most importantly, to **persist**.

Every audition taught me patience. Every rejection taught me resilience. Every performance reminded me why I started. That same fire that drove me to memorize monologues and rehearse scenes under flickering lights is the same fire that burns in my fragrance studio today.

Acting **showed me who I was. Perfume gave me the courage to share it with the world.**

## The Birth of My Why

So, what is my Why?

**My Why is to inspire.**

To remind others that no dream is too far, no story too small, no passion too peculiar.

I want to be the voice that whispers to someone when they're ready to give up: *"Don't. Not yet."*

I want to create moments—through scent, story, and soul—that make people feel seen, heard, valued.

**I believe in creating beauty with purpose.**

Every fragrance I launch carries a piece of my journey, and every bottle is a message:

**You matter. Your story matters. Your Why matters.**

## Passion: The Spark

When you're passionate about something, it's not work. It's joy! . It's a way of showing gratitude for the life you've been given.

My passion is fragrance and expression. It's creating something out of nothing and knowing that it has the power to shift someone's entire day. It's telling stories through scent. It's watching someone inhale one of my creations and say, "This reminds me of..." and knowing I've sparked a memory, a dream, a feeling.

I chase that moment. I live for that moment.

## Purpose: The Anchor

Passion can ignite you, but purpose grounds you. Purpose gives your path direction. It's not enough to love what you do—you must know why you're doing it.

My purpose is to create legacy through artistry. To help others discover their strength, creativity, and resilience. To remind them they are worth fighting for, even when life gets hard. Especially when life gets hard.

Every bottle I design, every note I choose, is an extension of that purpose. My perfumes are love letters to the world, to dreamers, to believers.

## Persistence: The Engine

Here's the truth no one tells you about chasing a dream:

It will test you.

There will be days you want to quit. Days when the world feels like it's shouting "No!" louder than your soul can say "Yes."

But this is where your Why becomes your power.

I have failed. I have cried. I have heard "not yet" more times than I can count. But I have never given up.

## Why?

Because I owe it to myself.

Because I owe it to that little girl who believed she could fly if she just ran fast enough.

Because I owe it to every person who might see my story and finally believe in their own.

Persistence doesn't mean never falling. It means always rising.

## Perfume: The Soul of My Story

Perfume is the soul I leave behind. A legacy you can feel with every breath.

Each fragrance I craft tells a tale:

- One of heartbreak and healing.
- One of dreams deferred and then delivered.
- One of boldness and vulnerability intertwined.
  - One that creates memories and reminds us of loved ones alive and those who have passed; our first kiss, our significant other and beautiful (and maybe sad) childhood memories.

It's not just about smelling good—it's about feeling good. Feeling powerful. Feeling unforgettable.

When you receive a compliment about the fragrance you wear it lifts your spirit it makes you stand up taller, smile more widely, and generates supreme happiness and confidence.

Perfume gave me a platform. It gave my creativity a canvas. It gave my voice a vessel.

## Acting and Advocacy

As an actor, I step into other people's shoes. As an entrepreneur, I invite people to step into mine.

I've learned that art—whether on screen or in scent—is about connection. It's about making people feel. It's about stirring something in the soul that says, *"I'm not alone."*

That's why I fuse acting and perfume together. Because both are storytelling. Both are art. Both are deeply, intrinsically human.

## Sharing the Light

The world needs more dreamers.

But more than that, the world needs more doers.

People who don't just wish, but work.

People who don't just survive but thrive.

If I can be a light for even one person—to inspire them to keep going, to find their Why, to believe in their own voice—then every sleepless night, every rejection, every sacrifice has been worth it.

You don't need to have it all figured out. You just need to know why you're starting.

## So, What's Your Why?

Maybe your Why is your children.

Maybe it's freedom.

Maybe it's art.

Maybe it's healing, or hope, or proving that your scars made you stronger.

Whatever it is—**find it.**

And once you find it, **honor it.**

Let it guide you when the road gets dark. Let it remind you who you are when the world forgets.

**Because your Why is your foundation.**

And when the storm comes—and it will—it will be the reason you stand.

## Final Words

My Why is perfume.

My Why is acting.

My Why is inspiring you to chase your dreams, even when they feel a thousand miles away.

I'm here to remind you that you are **powerful, beautiful, and full of potential.**

You are a masterpiece in progress.

And your Why is waiting for you to embrace it.

So, inhale deeply.

Sniff constantly.

Exhale fear.

And take the next step.

Remember ...**Perfume is the signature of your soul.**

## Sue Phillips

Sue Phillips is a globally recognized fragrance expert and Scentrepreneur (TM), celebrated for her innovative contributions to the perfume industry and her bespoke scent experiences.

Born in Johannesburg, South Africa, Sue Phillips initially pursued a career in theater before transitioning into the fragrance world. Her journey began at Elizabeth Arden as National Training Director, Lancôme as Marketing Director, eventually leading her to Tiffany & Co., where she served as Vice President of Marketing. At Tiffany, she developed and launched the company's first fragrances: TIFFANY and TIFFANY for Men .

In 1990, Phillips founded Scenterprises Inc., a fragrance consultancy that has crafted scents for prestigious brands like Burberry, Avon, and Trish McEvoy and Lancaster. Her expertise has also attracted a celebrity clientele, including Jamie Foxx, Katie Holmes, Zendaya, Susan Sarandon, and Laurence Fishburne .

Phillips is the author of The Power of Perfume: How to Choose It, Wear It & Enjoy It!, a book that delves into the art and science of fragrance, offering readers insights into selecting and wearing scents that reflect their individuality .

Beyond her work in perfumery, Phillips has contributed to academia as an Adjunct Professor at the Fashion Institute of Technology, where she taught Cosmetics and Fragrance Marketing . She is also known for her philanthropic efforts, particularly in raising awareness and funds for Alzheimer's research, inspired by her mother's battle with the disease. And she has helped over 250 people regain the sense of smell from Covid Anosmia.

Today, Sue Phillips continues to innovate in the fragrance industry through her New York-based atelier, offering personalized scent experiences that empower individuals to express their unique identities through custom-made perfumes, and she still continues to act with theatre groups and has appeared in several Off-Broadway productions. Passion, Purpose, Persistence Perseverance & Perfumes are words she lives by!

CONTACT:

Sue Phillips

Info@suephillips.com

917-449-1134

www.suephillips.com

Instagram:

@scentfullysue

@suephillipsfragrance

@Scenterprises

@therealSuePhillips

Hashtags:

#thefirstladyofScent

#FragranceQueen

#thefirstladyoffragrance

# My Big Why: A Passion for Uplifting and Healing Others

*By Dr. Susie Mierzwik (h.c.)*

From the very beginning of my life, I have been drawn to transformation—watching it, facilitating it, and ultimately experiencing it myself. There is nothing more fulfilling than witnessing someone step into their full potential. Whether it is a young child grasping the magic of reading for the first time, or an adult breaking free from years of pain and limitation; Transformation is my passion, my purpose, and my life's mission.

My early career as a kindergarten teacher was where I first saw the power of transformation in action. I had the privilege of nurturing my "embryonic student chicks" into confident learners capable of reading and writing. Seeing the spark of understanding in their eyes, watching them grow, and knowing I played a role in shaping their futures filled my heart with purpose. I realized then that my true calling was to nurture, guide, and empower others to reach their full potential.

But my journey didn't stop in the classroom. In 2009, an unexpected encounter led me to another level of transformation—this time, my own healing. A former student's mother noticed the painful swelling in my hands and introduced me to a drug-free wellness solution. At the time, I had spent decades relying on medications that never ever alleviated my suffering. Skeptical but desperate, I tried the technology. Within weeks, the swelling and chronic pain that had burdened me for years disappeared! It was as if I had been given a second chance at life, and I knew I had to share this gift with others. Then, the following month, my body was free from the chronic allergies that had plagued me for decades.

Now my heart and soul were on fire with the opportunity to change the lives of others, who were open to the possibility of relief and healthy living.

From that moment forward, my purpose became clear: to help others find healing, renewal, and vitality—without dependence on medication. The secret was a signal of light, called "PHOTOTHERAPY" that created positive changes in the brain and body. My husband and I started setting up a booth at street fairs and farmers markets, so that we could demonstrate the incredible potential of this twenty-first century technology. The joy of seeing people experience relief, sometimes within minutes, was indescribable. What started as a simple act of sharing grew into a mission to empower others to reclaim their health and live fully beyond what pharmaceuticals could ever do.

As new wellness innovations emerged, including stem cell regeneration technology, I witnessed countless people regain their strength, energy, and hope. I became devoted to not just relieving pain but inspiring transformation. Health is more than the absence of illness—it is the ability to live life vibrantly, with joy and purpose.

## Stories of Transformation

Every day, I am reminded why this mission is so important. I have been privileged to witness incredible transformations. Here are just a few examples:

- **Ray's mother**, once struggling in assisted living after a stroke, regained her strength and moved back home to reclaim her independence after using this solution.
- **Carol**, after years of battling severe pain caused by medications, found relief and freedom through these

phototherapy patches.

- **Annie**, a teacher recovering from cancer and chemotherapy, regained the stamina to return to the classroom and the following year welcomed a healthy baby girl into the world.

- **Josephine**, debilitated by years of chronic pain and fatigue, discovered renewed energy and a pain-free life using the phototherapy patches.

- **Bonnie**, once reliant on a CPAP machine, finally experienced deep, restful sleep with the help of the phototherapy products..

These stories—and so many others—fuel my passion. Each time I see someone regain their quality of life; it reaffirms my purpose. Healing is not just about alleviating physical pain; it is about restoring hope, empowering people, and helping them rediscover their potential.

## The IOU's of Transformation

My calling to uplift others extends beyond physical healing. It took a journey of self-discovery and transformation for me to fully embrace my mission. Along the way, I developed three essential guiding principles—my IOU's of transformation:

1. **Look In** – True transformation starts from within. I examined my past, confronted my emotional wounds, and committed to deep personal healing. I recognized the patterns that had kept me small and unfulfilled and took deliberate steps to change them.

2. **Look Out** – Growth does not happen in isolation. I sought support, knowledge, and opportunities to evolve. I pursued therapy, studied personal empowerment, and embraced lifelong learning to become the person I was meant to be.

3. **Look Up** – Faith has always been my foundation. In my most desperate moments, I turned to God for strength. Trusting that there was a greater plan for my life allowed me to move forward with confidence and purpose.

Through this transformation, I found my voice. I let go of fear, embraced my purpose, and committed my life to uplifting and healing others. My mission expanded beyond physical wellness—I wanted to help people break free from limiting beliefs, overcome adversity, and step into the fullness of their potential.

## A Life of Purpose and Service

Healing, in its truest form, is about more than just the body; it is about the mind, the heart, and the soul. My journey has shown me that when we heal ourselves, we create ripples that touch the lives of those around us.

Through my contributions to thirteen anthologies and my bestselling book, *SOW in TEARS, REAP in JOY*, I show my readers that wherever we find ourselves in life, healing, changing, and new possibilities are always present. But we must keep our own eyes and souls open to the miracles that are possible.

This is why I dedicate myself to service—not only through my healing practice but also through philanthropy and mentoring. I support charities like Samaritan's Purse, Compassion International, and Feeding the Hungry because I believe that true fulfillment comes from giving to others.

I also share my experiences with those who feel trapped in pain, whether physical or emotional. I teach them that healing is possible, that life can be rich and joyful again. My goal is to uplift, inspire, and guide others toward a life of vitality, resilience, and purpose.

## Embracing the Journey

Life is a continuous process of growth and transformation. I have learned that challenges are not meant to break us; they are opportunities to rise. We all face setbacks, pain, and loss, but we also have the power to choose how we respond.

Some people retreat into suffering, resigning themselves to a life of limitation. But I believe in a different path—the path of courage, perseverance, and faith. My mission is to help others see that they are not victims of their circumstances; they are capable of rewriting their stories.

If I have learned one thing on this journey, it is that healing and uplifting others is not just my passion—it is my life's calling. Every person I help, every life I touch, brings me closer to fulfilling that purpose. And so, I continue forward, sharing my knowledge, my experience, and my heart, with the hope that others will find the strength to heal and embrace the vibrant, joyful life they deserve.

Because healing is not just about eliminating pain—it is about reclaiming the power to live fully, with passion, love, and purpose.

## Dr. Susie Mierzwik (h.c.)

Since 2009 Dr Susie (hc) has helped her clients restore their health to a pain-free state, using phototherapy light patches that signal the body to create balance while removing toxins and inflammation. She is the bestselling author of Sow in Tears, Reap in Joy, A Transformational Journey. She also collaborated on thirteen other bestselling books, including The Impact of

One Voice Vol 1 and 2, It's All About Showing Up Vol 2 and 3, Maintain a Solid Mental Health and others. She retired from education after 26 years in the classroom. She has received numerous awards for her work and community service including Teacher of the Year in 2000, SIMA Global Award and her honorary doctorate in 2022. She is currently the co-director of the GSFE Virtual Network.

Dr Susie's clients are worldwide, and she is a frequent speaker on podcasts. Her topics include how to restore your life after traumatic events as well as the health benefits of phototherapy and stem cell regeneration.

Facebook https://facebook/SusanEMierzwik LinkedIn https://www.linkedin.com/in/SusieMierzwik

Since 2009 Dr Susie (hc) has helped her clients restore their health to a pain-free state, using phototherapy light patches that signal the body to create balance while removing toxins and inflammation. She is the bestselling author of Sow in Tears, Reap in Joy, A Transformational Journey. She also collaborated on thirteen other bestselling books, including The Impact of One Voice Vol 1 and 2, It's All About Showing Up Vol 2 and 3, Maintain a Solid Mental Health and others. She retired from education after 26 years in the classroom. She has received numerous awards for her work and community service including Teacher of the Year in 2000, SIMA Global Award and her honorary doctorate in 2022. She is currently the co-director of the GSFE Virtual Network.

Dr Susie's clients are worldwide, and she is a frequent speaker on podcasts. Her topics include how to restore your life after traumatic events as well as the health benefits of phototherapy and stem cell regeneration.

Facebook https://facebook/SusanEMierzwik

LinkedIn https://www.linkedin.com/in/SusieMierzwik

Instagram https://Instagram.com/SusieMierzwik

Website https://susiemierzwik.com

# What Is My Why?

*By Tonya Holley-Powell*

As I pondered this question—What is my why?—you'd think I could answer it in a heartbeat. But truth be told, I had to pray and reflect deeply.

I believe my "why" is to be a blessing to others by sharing my story, my testimony—how God covered me, pulled me out of the darkness, rescued me from the flames of fire... and I don't even smell like smoke! Praise God!!

That fire I walked through, it didn't consume me—it prepared me.

You see, my story might sound familiar to some, and foreign to others. But let's recap, shall we?

I was molested by a close family member at a very young age. No one believed me—or should I say, it was brushed under the rug, as happens in so many households. In turn, I became angry. I rebelled. I felt unloved. I felt like a black sheep.

Fast forward: I became addicted to drugs. I was running the streets, looking for love in all the wrong places. That behavior led me in and out of prison, drug programs, and into the pain of temporarily losing my children—and the connection with my family.

In 2010, I served what would become my final sentence behind bars. After 20 years of playing in the devil's playground, I was tired. Tired of being sick and tired. Exhausted of being whooped on by the demonic forces of the streets.

I remember sitting in my prison cell, asking God to please forgive me one more time. I begged Him to help me be a better person—not for the judge, the social worker, my parents, or even my kids. This time, I wanted to be better for Him.

Before, I was always trying to stay clean for someone else. But this time, I asked God to give me one more shot at this thing called sober life—so I could be used by Him. I promised that if He did, I would give it everything I had to keep my word.

Well... God did just that. He gave me another shot at life—the life He intended for me all along. A life with purpose. A life filled with love and happiness.

And I kept my word.

I've never looked back. I've let God lead and guide my every step and decision. And when I say God is faithful, loving, and kind—that's exactly what I mean!

As it says in Jeremiah 29:11 (NIV), "For I know the plans I have for you," declares the Lord, "plans to prosper you and not to harm you, plans to give you hope and a future."

That scripture is my anchor. My life is living proof that He does have a plan—and it's bigger and better than anything I could've imagined.

## Called to Give Hope

Part of my "why" is this: I am called to speak to troubled teens, to women in the prison system, in drug rehabilitation centers, and in the foster care system—to give them hope. Real, living, breathing hope.

Because if I can do it, they can too.

I know what it's like to feel lost, abandoned, misunderstood, and discarded by the world. I know what it's like to be shackled—whether by addiction, shame, trauma, or just life itself. But I also know what it's like to be set free. And not just physically free—but spiritually, emotionally, and mentally free.

That freedom came when I put God first.

It didn't come from a program or a judge's leniency or even the love of another person—it came from surrendering to God. That's where the healing began. That's where my restoration came from. That's where my true identity was revealed.

So now, it's my mission—my divine assignment—to pour into those who are still in the middle of the fire. To be a voice that says, "You are not alone. You are not beyond saving. You are not too far gone."

God is still in the business of redeeming lives—and I am living proof of that.

## The Power of Forgiveness

I can't tell my story without talking about my four beautiful adult children. Through all the ups and downs, all the chaos and heartbreak, they have been there—even when I didn't deserve it. During the years I was missing in action—in and out of their lives—they were angry with me, and they had every reason to be. I had caused a lot of pain.

Even after I got clean and sober, for years they still held guilt and hurt over my head like a weight. That kind of pain doesn't just disappear overnight. Healing takes time. Restoration takes time.

But God's grace and mercy... they're real. And they are powerful.

Through countless prayers and hard conversations, God has been softening hearts—mine and theirs. Today, our relationships are so much better. So much stronger. We're not perfect, but we are healing. Together.

I continue to pray for each of them—that their hearts be unhardened and unburdened. That forgiveness flows freely in every direction. That we can love each other unconditionally, the way God loves us. That we grow stronger together as a family because forgiveness is not just powerful for me—but for them, too.

God knows I love each and every one of them—with my whole heart.

## For So Many Years...

For so many years, I ran on self-will. I was chasing, chasing, chasing Jason-the nightmare—as they say—chasing the material things, A fast life in a slow lane.

I remember my dad telling me, "If you're tired of that merry-go-round, get off and find another ride. That one's not working for you."

And dad was right. May his soul rest in peace. Great dad he was!

And that's when I started searching for God's ride—one that wouldn't break down on me.

Today, I just want to be in God's presence. I want to know His purpose for my life. That means more to me than anything money could buy. Thinking I could do it my way, thinking I could fix it all myself—it never worked. I always hit a brick wall.

But once I surrendered—once I let God have His way—that's when it all started to change.

Yes, I'm grateful for the blessings I have today, but now I pray,

"God, what do You want me to do? What do You want me to have? How do You want me to move?" So, I stay prayed up.

## When God Sent My Husband

Quick testimony: When I purchased my first truck, I remember so many nights out there on the road alone. I was scared. I didn't know the trucking industry like that. One night on Interstate 40, I was crying out to God, "Father, I need a husband. I'm ready for a helpmate."

When I tell you God put him right in my lap—He literally did.

I met my husband on a dating site I rarely even used. He messaged me. Weeks passed before I replied. But when I finally did, I found out he was a truck driver, looking for a new opportunity.

I offered him a salary. He flew out. The rest is history.

He proposed to me at a rest area in Kentucky, and we've been together ever since. God did that!

My husband is a God-fearing, loyal, loving, respectful man. He's not perfect. Neither am I. But he has taught me so much about God, the Bible, and life. I surrender him to God daily, along with myself, my family, my business, and all aspects of my life.

And God keeps working it out.

## My Life Today

Today, I am happily married. I'm a business owner of a successful trucking company. I'm a homeowner. I'm a proud grandmother of twelve beautiful grandchildren and five bonus grandchildren—can you say a village?

God has also blessed me with amazing friends who have become like family. We pour into each other with love, encouragement, and grace.

He's given me vision after vision. One of those is to open a group home or senior care facility, where I can minister to others and pour into them what God poured into me.

I asked God: "If this is Your will, open the doors and the windows of Heaven. Make it possible for us to reach people through this testimony and build something that glorifies You." And I believe He will.

So, this is "MY WHY" I must give back for all the blessings that God has given me! I must keep going! He freed me from bondage, and I believe I must help others do the same through God's power within me. God loves me and has equipped me with what I need to be a blessing to others.

## Call to Action: Let's Connect

If my story touched you—if it gave you hope, clarity, or a sense of purpose—I want to hear from you. I believe in community, in building each other up, and in supporting one another on this journey called life.

Let's connect. Let's build. Let's walk in purpose together.

To support my vision, collaborate, or just say hello, reach out to me:

Email: HolleyTonya86@yahoo.com

Facebook: Tonya Holley-Powell

Instagram: tonya.holley.35

There is no pit too deep, no past too messy, and no heart too broken that God cannot heal.

Together, we can be a light in someone else's darkness.

With The Love of God,

Tonya

## Tonya Holley-Powell

Tonya Holley is a seasoned professional driver with over 30 years of experience in the transportation industry, including operating commercial trucks and buses across North America. She is the proud founder and owner of Fruits of Labor Trucking LLC, where she combines her commitment to safety, excellence, and service with a deep sense of purpose. Beyond the road, Tonya is a devoted wife, mother of four, and grandmother to seventeen. Her inspiring journey from addiction and incarceration to entrepreneurship and spiritual transformation has made her a powerful advocate for women in recovery, incarcerated mothers, and families seeking restoration. After surrendering her life to God in 2010, she has used her story as a message of hope, redemption, and healing. Tonya is passionate about mentoring women, speaking to at-risk youth, and pouring into underserved communities. She dreams of expanding her impact through faith-led outreach and long-term care services. Whether behind the wheel or behind the microphone, Tonya leads with integrity, authenticity, and a heart full of compassion.

Contact: HolleyTonya86@yahoo.com

(323) 326-7778 Palmdale, CA

Facebook: Tonya Holley-Powell

IG: tonya.holley.35

HH AMB. DR.
# WINFRED GITONGA

# Chronicles of a Village Girl from Mathakwaini Village
## A Journey of Resilience and Purpose
*By HH Amb. Dr. Winfred Wanjiku Gitonga*

I was born and raised in Mathakwaini village of Tetu Division, Nyeri County of Kenya. At the time of my birth, we lived in communal villages where every family had a mud grass thatched hut. Growing up in the villages involved being immersed into a deep connection of communal bonds and harmony. Village life was not just lived but shared. Neighbors were close knit extended family members who celebrated joys together with echoes of laughter. The unwritten village system was sharing and reciprocity.

Every child born belonged to the community. There is a proverb that says, "It takes a village to raise a child." Elders had a right to discipline, correct, admonish, and teach children good manners, morals, and respect to elders. This included teaching practical skills related to household chores. Boys were taught to graze cattle and hunt. Girls were taught to fetch water, gather firewood and tend the farms.

Village life had its own beauty. The evenings were full of adventure and events such as games, dance, drama, music and storytelling in the moonlight and evening bonfires.

## The Weight of a Title

My father was a scholar and had graduated as a head teacher. He later became a chief. He may have recognized that I had noticeable personality traits and qualities similar to his. I grew up as his favorite child and he didn't hide this affection. He openly showered me with praises and gifts. He had high hopes for my success and expected me to excel in life.

The villagers called me "The Chief's Daughter"—a title that sounded noble but felt like a burden. Mathakwaini village was tucked beneath the wide arms of Mount Kenya on one side and the rolling hills of the Aberdare Ranges on the other horizon. The village is where the red dust kissed our ankles and smoke curled from clay chimneys. The chief's daughter title should have meant privilege. But privilege does not fill an empty stomach or keep you warm at night.

By the time I was six, I was rising with the stars, not the sun, running barefoot to the seasonal Gatoto River before the village roosters stirred it with mud. There, amid the chaos of children jostling for muddy water, I learned my first lesson: survival does not wait for titles.

This is not just my story of survival. It is a journey of transformation—from a young girl whose worth was measured in water jugs she carried, and firewood bundles she brought home - to a woman who now measures her purpose in the lives she uplifts. This is a reminder that some of the deepest scars become the most fertile ground for purpose.

## Earth and Embers: The Making of a Fighter

I was born into a polygamous family. My father—respected, feared, and deeply traditional—had fifteen children with two wives. We were counted as blessings, but blessings that often had to do with bare minimal provisions. The misery of hand-to-mouth existence was nothing to romanticize about. It was merely a battle of survival.

Most of the time, polygamous families experience a lot of drama, confrontations, fights, verbal abuse, lots of gossip within the wives and children which create sibling rivalry and a very toxic environment for all. In our home, love was not spoken; it was endured.

Three memories shaped me:

## The Rhythm of Struggle

Before dawn, my sisters and I would dash down the river, our feet slapping the hard, cracked earth. The water was sometimes brown with mud. It didn't matter as we needed it. I learned that life demands our full effort, even for what should be basic rights.

The Silence of Shame

I was twelve when I had my first menstrual cycle. It came when I was at school. My dress turned crimson, and shame clung to me heavier than the wet cloth I stuffed into my undergarments. Boys laughed. Teachers said nothing. I stayed home for days. In our world, girls' education was an afterthought, not a priority.

## The Spark of Rebellion

My grandmother, educated and baptized "Charity Wangari," was different. She was one of the first village girls to be educated and converted by Scottish missionaries. She read her Bible aloud. Then, in quiet moments by the fireplace, she would whisper "Wanjiku," her fingers tracing scripture. She read to me the book of Genesis and the creation story and that "we are made in God's image." Exodus was a redemption story of God's grace. Her whispered truths cracked open a part of me which the world tried to bury.

Her lessons stayed with me. I began to look for opportunities to read, to speak and convert to Christianity. There was hope in this faith. I started teaching younger girls in the village about what I was learning—about womanhood, about choices and about dignity. It was then I began to find my voice.

## Illusions of Escape: My Fall from Grace

When I got a teaching job after high school, I felt the first breeze of freedom. My monthly salary—Ksh. 1,160—was little, but to me it was gold. I bought my first leather shoes, a dress with buttons, and held my head high. I thought I had escaped the village lifestyle.

But freedom is not always what it seems.

At 22, the night I discovered I was pregnant, my world unraveled and shattered. My father's response was swift and brutal. His eyes were red with fury, his lips shaking with rage. He unbuckled his leather belt and struck my back with all his strength. Blood filled my mouth as I bit my tongue. "You are dead to me," he spat. My mother was not spared and in equal measure received the same wrath and was chased away back to her own mother's home. She had failed to mentor her daughters too. I left home and sought refuge to my elder sister who lived in the city. I thought I could lean on her. She slammed her door shut and threw my belongings out.

A stranger, seeing me crying near a bus stop, offered me a bed for the night. That act of kindness lit a flicker of hope, and I proposed to pay forward in future.

And in that darkness, I discovered two truths:

- Pain is a ruthless teacher, but it carves lessons into your soul.
- The human spirit bends, but when it does not break, it becomes unshakable.

For weeks and months, I wandered—sometimes sleeping with migraine headaches and ulcers unable to eat. Sometimes l wondered what to do next - with nowhere to call home. This exile triggered a range of emotions, grief, confusion, and loss of identity. I felt lost, disoriented, and isolated. I was in a wilderness. I felt guilty. I had sinned against my father. But my baby kept growing inside of me, and so did my resolve.

I began looking for extra activities to earn me extra money to take care of my unborn child. I learned to negotiate, to persuade, to endure. Life became my classroom. I got a better paying job with an insurance company. At least I could afford to support my baby at birth.

When I gave birth to my daughter, I developed a very strong desire and purpose to safeguard and protect her from similar situations. My baby was all I had.

Banishment and isolation were significant life lessons. Amidst perceived punishment, I learned to confront difficult situations, I learnt to adapt to new environments; I learnt to develop resilience even in adversity. All these became my catalyst for growth, adaptation, change and self-discovery. It necessitated a process of self-reflection and re-discovery of my worth. I found my purpose.

## Summits and Salvation: Rising from the Ashes

Redemption did not come all at once. It came in the form of peaks climbed and valleys crossed:

## The Physical Summit (1979)

During my high school adventures, I climbed Mount Kenya. When I climbed the Mount after a long trek, I stood at Point Lenana. Frost biting my fingers and my breath stolen by altitude. I felt the African sky above and a lifetime of uncertainty below. Reaching the mountain peak evoked a range of emotions, a sense of accomplishment, awe, and gratitude. I felt a connection to something larger than myself. Mountains are not conquered in leaps, but in small steps. I had conquered a challenge of the climb. That truth became my compass of my transformative change.

## The Professional Summit (1990-1993)

Armed with years of training as an underwriter in the insurance industry for nine years, I sought to register for my own independent insurance brokerage firm. By then insurance broking firms in Kenya were a male-dominated industry. Men laughed at the idea of a female broker. I knocked on doors at dawn, pitching to shopkeepers and market women. Before I knew it, I had graduated to insuring corporate organizations, bank mortgages, finance institutions and government parastatals. While the men played golf, I built trust. By 1993, I was a self-made millionaire. But what mattered most wasn't the money—it was reclaiming my dignity. My father, once a judge who had condemned me, now called me his daughter with pride.

## The Emotional Summit

The day my father embraced me again, his calloused hands trembling on my back, is the day I understood that forgiveness doesn't erase history—it transforms it.

My elder sister continued to keep her distance, nursing old

rivalries, sowing seeds of discord whenever an opportunity presented itself. But all that mattered was that I made peace with my father and had found peace within.

After my father died, there was an escalation of family rivalry and never-ending conflicts especially fueled over inheritance disputes. I made a tough decision to surrender my inheritance rights. I chose peace and sanity rather than go through pain and agony. That was no longer my portion.

Fast forward, one of my kid sisters in conspiracy with some other family members isolated my mother from the rest of us in the name of care giving. They got her to assign property to themselves after fraudulently forging signatures to secure grant letters of administration. The administration letter had been granted to one of her sons – with a lawyer on record. All this happened when I was abroad. When I came back, I applied for the court file and an objection after establishing forgery of signatures. Hell broke loose. Once again I was banished by my mother. I had disobeyed her wishes as she had all the rights to property rights to give to whoever she wished - or so she thought.

Today I advocate for social justice and laws that violate natural as well as constitutional justice.

## The Spiritual Summit

I came to realize that the pain I endured had prepared me for the purpose I was destined to pursue. My faith deepened. I saw God's fingerprints in the strangers who helped me, in the women I mentored, the children I helped pursue education and above all, in the healing of my own heart.

## The Calling: Lifting as I Climb

I found purpose in more than personal success. Through Leaders of All Nations International (LOANI), I now endear to build ladders for others to climb. Our flagship project is styled "Centre of Excellence". It will serve as an empowerment centre including a football academy, innovation hubs, skills training, and mentorship facilities. It is proposed to be established at Paradise Lost Gardens near Nairobi, Kenya.

It's more than buildings. It's a beacon of hope. The facility will offer space for;-

- Knowledge Sharing and Transfer by global Experts
- Diaspora Partnerships and Investment to advance Innovation Hubs and Incubation Centres
- Digital Centres and Libraries – opening doors to STEM
- Training Life Skills to advance adaptation of ideas and concepts to Entrepreneurship
- Outreach programs for Dignity Kits with reusable pads and menstrual cups, so girls never miss school again;- Outreach Programs for Rainwater Harvesting Systems to end daily treks for dirty water;- Outreach Programs for Mentorship Forums, helping girls and young women find their voice and vision.

This is not charity. This is justice. This is the legacy of every grandmother who whispered truth, every mother who wept silently, and every girl still kneeling by a river.

## What Life Has Taught Me – Nuggets of Wisdom

- You are more than your circumstances. Where you come from is a starting point, not a sentence.

- Pain can birth power. Let your scars become the roadmap for others.

- Forgiveness is freedom. Not for those who hurt you, but for your own soul to breathe.

- Purpose transforms survival into service. It is not enough to rise; we must reach back and lift.

- The world may not offer you a seat at the table—build your own and bring a bench.

- Your voice matters. Even if it trembles, speak.

- Education is a sacred weapon. Arm yourself and others with it.

- Kindness is never wasted. Sometimes it's the bridge between despair and destiny.

- Never underestimate a village girl. She may grow to change the world.

## Epilogue: The Circle Remains Unbroken

When I stand before the United Nations agencies, the African Union or multinational organizations or receive honorary doctorates, I still feel the dust of Mathakwaini village beneath my feet. The pain and agony I have had to endure reminds me that true elevation isn't how high you climb, but how many hands you pull up with you.

To every girl reading this—whether you live in a hut, an apartment, or a mansion—hear me clearly:

Your current location is not your final destination. Your pain has purpose. Your story matters.

The process of finding your WHY often involves a journey. A journey of self-discovery; a deeper awareness of values that matter most. And when you find your WHY, you will ignite a fire that no wind can quench; you will experience something larger than yourself, a desire to live a life of purpose and meaning.

As for me, I embarked on a journey of learning, engagement, critical thinking, and purpose where I strive for a more just and sustainable planet.

I was born a village girl. I became the chief's daughter. I became a first in many situations. I became a woman of vision. I became a global change maker. I became a global citizen. And now, I live to empower others.

**HH Amb. Dr. (H.C) Winfred Wanjiku Gitonga**

LOANI Africa Chairperson/Board of Trustees
Co-Founder and Vice President, VisionAfric Development
+254 738013405
winfred.kenya2063@gmail.com

# Raising the Collective Vibe:
# Finding the Divine Within

*By Dr. Zulmara Maria (h.c.)*

*"We teach best what we most need to learn." Richard Bach,*
*Illusions: The Adventures of a Reluctant Messiah*

Answering the call to become a Ceremonial Priestess has been the single most important thing I have done to answer my deepest WHY, Raising the Collective Vibe. My why, my raison d'etre, my soul's purpose, is to help raise the collective vibe as I develop and influence communities to be kinder, gentler, and shine a light for themselves and others. My deepest why is to be of service to mankind by creating and holding a high frequency vibration for the collective. As I raise my own vibration, I help raise the vibrations of others and raise the planet's vibration as a whole. When your own energy is elevated, you elevate the energy of those around you, whether they consciously feel it or are aware of it or not. The more you practice expanding your energy, the more elevation and expansion you provide for the collective.

My call to become a Ceremonial Priestess came during my 2nd Saturn return in December of 2017 when I was fifty-seven and went to Peru. There, I had a transformational experience and was sent a channeled message that I was to become a ceremonial priestess and as a priestess I would be expanding my energy, my influence, and helping to raise the collective vibe. At that time, I was working on three signature programs, which have become the cornerstone of my practice in an ever-expanding cycle of positivity and thriving.

I was also guided to find guides and mentors in shamanism, crystal healing, magical practices, and celestial integrations. And these guides and mentors magically showed up–as I worked on my own healing and opening up my chakras to be able to receive divine guidance, guided messages, and expanded knowledge. As I continue expanding my energy, the more I am able to expand the energy of others, who then expand the energy of others in a never-ending cycle of expansion, healing, and raising the collective vibe.

*DIVAS\*ABRAZOS\*DIVINITY*

My logo says, DIVAS\*ABRAZOS\*DIVINITY to represent my three signature programs that make up how I live my deepest WHY–to raise the collective vibe using my gifts, talents, and abilities. These three programs have helped me to creatively unite many magical practices and healing modalities, with my talents and abilities to live my deepest why: to raise the collective vibe.

These three programs form the foundation and the core of my deeper WHY. As I keep working on expanding these offerings, I keep getting deeper and deeper into my own WHY as I find more and more ways to be of service.

## Millionaire DIVAS: Millions of DIVAS Manifesting Millions
*My object in life is to unite my avocation and vocation...*
*Robert Frost, Two Tramps in Mud Time*

My Millionaire DIVAS program is my signature money manifestation course. This program was primarily designed to help women gain financial independence, especially, when they are in untenable situations. It was born from my lived experiences with both my mother and my sister being in situations that were unimaginable, and them feeling stuck because of all the limiting beliefs about money they had been conditioned to believe and how these beliefs guided many of their life decisions. I realized that I wanted to help a Million DIVAS Manifest Millions as a way of helping women out of untenable situations.

This is the program you take when you have tried everything else, and money is still not flowing to you easily and effortlessly. In this divinely channeled program, we get to the very core of what you believe around money and how to instill different beliefs based on what you want to create. I say divinely channeled because in less than 6 hours, I had a full Millionaire DIVAS program. It was surreal. I was thinking of my next signature program and Millionaire DIVAS appeared, seemingly out of nowhere, to teach me what I needed to learn and to help me be of service to the women within my sphere of influence.

Millionaire DIVAS is a three-part program that embodies all that we know about manifesting, abundance, creating a life of our dreams, and being financially independent.

The first part of this program is BAM-BLAST-BLISS-BLESS which is a quick understanding of how money manifestation works and how our childhood conditioning keeps us in a cycle of lack, how our beliefs limit our potential, and what we need to do to break the cycle of lack and despair around money. This program makes apparent our cultural, personal, and societal conditioning around abundance.

The second part of this program is Millionaire DIVAS where we delve deeper into what we believe, how to recognize those beliefs, and how to instill the beliefs that serve our best interest and our highest good. This is where our avocation unites with our vocation, and we start finding ways to make money doing the things we love to do.

The third part of this program is Your Money Story. In this part of money development, I help people understand the money story they are living, the money story they want to live, and how to bridge that gap. We all live the money story we are telling ourselves and if you want to live a different money story, you must tell yourself a different money story first.

Millionaire DIVAS is a fast paced, fun, and engaging course that allows you to align your avocation with your vocation. Align what you are here to do in this lifetime with your way of earning a living, giving back, having fun, and making a difference.

Millionaire DIVAS help you to get an understanding of how money flows, how money gets blocked, how to unlock the blocks and how what you believe impacts what and how you manifest.

The program helped me not only with money manifestation, but also with teaching others about understanding their money stories and how those money stories are impacted by the conditioning you received from your parents, the beliefs you currently hold, and the thoughts you have regarding money. Once you understand all of this and make the changes necessary to align what you have- to what you want, you will be in quick and easy money flow. My goal is to change the collective vibe and feminine energy to help Millions of DIVAS Manifest Millions!!!

## ABRAZOS: A Hug from Your DIVINE Self

*Aspirations fuel our soul's purpose, our heart's desires, and our spirit's whims.*

*What are you aspiring to today?*

*Un abrazo,*

*Your Divine Self*

All of my life, I have been drawn to quips & quotes and anything notes. I have collected quotes, written a number of inspired poems as a part of my creative outlet, and kept quote journals. In June of 2013 as I was being guided on this journey of my deepest WHY to raise the collective vibe, I started getting downloads of ABRAZOS from your Divine Self. These hugs from your divine self are a quick, positive pick me up that make you smile, pause, nod, or breathe. They are a quick way to just get into a better feeling space, a great way to raise your own vibe, and thus raise the vibe of others.

I have written one ABRAZO a day since June of 2013 and each one has a unique message that resonates with someone. There is someone who needs to hear the message on that day and the message will come across their feed through a friend, social media, or just by chance or happenstance. When you need a quick pick me up, when you need to get into the zone, an ABRAZO is just the thing to get you there.

Within the ABRAZOS there is a special Gratitude program that is geared toward helping to improve and expand your gratitude practice. ABRAZOS of gratitude and appreciation is a special set of ABRAZOS focused primarily on gratitude designed to help individuals deepen their gratitude practice.

These ABRAZOS for Gratitude and Appreciation come with affirmations, afformations, and journaling questions in which individuals gain a deeper understanding of how gratitude, manifestations, and co-creating the life of your dreams go hand in hand with raising the collective vibe. As you vibe higher, those around you will also vibe higher to match your level of excitement, positivity, and zest for life.

In my quest to raise the collective vibe, the ABRAZOS program has been a cornerstone of my practice. ABRAZOS are filled with positivity and help individuals vibe at a higher level, which helps to raise the collective vibe. Give yourself a hug and grab an ABRAZOS book for yourself on AMAZON and join me in raising the collective vibe.

## Reclaiming Your Divinity: Honoring the DIVINE Within

*As above so below, as within so without*

*Hermes Trismegistus. A maxim from Hermeticism,*

Reclaiming Your Divinity is a wonderful and rich program that helps participants understand the divine within and claim it for their own. It is a divinely inspired program to help individuals connect with the magic of the universe, the divine within, realizing dreams, and living a life aligned with their personal goals and ambitions.

This wonderful and rich program emphasizes that how you feel within will determine how you feel without. That what lies within you is divine and worth exploring. Reclaiming Your Divinity provides opportunities for you to explore your soul's purpose, your heart's desires, and your spirit's calling as you engage in magical activities that help you to connect the person you are and the person you are meant to be.

First and foremost, the program asks you to accept that you are a divine being. You are a manifestation of the divinity and within you lies a divine self that loves you and guides you through life. This acceptance comes when you are done with, "yeah, but…" and ready to embrace, "yes, and…," because once you have embraced, "yes, and…" you are ready to say "Yes!!" to your divinity and accept that what you have to offer is uniquely you and only you can offer it. It is an opportunity to explore how fun life can be when you are not saddled with living a life that does not excite you or bring you comfort and joy. As you live a life that excites you, you will also encourage others to start living a life that excites them, creating a positive collective energy around you and those who are in your presence.

In Reclaiming Your Divinity, magical practices are infused into the program as individuals start on a journey to deepen their spiritual practices and get in touch with the true meaning of life for them, their raison d'etre, and their way of knowing and being in this world. The activities are fun and offer an opportunity to raise the collective vibe. As you reclaim the divine within, you will begin to radiate a divinity that will impact and affect all of those around you, thus raising the collective vibe just with your presence, your essence, your being.

## Deepening My Why: Oracle-Crone-Priestess

*Each of us has the power to raise or lower the collective vibration. We do this by raising our own individual vibrations. When we are loving, compassionate, and understanding, we are contributing to a more positive and harmonious world.*

*Whisper Moore*

As I transition fully into my role as an Oracle-Crone-Priestess, I will be deepening my WHY on multi-dimensional levels. I am creating a space where individuals can grow, learn, feel safe, and co-create the lives of their dreams. A space that will allow you to raise your vibration and contribute to raising the vibe of the collective.

As an oracle, I provide guidance and advice for individuals as they discover and develop their gifts. We all have gifts that are waiting to be shared and the more of us who access and share those gifts, the more we raise the collective vibe. As we discover the healer within, we are able to not only heal ourselves but help others to heal themselves as well.

The crone, defined as the third phase of the Goddess, symbolizing wisdom, and the final stages of life, represents a powerful, wise, and often transformative figure. For me, the crone state is an opportunity to live my deepest why as one who has lived this path, healed in this and in previous lifetimes, and is ready to share my wisdom, advice, knowledge, and gifts with the collective.

As a Ceremonial Priestess, I am prepared to hold sacred space for self and others. To curate beautiful experiences for transitions, for new beginnings, to preside over endings, and to help with transmutations. I am looking forward to opening a sacred space that will harness the energy of the Oracle-Crone-Priestess as I create a center to coalesce the energy and keep it flowing as we collectively raise the vibe of the planet.

The Center for Renewal, Rejuvenation, and Relaxation will be a sacred space where individuals come and raise their vibe in a number of different ways. They can receive a blessing, a cleansing, or a card reading, chakra alignment, crystal healing or just be in a sacred space that raises their vibe and offers an opportunity for self-healing, meditation, sound baths, or salt bathing. A place

to come together for drumming, prayer, healing events, retreats, and classes. It will be a space where individuals can come to shine their light for others, to be seen, be a beacon of light for their community, and feel safe as they continue on their journey.

Raising the collective vibe starts with us and begins within. It is the process of learning and understanding the gifts we have to share and honing in on those gifts so we can share them fully with our family, friends, and community. As we share our gifts, we help others feel better, find their own gifts, and spread good cheer and positivity. This good cheer and positivity creates a beautiful never-ending cycle for the collective.

My three signature programs have allowed me to live my soul's purpose and as I expand them, I expand the vibrations of the planet...and raise the consciousness and awareness of humanity toward compassion, understanding, and overall love and expansion.

Join me on this wonderful journey as I continue to live my deepest why in service to the community, the collective, and to humanity as a whole.


Con un pan y cafecito,

Seguimos adelante

Zulmara Maria

# Dr. Zulmara Maria
## Holding a Sacred Space for Your Spiritual Growth and Development

Award winning Latina, Dr. Zulmara Maria is a ceremonial priestess who holds sacred space for your financial abundance, physical healing, and healthy relationships. She is available for readings, blessings, cleansings, and ceremonies. Dr. Zulmara hosts wellness events, retreats and private parties for groups and individuals. She will do blessings and cleansings of home and workspaces that are specifically cultivated for you and your needs.

In 2003, Dr. Zulmara Maria founded Roots and Wings and started offering personal, professional, and spiritual growth programs to help individuals find their voice, their strength, their identity, and their purpose in life. Her inspiring workshops focus on achieving dreams, celebrating humankind, healing the collective, developing as self-actualized individuals, and living a purpose informed life.

Dr. Zulmara Maria is currently the Director of the Long Beach Chapter of the Global Society of Female Entrepreneurs (GSFE), past-president of the Long Beach Holistic Chamber of Commerce, certified leader for Infinite Possibilities, co-founder of the RiseUp Leadership Series, founder of Latina Gratitude Month, and a featured author in Chicken Soup for the Latino Soul. She has authored three signature programs: Millionaire DIVAS, ABRAZOS of Gratitude and Appreciation, and Reclaiming Your Divinity.

She has been recognized and honored as a Woman of Distinction from CA Assembly District 70, Woman of Distinction from CA

Senatorial District 33, received the Latina of Influence recognition, and honored as a Ms. Long Beach Women of Achievement. She has been featured in VoyageLA as a person to watch.

She specializes in helping others reach peak performance spiritually, professionally, and personally as they cultivate gratitude and appreciation in their lives.

Zulmara Maria is an Educator, Inspirational Speaker, Author, Blogger, and Entrepreneur--Inspiring women to soar while being grounded in their ancestral roots. As the Founder at Roots and Wings, Dr. Zulmara Maria endeavors to inspire others to grow personally, professionally, and spiritually for peak performance.

Zulmara Maria can be contacted at: zulmaramaria@gmail.com or through her website at http://zulmarmaria.com

**Zulmara Maria can also be found at:**
- Amazon: Zulmara Maria Teixeira de Lima
- Facebook: http://facebook.com/zulmaramaria
- Instagram: https://www.instagram.com/zulmara.maria/
- LinkedIn: http://linkedin.com/zulmaramaria

## Testimonials

### A Heartfelt Journey to Purpose and Clarity

"What's Your Why? Unlock Your Desired Life by Finding Clarity" is an inspiring and heartfelt anthology that guides you on a journey to intentional living. The diverse stories evoke a full range of emotions and remind us that we are never alone in our pursuit of purpose. You may see yourself in many of the chapters, finding echoes of your own experiences and dreams. With each story, you'll find encouragement and practical insights to help you clarify your vision and live your life to the fullest. A must-read for anyone ready to embrace their true potential!

--Amb. Rev. Dr. Christine Park, DD (h.c). is an international and US bestselling author, speaker, pastor, and Director of GSFE Menifee Network. Email: menifeegsfe@gmail.com

## Supporting Women and Finding My Own Why

As a man reading "What's Your Why?" I found it to be a powerful collection of stories that truly resonated. The chapter with a male perspective offered valuable insights into understanding purpose and supporting the women in our lives—mothers, daughters, sisters, wives, and granddaughters. This book is a must-have for anyone looking to strengthen those relationships and encourage intentional living. Whether you're seeking your own clarity or looking to uplift the women around you, this anthology is a compelling and inspiring read.

--Randy Grove is an American Hazmat driver who encourages and supports the women in his life.

## A Life-Changing Masterpiece

"What's Your Why?" is more than a book — it's a life mirror. Each story offers a window into the soul of purpose, guiding readers to reflect, refocus, and reignite their own passions. I walked away feeling deeply inspired and ready to make clearer, more intentional choices. This is a must-read for anyone seeking to live a purpose-driven life.

— Ambassador Jean Olexa, Professional Organizer and Youth Advocate, USA  Email:gigi8247@gmail.com, 858-357-7295

## A Global Movement of Purpose

Lady Amb Dr. Robbie Motter and her co-authors have once again created a timeless masterpiece. With fifty-three voices united, this book reminds us that when women come together not to compete, but to complete, mountains move. "What's Your Why?" is not just a title — it's a global call to action.

— Ambassador Nicole Fournier Farrell, Singer, DJ and #1 Award Winning Author, nicolefarrell123@hotmail.com, 760-807-4300

## A Guiding Light for Generations

Whether you're at a crossroads or simply seeking clarity, this anthology will be your lighthouse. It gently pushes you to ask the hard questions and provides stories that spark courage. "What's Your Why?" isn't just a book — it's an experience that stays with you.

— Amb. Dr. Violet Williams, Professional Speaker, Transformational Coach, Award Winning Author, Chaplain and Show host. yourbestspirit@gmail.com, 951-691-6517

## A Legacy of Impact

This historic book launch in Africa marks a powerful turning point. "What's Your Why?" offers transformative wisdom and soulful insight. Each chapter is a reminder that intentional living is within reach, and that your 'why' has the power to change the world.

— Ambassador Dr. Cheri Reynolds, Solar Pro, and Award-Winning best-selling Author cherisenergysolutions@gmail.com, 909-238-6790

## Uplifting With Grace

"Knowing our 'Why' is the foundation of how we serve, how we lead, and how we show up for others with love and grace. This book serves as the guiding force behind every step we take as women entrepreneurs. I am deeply grateful to be part of the Global Society of Female Entrepreneurs, a beautiful community that not only uplifts women but empowers us to thrive, honor our purpose, and serve the world with passion and heart."

Amb. Briana Rice BSC. - Loveandlightmovement@gmail.com www.brianarice.com

Briana Rice

Meet Briana Rice biologist, entrepreneur, beauty queen, and disability advocate

(951) 314-5406

## Finding My Why

For much of my life, I made decisions two ways: sometimes impulsively, other times with careful planning. While neither way was necessarily wrong, I learned something powerful along the way. People who truly know their "Why" move differently. They live differently. Their decisions are not just reactions; they are guided by purpose. And with that purpose comes fulfillment, not just survival.

When you have a "Why," you don't just wake up and tolerate life. You wake up with joy, with vision, and with the fire to pursue what sets your soul alive. You are not just working to pay the bills; you are working in alignment with what you love. There is a huge difference!

Think about it this way: would you get in your car and start driving aimlessly with no destination in mind? Of course not. You would set your GPS, you would know exactly where you are headed. It is the same with life. When you know your "Why," you can navigate with clarity. You waste less time wandering, and you move toward your goals with conviction.

In the powerful anthology, "What's Your Why," Lady Dr. Robbie Motter (h.c.), not only shares her own journey of living her passion but also inspires countless others to do the same. Through her nonprofit, the Global Society of Female Entrepreneurs, she has encouraged women to step out of their comfort zones, to dream bigger, and to claim their true purpose. She knows firsthand the power of showing up and the strength that comes from simply asking for what you want.

In this book, she invited each co-author to share their personal "Why," not just the polished version, but the real, raw stories of how they aligned their dreams with their decisions. The authenticity shines through every page. It is not just inspiring, it is transformative.

If you are standing at a crossroads, choosing a career, entering a relationship, starting a new chapter, your "Why" should be your compass. A career is not just a job; it is a long-term commitment! Without passion, it becomes just a paycheck. The same is true for relationships: shared values and visions for the future matter more than fleeting emotions.

I have learned that no one else can define your growth for you. It is personal. It is sacred. It must start with your "Why."

Because when you know your "Why," your life isn't something you simply endure, it becomes something you build with intention, courage, and faith.

And that, my friend, makes all the difference!

-Amb. Dr. Joan Wakeland (h.c), Award winning International & US Author, Speaker, and advocate for women. joanewakeland@ gmail.com,

909-721-7648

# REFLECTIONS

www.ingramcontent.com/pod-product-compliance
Lightning Source LLC
Chambersburg PA
CBHW051504120626
46551CB00012B/765